Object Technology Strategies and Tactics

Managing Object Technology Series

Charles F. Bowman
Series Editor
Editor
The X Journal
SIGS Publications, Inc.
New York, New York

and

President
SoftWright Solutions,
Suffern, New York

1. What Every Software Manager Must Know to Succeed with Object Technology, *John D. Williams*

2. Managing Your Move to Object Technology: Guidelines and Strategies for a Smooth Transition, *Barry McGibbon*

3. The Object Primer: Application Developer's Guide to Object-Orientation, *Scott W. Ambler*

4. Getting Results with the Object-Oriented Enterprise Model, *Thornton Gale and James Eldred*

5. Deploying Distributed Business Software, *Ted Lewis, Ph.D.*

6. The Blueprint for Business Objects, *Peter Fingar*

7. Object Technology Strategies and Tactics, *Gilbert Singer*

8. Upgrading Relational Databases with Objects, *Robert Vermeulen*

Additional Volumes in Preparation

Object Technology Strategies and Tactics

Gilbert L. Singer
Object-Oriented Computing Solutions
Naperville, Illinois

SIGS
BOOKS & MULTIMEDIA

New York • London • Paris • Munich • Cologne

Library of Congress Cataloging-in-Publication Data
Singer, Gilbert L.
Object Technology strategies and tactics / Gilbert Singer.
p. cm. — (Managing Object Technology series : 7)
Includes bibliographical references and index.
ISBN 1-884842-38-0 (pbk. : alk. paper)
1. Object-oriented methods (Computer science) I. Title. II. Series
QA76.9.035S56 1996
005.1'2—dc20 96-2839
CIP

PUBLISHED BY
SIGS Books & Multimedia
71 W. 23rd Street, Third Floor
New York, New York 10010
http://www.sigs.com

Design and composition by Kevin Callahan.
Cover design by Beth Scalafani.
Printed on acid-free paper.

SIGS Books ISBN 1-884842-38-0
Prentice-Hall ISBN 0-13-261132-5

Printed in the United States of America
00 99 98 97 96 10 9 8 7 6 5 4 3 2 1
First Printing July 1996

To my wife, Carol

About the Author

Gil Singer is the owner of Object-Oriented Computing Solutions, an independent consulting company specializing in object technology. His services range from strategic planning of object-oriented development projects to object-oriented analysis and design to Java programming. For more information about the author, check out his website at http://www.oocs.com/~singer or email him at singer@oocs.com.

Foreword

Let me introduce this book by citing one of Singer's many compelling analogies. In distinguishing between the procedural and the object-oriented approach to software development, he likens the procedural approach to giving someone driving directions: Turn right on this street, continue through four traffic lights, then bear left at the Y intersection, and so on. The object-oriented approach, by contrast, is more like handing the person a map: you are here, your destination is there, and this is a pretty good route to take.

As Singer points out, both techniques can get you where you want to go, but the procedural approach assumes stable requirements and an unchanging environment. What if you start from a different point, or change your mind about your destination? What if a road is closed, or an accident backs up traffic and forces you off your predetermined route? In each of these cases, any fixed set of directions you started with quickly becomes useless. But the map only increases in value as your situation changes.

So it is with software. In the days when companies had stablepositions and goals and the business environment changed slowly if at all, procedural programming worked just fine. Today, as you probably know from painful experience, the only constant is change; the pace of change is increasing all the time. No matter how diligent and skillful you might be, you can no longer formulate a set of directions that will get you where you want to go. You need maps to keep your bearings and to allow you to constantly change your course in response to real-time feedback from your environment. In short, you need objects.

Ironically, many books on object technology are splendid examples of the procedural paradigm at work. They offer directions. They assume a known starting point, prejudge your destination, and then give you precise directions for getting from where you are to where they think you should be. There is a comfort in such books. If you just follow this one special methodology, use these particular symbols to diagram your design, and translate the design into code in just the right manner, everything will be okay. Would that life were so simple!

The book you hold in your hands is object-oriented in the deepest sense. Rather than giving you a sequence of directions for using objects, it provides a map of the terrain and offers experienced counsel on how to proceed. Start from where you are, select your own goal, and move forward at your own pace; this book will help you keep your bearings at every juncture. Trying to decide on a methodology? This book doesn't offer one. Instead, it surveys the existing methodologies, then provides systematic guidelines to help you select the one that best suits your needs. Considering an object-oriented DBMS? Here again, Singer provides a detailed map of the terrain, then offers a set of decision criteria for selecting the most appropriate product.

Despite its increasingly widespread acceptance, object-oriented technology is still foreign territory for most companies. If I were venturing into an unknown region, uncertain of my starting point, my destination, or the condition of the roads I would face, I would want a very good map indeed.

This book is such a map. It will help make your journey into objects more manageable, more enjoyable, and—ultimately—much more profitable.

David A. Taylor, Ph.D.
May 1996

Preface

Switching to object technology requires innumerable decisions ranging from a manager's decision to select a methodology to a developer's decision on how two objects will communicate with each other. Making effective decisions at all levels of management is essential for the success of object-oriented projects. Making effective decisions at the implementation level is essential to creating high-quality software. This book is designed to help the reader make more effective decisions in managing and implementing object technology.

Audience and Purpose

This book is intended for managers who must understand how object-oriented software capabilities affect management decisions in object-oriented projects. The entire book is appropriate for technical managers. Most of this book should interest high-level project managers; however, upper management is expected to skip the technical material in Appendix A. This book is also intended for software developers who seek a broader view of object technology and who wish to better understand object-oriented concepts so that they can make intelligent analysis and design decisions.

When object-oriented projects succeed, they frequently achieve an unparalleled level of quality and results virtually impossible without object technology. Nevertheless, object-oriented projects appear to fail as often as non–object-oriented projects. Object technology is a proven technology; what is not proven is the ability of organizations to handle the technology effectively. Readers should gain an understanding of both the risks as well as the benefits of the technology, as well as how to minimize the risks and maximize the benefits.

I wrote this book in part because I have faith in object technology and do not want projects using the technology to fail for lack of understanding of the relationship between object-oriented concepts and the managing of software development projects. Software methodology and software management should not be viewed as separate domains and pursued independently by different people if object technology is to meet its full potential. In fact, separating the two is a sure recipe for disaster.

Managing object technology presents unique challenges that differ from those of traditional software technology. To met these challenges, managers need to understand the new technology. Some will argue that good managers can manage anything well; perhaps, but good managers who are technically qualified can manage even better. This book is intended to help provide managers with the technical foundation for managing object-oriented projects. It is also designed to help software engineers understand object-oriented concepts and how they relate to creating a successful object-oriented project. Managers and developers need to understand one another's responsibilities better if they are to communicate to the degree needed to make projects successful.

Additional specific goals of this book include the following:

- To provide an overview of object-oriented concepts
- To provide a broad understanding of the approaches taken by various object-oriented methodologies and to assist in selecting one
- To provide a method to help in the selection of an object-oriented database management system
- To provide a broad view of the uses of object technology
- To provide specific analysis and design techniques for software developers

Everyone loves to give advice, and since this is a legitimate purpose of a book such as this I have freely indulged in sharing what I have learned during more than three decades of developing software. Advice is provided on such topics as changes needed in the software life-cycle model, how to manage for reuse, how to create specialization hierarchies, how to make most effective use of a training and consulting budget, how to select an object-oriented methodology, and how to select an object-oriented database management system, to name a few.

Organization and Content

This book focuses on topics that are of interest to both managers and developers. Since the nature of object-oriented analysis and design greatly affects how a project should be managed and since both software developers and managers need to understand these topics, analysis and design are included. On the other hand, the actual implementation of the design is of interest mainly to programmers, not managers, so this topic is virtually ignored except as it relates to language selection and the design of the software. Therefore, while there are many references to the capabilities of object-oriented programming languages to assist in understanding of the implementation implications of the design, the book does not depend on knowledge of a programming language.

While some originators of methodologies have an understandable tendency to promote the merits of their methodology and emphasize the deficiencies of others, I have no methodology I am particularly interested in promoting. Therefore, I hope I am able to objectively describe the merits and deficiencies of the various methodologies. I distribute my attention to methodologies roughly in proportion to their popularity, although the degree of attention was actually determined by the concepts I wished to present. The methodologies receiving the most attention are, in descending order, OMT, OOSE/Objectory, Wirfs-Brock, Booch, Fusion, Shlaer-Mellor, and Coad-Yourdon. The Unified Method is also discussed because of its importance, despite the fact that it was not released at the time of this writing. Additional methodologies are discussed very briefly. While the recent mergers of methodologies affects the selection of a methodology, understanding the evolution of the concepts provides considerable insight into the technology. Thus the methodologies are approached from a historical as well as conceptual framework.

Many techniques that some methodologists discount as not being generally applicable are still quite valuable for specific applications. No methodology has yet been devised that handles every situation well, so understanding a wide spectrum of object-oriented and traditional methods is needed for many applications. To provide a consistent foundation for the discussion of numerous diverse methodologies, I present a prototype object-oriented life-cycle that spans multiple methodologies.

This book covers a wide spectrum of topics related to understanding object technology. It ranges from fundamental principles to specialized topics such as selecting a methodology for a neural network application. It encompasses the needs of software engineers and managers. It covers a wide variety of object-oriented methodologies and a wide range of other topics in object technology and should, therefore, contain much of interest even to those with considerable expertise in the field.

Every book must repeat some foundation material upon with object technology is based or else risk making the book incomprehensible to many readers. For those already familiar with the foundation material, I have striven to create new examples and a broader perspective on this material by comparing the views of various methodologists and adding my own insight. I hope this will make the foundation material of interest even to experts.

To cover such a wide spectrum of topics, something must be omitted. The most notable omission is in describing the details of any particular methodology. This is best left to the originator of the methodology anyway. In addition, the book practically ignores graphical notation to avoid the notation wars and concentrate on the concepts. The value of a methodology is only slightly affected by the quality of the notation since most are of about the same quality. Concepts are emphasized because most apply to all methodologies. Another casualty of covering topics for both managers and engineers is that the topics of testing, patterns, and CASE tools do not get the attention they deserve.

Chapters 1–4 provide an overview of the technology, help the reader decide whether the technology is appropriate for a particular situation, explain basic object-oriented concepts, and describe the object-oriented development process.

Chapter 5 addresses object-oriented analysis and design specifications. Chapter 6 describes methodologies by focusing of the important concepts they have contributed. Chapter 7 provides a method to assist in the selection of a methodology and information to help with the evaluation process. This chapter is important to read even when a methodology has already been selected. By systematically evaluating one's methodology, one can better understand its capabilities and can recognize and compensate for any deficiencies. Chapter 8 covers the object-oriented database management system (ODBMS). Chapter 9 describes a method to assist in selecting an ODBMS. Specific criteria are provided to assist in the selection with the goal of reducing the cost of the evaluation process. The chapter is of value even to those who have already selected an ODBMS because it explains important features of ODBMSs. The inclusion of Chapter 10 on distributed computing is motivated by the unique utility of object technology in the field of distributed computing. Chapter 11 summaries the management implications of the use of object technology and includes advice on how a company can get the most for its training and consulting investment.

Appendix A helps the reader understand the meaning of some confusing object-oriented terms and concepts. Appendix B provides a sampling of application experiences with object technology.

Some managers may wish to read the conclusions without reading the background material. The only problem with this is that the reader may not understand the reasoning behind the conclusions and may therefore not accept the conclusions. Nevertheless, this approach may be worthwhile for managers who wish to collect a wide sampling of opinions on the management of object technology. Object-oriented concepts are a fascinating topic, and I urge managers to spend as much time as they can afford in understanding the conceptual foundation of the technology. Object-oriented concepts do affect management decisions.

Object technology is a proven technology. Companies that ignore the opportunities provided by the object-oriented approach to developing software will find themselves at a competitive disadvantage to those who adopt the new technology. The risks of switching are significant, but the rewards of an effective transition can be enormous.

I welcome comments about this book. I may be reached at Object-Oriented Computing Solutions, 363 S. Wright, Naperville, IL 60540; e-mail: singer@oocs.com.

Acknowledgments

I wish to thank Nathan Singer for his major contribution to the chapters on object-oriented database management systems. I wish to express my profound appreciation for the invaluable comments and astute advice that I received from Charles Bowman, Donald Jackson, Brian Nolan, Wulf Rehder, and David Taylor during the creation of this book. Thanks also to Peter Arnold and Mike Blum for their production assistance.

Contents

Chapter 1

Introduction

If you are a manager, you may know that your competition is using object technology or may soon be using it. If you are a software engineer, you may know that object technology provides a less labor intensive and more enjoyable way to develop software than traditional techniques. If you are a student, you may wish to ride this wave of software technology advancement. This book serves a broad range of readers who already know the basics of software engineering but want to understand more about object technology. It provides a conceptual framework upon which to base critical management decisions and everyday analysis and design decisions.

The history of object technology (OT) is brief, its growth has been rapid, and its potential is enormous. A look at the status of object technology will provide an intuitive feel for what is unique about this fascinating technological opportunity. This chapter introduces object technology and should further whet your interest in the topic. Subsequent chapters will provide a deeper understanding of the technology and a guide to its use.

1.1 Object-Oriented Computing Today

Sellers of object-oriented products and services enthusiastically describe the advantages of object technology and, consistent with their vested interests, rarely alert their customers to potential pitfalls. Practitioners, including this author, are excited about seeing solutions to problems that have long plagued software projects. However, sometimes object-oriented advocates are so busy describing how great the view is from the top of the mountain that they forget to mention that the climb was lengthy, risky, and exhausting (Figure 1.1). This book will balance explaining the benefits of OT with describing the problems inherent in converting to it.

The following parable explains one aspect of the transition to object technology. If you are familiar with the history of object-oriented computing, you may understand the meaning of the parable before the interpretation.

> Kent goes into a computer store and a salesperson shows him the latest computer. She tells him honestly that this is the best PC ever made. Compared to its competition, it runs 5 times faster, costs half

Figure 1.1 *Remember the risks.*

> as much to buy, and because of its low power requirements, costs 1/10 as much to run. Not only that, all parts can be upgraded and used in subsequent versions. Kent is really impressed, but he looks at the keyboard and wants to know why the keys on the keyboard aren't in the standard positions. The salesperson tells Kent that the computer only works with a new type of keyboard with nonstandard key positions. However, if he doesn't like this keyboard, the computer does come with 39 other nonstandard keyboards. Everyone in his company can get the same nonstandard-version keyboard so that everyone in the company can learn the same new way of typing. Of course, anyone going to another company that chose a different new keyboard will have to learn to type again.

This little parable is analogous to object-oriented analysis and design in the early 1990s. We had a great new technology with well-defined concepts, but the implementation of the technology lacked standardization. There were scores of object-oriented methodologies that did not use the same terminology or the same graphical notation. Despite this problem, the technology had so many obvious advantages over its predecessors that growth was rapid even before efforts were undertaken toward standardization. Fortunately, many methodologies contributed some good ideas to the technology and then were obscured by the major methodologies. In addition, the principal contributions of Rumbaugh, Booch, and Jacobson have coalesced, giving customers for whom standardization is important the ability to choose a widely accepted methodology.

1.1.1 Project Experiences

Developers and users need to accumulate sufficient experience with object technology to separate the hype from the benefits. In the absence of such experience, one can look at the products they have been creating using the new technology to get a feel for the value of the technology.

Success with using objects in software development projects began back in the 1970s. Ericsson, the now giant Swedish telecommunications company, created one of the most noteworthy of these early major projects. Jacobson attributes much of the success of the company to the use of object technology in the AXE switching system (Jacobson, 1996), giving it a competitive advantage in central office telephone exchanges and mobile communications. Despite the huge size of the system (it represents over 1000 person-years of effort), the software demonstrated reliability, flexibility, and easy of modification. Tom Love's book, *Object Lessons,* provides detailed descriptions of some quite successful and other not so successful projects using object technology (Love, 1993). The following is a summary of a few of these.

In the 1980s when object-oriented programming languages became available, there were many successes in companies such as Apple, Hewlett-Packard, and Lawrence Livermore Laboratories. This is not surprising. However, one of the first outstanding successes with an object-oriented approach was accomplished by Brooklyn Union Gas, not a company one would immediately associate with sophisticated software technology. It successfully used object technology to construct a system that manages the entire revenue cycle for all of its operations, part of which includes dealing with more than a million customers.

Not all object-oriented efforts have been unqualified successes. Mentor Graphics essentially bet the company on switching from C to C++; it survived the experience but not without considerable pain. The effort was mainly a programming conversion effort and was short in analysis and design, so the project achieved limited reuse of code and even less of analysis and design. One person who worked on the project told me they didn't really understand the implications of the use of inheritance until it was too late to avoid the problems of overly complex inheritance structures. This is one of many possible mistakes in applying object technology that I hope this book will help you avoid.

Another company that bet the company on object technology is NeXT Computer Inc. They were an unqualified technical success. Pinson describes NeXT as "several years ahead of other OO systems" (Pinson, 1994). NeXT did have marketing problems with its hardware, but its operating system was too good to die and is continuing to evolve into an operating system-independent object-oriented development environment in a joint development effort by NeXT and Sun Microsystems Inc. ("Executive Brief," 1995).

Of the companies Love is familiar with that have created products successfully both ways, none have ever gone back to traditional methods after using object technology. (This does not count a few acquired companies that were forced to give up OT to conform to the new parent company.) Others have commented about the problem of getting anyone who has learned object-oriented techniques to go back to traditional ones; I certainly cannot imagine doing it myself.

Many successful applications of object technology are hidden from view. Booch explains why: "It's politically incorrect to mention any of these companies by name because, not surprisingly, most of them view their efforts as strategically very important and, hence, offering a competitive advantage" (Booch, 1993). Appendix B provides summary information on a selection of projects for which information has been made public. For a more extensive discussion of case studies see *Succeeding with Objects* by Goldberg and Rubin (1995); these authors have extensive experience with object-oriented projects going back to the early days of creation of the Smalltalk language.

1.1.2 The Software Industrial Revolution

Object technology is inevitable, so you might as well get used to it. As Brad Cox put it, "The software industrial revolution will occur, sometime, somewhere, whether programmers want it to or not, because it will be the software consumers who determine the outcome" (Cox, 1990). By "software industrial revolution," he is referring to a change from creating customized products to building items from reusable off-the-shelf components. OT has made the software industrial revolution possible; it is taking place now, but it is still in the early stages. The full potential of structured techniques has been essentially achieved. The full potential of object technology is yet to be realized.

Object technology is inevitable because the software industry is undergoing a fundamental technology shift to better meet customer needs. This shift includes client/server systems, distributed processing systems, and systems based on a graphical user interface (GUI, pronounced "goo' ey"). The only currently available software development technology that can adequately handle all of these new needs is object-oriented technology. The competitive nature of our economic system ensures that improved cost effective technologies will eventually supplant less effective ones. There is nothing like the success of one's competition to get management's attention.

1.1.3 Career Implications for Individual Software Engineers

A conversion to OT means that a software engineer will spend more time understanding the development process, will spend a greater proportion of time doing analysis and design, less time doing programming, and much less time doing maintenance. In the long term, even greater changes will occur. OT is helping advance technology to the point where programmers may become a vanishing breed. Anyone expecting to be doing programming in the next ten years should read Ed Yourdon's *Decline and Fall of the American Programmer* (Yourdon, 1992). Reading this book may help prevent "graffiti dyslexia"—the inability to read the handwriting on the wall. In addition to the economics that make it cheaper to hire programmers abroad, technology is coming closer and closer to being able to automate the programming process out of existence. The mechanism for this is the creation of tools that allow analysis and design specifications to automatically generate code. The process has been demonstrated (Lato and Parks, 1995), but the efficiency of the code produced is sometimes a problem.

Besides the trend toward the automation of the programming process, there is a trend toward the creation of ever more sophisticated software tools. Object-based environments are already creating tools that can assemble complex programs in specific areas such as graphical user interface (GUI) and database applications. This requires little programming in the traditional sense of the word, but requires considerable knowledge about the capabilities and use of specialized tools. This implies an alternative view to the idea that future needs will require more analysts and designers and fewer programmers. Rather, tools will become so sophisticated that formal design will be unnecessary.

Thus there are a couple of antithetical alternatives for forward-looking programmers. If the need for traditional programming is shrinking, one could become an analyst, a designer, or an analyst-designer. The combined role of analyst-designer is more feasible now because the distinction between the two is diminishing with the smoothing of the transitions between analysis and design. However, if the second view is correct, one should become a software tool specialist. GUI specialists will be needed in either case to use the specialized object-oriented and object-based tools that make program interfaces easy to create and use. Programmers will still be needed, but programming work will be a continuously shrinking piece of the development cycle.

1.1.4 A Short History of Object-Oriented Methodologies

The roots of object technology extend back to the creation of Simula in Norway in 1967. The development of object-oriented languages continued with the creation of Smalltalk in the 1970s. Object technology remained limited mostly to the implementation phase for two decades. It was not until 1988 that a widely read book describing the philosophy behind developing software in an object-oriented manner was produced. This book, *Object-Oriented Software Construction* by Bertrand Meyer (1988), is a classic that is still well worth reading and can be considered the starting point of the development of object-oriented methodologies. These methodologies quickly diverged during the short life of object-oriented analysis and design. Let's look at this divergence and then the more recent convergence of various methodologies.

1.1.4.1 The Divergence

Because of the growing popularity of object-oriented languages and the lack of information about how to perform analysis and design for object-oriented software, books on object-oriented methodology finally started appearing around 1990. That year brought Coad and Yourdon's *Object-Oriented Analysis* (Coad and Yourdon, 1990), an excellent book for beginners (which practically everyone was then). However, it wasn't really an industrial-strength product; the following year, Coad and Yourdon added *Object-Oriented Design* (Coad and Yourdon, 1991). The year also saw the publication of Wirfs-Brock's *Designing Object-Oriented Software* (Wirfs-Brock, et al., 1992), which extended and popularized the idea of describing class interactions using contracts, as earlier described by Meyer. Software developers welcomed the publication of Booch's and Rumbaugh's books in 1991 (Booch, 1991; Rumbaugh, 1991). The following year brought an acceleration of books on analysis and design, the most notable of which, in my opinion, was Jacobson's *Object-Oriented Software Engineering* (Jackson, et al., 1992). By 1993, we had an avalanche of new books, with a plethora of methods and graphical notations.

Some of the divergence in methods is both unavoidable and desirable when new ideas are being introduced into the technology. However, some of the divergence is difference for difference's sake, particularly when it comes to graphical notation. Much of the divergence appears to be driven by the desire to show originality rather than to use the work of others. However, the development of object technology has reached the point at which there is a greater need for standardization than for originality, at least when it comes to notation and terminology.

The most glaring divergence among the various methods is in graphical notation, with divergence in terminology being a runner-up. Let's look at the more significant conceptual differences among the various methods. The divergence is typified by the difference between Wirfs-Brock's responsibility-driven approach and Rumbaugh's Object Modeling Technique (OMT). Don't let anything about the differences in object-oriented methods described here give you the idea that the object-oriented paradigm is not well defined. Regardless of the differences in the methods, they are more similar than different, and they are distinctly different from the structured analysis and information engineering approaches.

OMT is an evolutionary approach in that it builds on the tools of structured analysis. It uses three complementary views of a system. The object model is an extension of Chen's entity relationship model (Chen, 1976); the dynamic model is based on state transition diagrams, and the functional model is based on data-flow diagrams. There is a transformation step in which the three analysis models determine the object design relating to class behaviors.

While Rumbaugh developed an evolutionary approach to OT, Wirfs-Brock adopted a revolutionary approach, called responsibility-driven design. Wirfs-Brock's method is revolutionary in the sense that it is an abrupt change from structured techniques. Her responsibility-driven approach is based on a single model where static relationships among object classes are described in terms of contracts.

The responsibility-driven approach, with a single object model and a client/server focus on relationships between classes, and OMT, with its three models and a focus in the object model on the general nature of associations, represent two ends of the object-oriented spectrum. However, talking about a spectrum with something as multifaceted as object-oriented methods probably is not very accurate.

1.1.4.2 The Convergence

The methods that came out during the first few years of the decade were all relatively unique and had limited overlap. The second generation of object-oriented methods overlap considerably. We are now seeing a strong trend toward convergence in object-oriented methods, not in an agreement on using a unary or a ternary methodology or in the process used (these are discussed later) but in the critical area of an agreement as to what content is needed in a methodology. Let's look at the forces promoting this convergence.

The main reason that we can expect a convergent trend is that the users of object technology are demanding it. Users do not want a choice of 40 different methods, they want one that will work for them. This influence tends to make the most popular methods more popular and the less popular even less popular regardless of merit. Customers want assurance that the method will last; this favors methods with significant corporate backing, and it encourages small consulting organizations to be as mainstream as they can.

The CASE (computer-aided software engineering) tool vendors are another force toward convergence. A method is doomed unless it is supported by at least one CASE tool. A method really needs CASE tools on a variety of platforms to be viable, therefore the need for CASE tools will cause convergence by attrition.

The basic modeling of the various methodologies has been visible long enough now that the producers of methods have had the opportunity to incorporate the ideas of others into own their methods. Good ideas have had irresistible appeal to methodologists who might otherwise be expected to prefer to use what they invent themselves rather than borrowing the ideas of others. As long as there is some agreement as to what is "best," the desire of practitioners to improve their methods will be a strong force toward convergence.

The convergence is evident in books that advertise themselves as second-generation methodologies. One methodologist advertises his method as fourth-generation object-orientation, so obviously the term *generation* is not very meaningful. Let me define second-generation object-orientation as methodologies that borrow significantly from the work of others. Books like Booch's second edition (Booch, 1994) and the Fusion book (Coleman, 1994) integrate many of the ideas presented in the books of 1990–1993. The incorporation of the core idea of Jacobson's use cases into most methodologies furthered the convergence.

It is more than just the theories that are converging; people and companies are merging their efforts. The most notable evidence of this consolidation is that the originators of three of the most popular methodologies, Grady Booch, Ivar Jacobson, and James Rumbaugh, now all work for Rational Software Corporation. The most notable event in the consolidation of methodologies is the creation of Rational's Unified Method, which merges the OMT and Booch methodologies and includes the key element of Jacobson's methodology (Booch and Rumbaugh, 1995). By the time you read this book, even more mergers of methodologies will have occurred and standards for object-oriented fundamentals should be well developed (Henderson-Sellers, 1995).

1.2 What's the Difference?

It is not easy to precisely define the object-oriented paradigm. Tim Rentsch's famous quotation reflects this:

> My guess is that object-oriented programming will be in the 1980's what structured programming was in the 1970's. Everyone will be in favor of it. Every manufacturer will promote his products as supporting it. Every manager will pay lip service to it. Every programmer will practice it (differently). And no one will know just what it is! (Rentsch, 1982)

Actually, the essential features of the object-oriented approach are reasonably well defined. The object-oriented paradigm represents a new philosophy of how software should be developed. The object-oriented paradigm's predecessor is called the *procedural paradigm*. The procedural paradigm separates the data from the operations on the data. It describes a set of steps to solve a problem. The object-oriented paradigm combines and encapsulates data with the operations of the object. This allows realistic modeling of real-world entities in a more natural way. The example later in this section will describe the differences between the paradigms in more concrete terms.

The fundamental difference between the object-oriented approach and traditional approaches to software development is significant enough to term it a paradigm shift. A paradigm is a pattern, a way of thinking about something. The impact of some paradigm shifts on science has been immense, as witnessed by the contributions of Galileo, Newton, and Einstein. All of these paradigm shifts required people to think in a new way, all met with considerable resistance because of this, and all resulted in technological advancement.

The impact of the object-oriented paradigm on software development is not as momentous as the these historical examples, but it does require a new way of thinking, it certainly has had its detractors, and it does represent a major advancement in software engineering technology.

What is this fundamental difference? The next three sections demonstrate the difference by solving the problem of driving a car to a destination in two different ways and comparing the solutions.

1.2.1 The Procedural Paradigm

The idea of the procedural paradigm is to describe a set of steps to solve a problem. The procedural solution to the problem of going from one location to another would be something like the following. Go straight for 2 blocks then turn left, go 3 blocks and turn right, continue to the second stop light, turn right, and stop after 5 blocks. A good procedural solution might well be the most efficient solution to this problem.

1.2.2 The Object-Oriented Paradigm

The object-oriented approach is as follows: Here's a map. You're here; your destination is there. You figure out your turns. Your car is an object that interacts with other objects shown on the map, particularly streets. The car will proceed in a northerly direction if south of the destination and vice versa and in an easterly direction if west of the destination and vice versa. A good object-oriented solution would likely result in the same or equivalent route as for the procedural solution. The difference is that the map provides an object-oriented conceptual foundation for the problem that is relatively stable over time. The effect of this difference is in the relative adaptability of the solution to changes in the requirements.

1.2.3 Comparing Object-Oriented and Procedural Solutions

Which way would you prefer to get your directions? You say you're not good at maps and want to try the first way? Okay. So you go 2 blocks, turn left and after one block you run into a sign that says "Bridge Out." Want that map now? Procedures are not easily adaptable to change; they are not stable. Things like city blocks are relatively stable;

programs based on fundamental objects can adapt to changes.

With the object-oriented approach, if the car encounters obstacles, such as a bridge out or a one-way street, it can adapt to the situation by minor changes in its behavior. The solution is based on the nature of streets and the relative locations of the car and the destination, not on a sequence of steps where the correctness of each of the later steps depends on the correctness of the earlier ones. The object-oriented solution adapts easily to different starting and ending locations. The procedural solution is totally useless for most other starting and ending locations. *A sequence of steps is not a stable foundation for a program.*

Procedures are still used within the object-oriented paradigm, but they are used at a local level and are based on objects and object relationships. The starting point is to determine the objects (car and street) and build on their basic stability.

1.2.4 An Evolution or a Revolution?

Is there anything revolutionary about what we have been talking about? Is object technology revolutionary or evolutionary? Certainly, the object-oriented paradigm was preceded by decades of work that was prerequisite to its existence. Encapsulation (information hiding) and abstraction are long-standing principles of software development that form a key part of the object-oriented paradigm; Parnas described the principle of encapsulation in 1972. Therefore, we could conclude that object technology is simply an evolution that added the concept of using polymorphism to the existing principles. However, a lot of experts do not feel this way about it.

Bertrand Meyer begins *Object-Oriented Software Construction* with "Born in the ice-blue waters of the festooned Norwegian coast; amplified . . . along the much grayer range of the Californian Pacific; viewed by some as a typhoon, by some as a tsunami, and by some as a storm in a teacup—a tidal wave is reaching the shores of the computing world" (Meyer, 1988). He was talking about object-oriented computing, of course, which did indeed start in Norway with the Simula language, and became popular with Smalltalk, which was developed by Xerox in California. Clearly, he feels that it is revolutionary.

Why does object technology seem like a revolution to so many people? It is because what some might consider a relatively minor addition to the technology has a major effect on the entire development process.

Conceptually, it was a small step from viewing the earth as flat to viewing it as a sphere, but the practical effect was enormous. It is the anticipation of the eventual effect of the object-oriented paradigm that has people so excited about it.

Changing from a procedural mindset to an object-oriented mindset is a fateful event for most software engineers. Whether individual software engineers start on the road to Damascus from experiencing software disasters or simply from longing for a way to make code more maintainable, it creates for them a new vision of how software should be developed. Whether the paradigm is evolutionary or revolutionary, object-oriented computing is causing a revolution one individual at a time.

1.3 Benefits and Challenges of Object Technology

The increasing popularity of the object-oriented approach is a result of its success in the following areas:

- Customer communications
- Extensibility and maintainability
- More efficient development process
- Increased reliability
- Increased reuse of analysis, design, and code
- Decreased time to market
- Increased productivity

All of these items have been successfully demonstrated on real projects, but they are by no means guaranteed for all projects. Increased reuse is potentially the most valuable benefit, but it is also the easiest benefit to miss because it requires more forethought, company-wide cooperation, and more initial investment. While to some extent the other benefits arise naturally from doing a reasonably good job of object-oriented development, some challenges must be overcome to achieve each benefit. Chapter 11 will discuss the challenges and how to surmount them.

1.3.1 Customer Communications

For a customer to effectively communicate what he wants a software product to accomplish, he needs to communicate the same way he is used to communicating. This communication is in natural language plus a fair amount of jargon. Both the everyday words and the jargon describe real-world things and concepts. Traditional approaches to analysis (the process of describing a problem) used either natural language or a representation based on computer software constructs.

Natural language is reasonably good at facilitating communication between the customer and the software analyst, except that it allows the ambiguity common to English and every other language. Specifications based on natural language tend to be ambiguous, verbose, and inefficient. The representation of computer software analysis prior to the object-oriented approach avoids ambiguity by using software modeling constructs such as data flow diagrams to describe the flow of data within the software. However, this method relates very poorly to the customer's natural mode of communication and creates abundant opportunity for misunderstanding between the customer and the analyst.

In the object-oriented approach, the customer's terminology and concepts provide the foundation for both communication between the customer and the analyst and for the representation of the problem specification and the implementation. Not only do the customer's application objects and the software's objects correspond closely, but the entire way that the customer naturally thinks about his application is mirrored by the software.

People think in terms of whole-part relationships (e.g., the gear is a part of the conveyor system). We think in terms of specialization relationships (e.g., the Taurus is a kind of a car). If we know something about cars and we know that a Taurus is a kind of a car, we know a lot about a Taurus even if we have never heard of the model. The ways that we naturally think about real-world objects are reflected in an object-oriented specification.

Because the software specification uses the same language as the customer and describes the problem in the same way he or she thinks about the application, communications are greatly simplified. The customer no longer has to become part software engineer to understand the specifications. Since an object-oriented model describes the problem in terms of the customer's application, the developer and client communicate more effectively; analysis errors due to misunderstandings are less likely—clients can understand the object model better because it is expressed in terms of a real-world application, not in terms of esoteric software specifications.

1.3.2 Extensibility and Maintainability

Extensibility is a measure of how easy it is to add additional capabilities to software. *Maintainability* is a measure of how easy it is to locate and repair software errors or to modify software to sustain existing capabilities despite environmental changes, such as a change in the operating system. The extensibility and maintainability of software is improved by creating coding that has low coupling and high cohesion. *Coupling* is a measure of interdependence of the programming units (e.g., subroutines, procedures, or objects) in a computer program. *Cohesion* is a measure of the degree to which the tasks performed by a programming unit are functionally related. To maximize the extensibility and maintainability of software, one strives for low coupling and high cohesion.

Making software more modifiable is what sold me on object technology much more than productivity or anything else, because I have seen the rippling effect in action. The rippling effect is the tendency of one change to generate the need for other changes; correcting an error in one part of the code may generate more than one error elsewhere in the code. I have seen codes that used variables visible throughout the program (called global common) for most communication and other codes that commonly used arguments of 63 parameters. The only reason they didn't use more arguments was that the compiler limited them to 63. The extensive use of global common or many arguments causes high coupling between various parts of the code. Therefore, with this type of structure, a change in one part of the code can have disastrous consequences in very remote locations.

Good coding practices can reduce this problem considerably even without the object-oriented paradigm, but the abstraction and encapsulation capabilities exhibited by objects and classes greatly enhance one's ability to reducing coupling. Less coupling makes it easier to add enhancements because fewer parts of the code require modification.

Objects are more stable than independent data and methods because they model real-world entities that are relatively stable.

Sequences of operations are situationally dependent and may need major changes to respond to minor changes in the requirements, as shown by the earlier example of driving a car in Section 1.2.

The inheritance capability, which is a requirement for a language to be considered object-oriented, also makes it very easy to add specializations of existing objects. It does this by creating a child object that is a specialization of a parent object. The child object uses the data and behavior of the parent object, plus whatever additional capabilities that the child object may wish to add. So inheritance allows the parent object to remain unchanged and the child object to contain only the new properties and behavior needed for the specialization represented by the child object.

Extensible software is also maintainable software. The reduced coupling among program units that makes software extensible also makes it more maintainable. The object-oriented approach reduces coupling through encapsulation and this means changes will be predominantly local rather than global.

Theoretically, the object-oriented approach makes it easier to maintain software. However, theories do not always check out in practice, so let us consider an actual study that was designed to test the theory. Henry and Humphrey (1993) conducted a study that compared the effort involved in performing a set of maintenance tasks on two functionally equivalent programs. One program was designed with structured design techniques and used the procedural language C for implementation. The other was designed using object-oriented design techniques and the object-oriented language Objective-C. The study was well designed. It used statistical analysis to show that the results were free of bias in areas of concern. The study concluded that "the experiment supports the hypothesis that subjects produce more maintainable code with an object-oriented language than procedure-oriented ones."

Anything that significantly reduces maintenance is a major cost benefit because a large fraction of the total cost of software is due to maintenance. Numerous studies have been done to determine what this fraction is in non–object-oriented projects. Rather than quote a particular study, let me present some snippets from an unscientific sampling of books and articles in my office that give a general idea of the value of this fraction: "is between 50% and 75%," "up to 70%," and "85%."

The numbers are not consistent, presumably because of differences in the nature of the applications sampled and numerous other factors, but the significance of reducing the cost of maintenance is apparent.

1.3.3 More Efficient Development Process

The object-oriented approach improves the efficiency of the development process both by enhancing comprehension and streamlining the mechanics of the process. Comprehension is enhanced by the better cognitive model that the object-oriented approach provides. The streamlining of the mechanics is due to smoothing the transition between the phases of the software life cycle. This simplifies maintaining software traceability.

1.3.3.1 A Better Cognitive Model

Not only does the object-oriented approach improve the efficiency of customer and analyst communications, it provides a better cognitive model for the analysts and designers to represent, visualize, and manipulate the entities and ideas needed to model a problem and its solution. It allows developers to be more creative by working at a higher level of abstraction. Thinking in terms of relatively large abstractions such as objects or types allows the analyst-designer to focus on the most important issues instead of getting bogged down in the details.

The object model is more natural and easier to understand, at least for those who are not ingrained in using another model. New developers learn the object model quickly; but experienced software developers may have to do some unlearning before they can relearn.

The object model mirrors the way kids learn language. They first learn nouns and then verbs. They recognize that objects consist of physical properties plus what they can do. For example, a doll has properties, such as brown hair, and behavior, such as flexible knees and elbows. Kids recognize the connectedness of properties and behavior very early. You can see that they recognize the significance of the function that an object serves as being part of the essence of the thing, because they will take a piece of wood and treat it as a gun or a boat according to what they decide to do with it. They learn to generalize from the idea of a doll and building blocks to the idea of toys within two years of life. We can learn a lot from kids—software developers took decades to take advantage of these basic ideas.

1.3.3.2 Efficient Traceability

Every software development effort needs to maintain traceability from the requirements through the implementation and vice versa. Otherwise, the programming may not actually satisfy the requirements and some of it may have a purpose other than satisfying the requirements.

In the structured techniques, the representational mismatch between analysis and design makes traceability difficult. The network representation of the system in analysis (e.g., data flow diagrams) is converted to a hierarchical representation of the code structure during design. The transform and transaction analysis techniques used to accomplish this are more of an art than a science, making it difficult to trace a requirement from analysis to design. The structured technique of functional decomposition further complicates the problem by scattering one requirement over many implementation functions.

With the object-oriented approach, it is easier to trace the specifications between life cycle phases because of the constancy of representation between analysis, design, and programming. Types and objects provide a common unifying means of model representation for all three phases. Because there is no representational mismatch between the phases, there is a smooth transition that greatly simplifies the traceability problem. Requirements are rooted in real-world objects and concepts that end up with counterparts in the coding, so one requirement does not tend to become scattered over numerous programming units.

1.3.4 Increased Reliability

If the companies developing the software had to pay their customers for the time they wasted due to errors in the software the companies sell, most software companies would be bankrupt. If we can't come up with a more reliable way of developing software, Ed Yourdon will be proven right about the thesis represented by the title of his book, *The Decline and Fall of the American Programmer.* Reliability is a survival issue for the U.S. software industry, and it is being addressed, in part, by object technology.

Having a better cognitive model is as much a reliability issue as a process efficiency issue. Having a model that allows both the developers and the customer to communicate in the common terminology of application objects helps prevent specification errors. Various studies have shown that the cost of finding errors late in the life cycle or after delivery is vastly greater than finding them early, even without counting the cost to the customers of using a buggy code. The use of inheritance with an object-oriented language can improve reliability because it allows extending existing well-checked-out coding without modifying any of it. Nevertheless, the added coding has all of the functionality of the existing code plus whatever additional functionality is added. Exactly how this is accomplished is explained in Chapter 5.

1.3.5 Reuse: Violating Brook's Law

Modern life cycle models in conjunction with object technology allow the violation of Brooks' law. Fred Brooks was in charge of large IBM projects and wrote the classic book, *The Mythical Man-Month,* to document the frustrations he had in managing these projects (Brooks, 1982). This book is a must-read for anyone who is managing large software projects.

The book is very well written, as indicated by the first paragraph of the first chapter, "The Tar Pit," which is quoted here:

> No scene from prehistory is quite so vivid as that of the mortal struggles of great beasts in the tar pits. In the mind's eye one sees dinosaurs, mammoths, and saber-toothed tigers struggling against the grip of the tar. The fiercer the struggle, the more entangling the tar, and no beast is so strong or so skillful but that he ultimately sinks.
>
> Large-system programming has over the past decade been such a tar pit . . .

This should give you a feel for Brooks' frustration in managing large software projects using traditional technology and presumably why he became a university professor. Brooks goes on to describe how people working on large-system software development are just like the animals in the tar pit; no matter how good they are or how hard they try, they are doomed, if not to failure, to schedule and cost overruns.

Brooks' law states, "Adding manpower to a late software project makes it later." There are a couple of reasons for this. First you have to train the new people, which means you have to take people currently working on the project away from it to do the training. Second, communication problems between people and between units of software grow rapidly with the increasing number of people working on the project.

Suppose, as an unrealistic but instructive example, each person needs to spend half an hour a day talking to each person on the project, and the project expands from 5 people to 21 people. This would expand two hours devoted to communicating into a ten-hour day, even without doing any "real" work. The total numbers of hours spent by all members in communication within the group of five is 5 times 2 hours, or 10 hours. The total for the larger group is 21 times 10 hours, or 210 hours. Increasing the number of people by a factor of 4 increased the time spent by a factor of 21. The numbers may not be realistic, since not everyone has to talk to everyone else, but the problem is obvious.

I said the object-oriented approach allows violating Brook's Law. Actually it can't do much about the training problem, but it can have a major impact on reducing communication problems. It allows a much greater degree of decoupling of the parts of the problems and allows work to be conducted in parallel with other work. With greater decoupling of the tasks, each person needs to talk to fewer people. Let's look at a graph (Figure 1.2) using a typical cost estimate formula, Effort = k $size^x$, that shows the violation of Brook's law, where k and x are empirically determined constants. Traditionally, x has been greater than one. Whenever x exceeds 1, effort increases more than proportionally to the size of the program. We have grown to expect that doubling the size of a program will more than double the effort required. However, it is quite possible for x to be less than one for object-oriented projects. How is this possible? The answer is reuse. The larger the project, the more opportunity there is for reuse, and object technology provides the means for increasing reuse.

The reason reuse is easier to achieve with the object-oriented paradigm is that it allows users to model real-world objects instead of creating software models that reflect the steps the computer is going to take to solve a problem. Since the nature of the real world, such as the laws of physics, are more stable than sequences of procedures, objects can be reused in more situations than can a series of steps. Also contributing to reuse is the encapsulation of data and behavior, which gives objects all the ingredients they need to be realistic models. This decreases inter-module coupling, so that reuse is enhanced by improv-

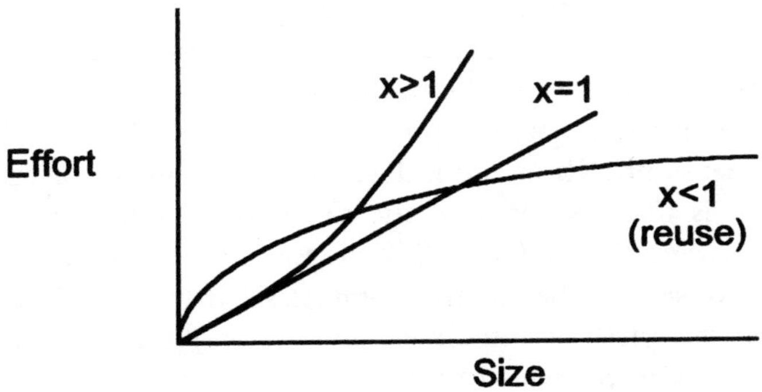

Figure 1.2 *Effect of reuse on the relationship between program size and effort required.*

ing the software architecture. Thus classes constitute a programming tool for reuse by creating encapsulated objects.

Inheritance is another programming tool for achieving reuse. Inheritance implements analysis and design generalization/specialization hierarchies. In a generalization/specialization hierarchy, a specialized class of objects can be created simply by extending the capabilities of a more general class of objects. Therefore, by using inheritance one can reuse the data and functions of a more general class rather than starting from scratch. Subsequent chapters explain inheritance more fully.

Reuse also will be enhanced by the maturing of the object-oriented industry and adherence to standards, such as those being promoted by the Object Management Group (OMG), the Object Database Management Group (ODMG), and others. Potentially, the most valuable bene fit of OT is reuse, but achieving it is problematic since it involves company-wide cooperation to maximize benefits. Reuse requires a high-level management commitment to support the extra effort required to write reusable code.

Reuse applies not only to reusing code but to reusing analysis and design. Therefore, we use the term component reuse to include other forms of reuse besides code reuse. Well-designed object-oriented components are sufficiently decoupled to make the reuse of the specifications feasible. Since specifications are more costly to produce than code, the potential savings are greater in reuse of the products of analysis and design than in the reuse of code.

There are two approaches to achieving reuse. One is creating small, versatile object-oriented software components that can be used to help assemble a wide variety of programs. The other is to create object-oriented frameworks that are specific to an application domain and are specialized to handle the specific needs of one type of application.

The former method was first promoted by Brad Cox, who saw the object-oriented approach as the industrial revolution of software engineering. Cox is the developer of the Objective-C language, which is used by the NeXT computer's NEXTSTEP object-oriented operating system. Cox observed that in the computer hardware industry, if we want a part, we pick an integrated circuit (IC) off the shelf (Cox, 1986). In the software industry there was never much on the shelf, so we built almost everything from scratch. Cox proposed developing the software counterpart to integrated circuits, and he pointed out that the object-oriented paradigm provides the tools needed to create these reusable "software ICs." Companies such as Rogue Wave of Corvallis, Oregon, have now developed extensive libraries of general-purpose and mathematical applications.

The second way to achieve savings is by developing domain-specific object-oriented frameworks. It is certainly not feasible to analyze the entire universe and reuse the analysis for all projects. However, as experience with GUI development has shown, it is feasible to create frameworks domain by domain. Frameworks may limit what you can do without going outside of the framework, but within the framework they improve one's efficiency tremendously. Borland's Paradox for Windows is a well-known example of an object-based framework for both GUI and database applications. It allows the user to assemble a database program by dragging and dropping icons with little or no programming involved. It also has a programming language to allow the user to extend the built-in features. Additional examples of frameworks are provided in Section 11.3 when this important topic is revisited.

A debate currently exists about which of the two approaches will result in the greatest improvement in productivity. Those who favor the component approach point out the effect of the need for distributed object computing. The same effort that will make objects distributable over a variety of platforms, by making small highly reusable classes that can be linked together in a standard way, will promote reuse of small highly reusable classes. A standard to promote this has been developed by the Object Management Group. It is known as the Common Object Request Broker Architecture (CORBA) standard (see Chapter 10).

This effort is critical to the future of distributed object computing. However, it is unlikely that the creation of a lot of small reusable objects will have nearly as much impact on improving productivity as frameworks will. Nice, neat classes that can meet the needs of different application domains are very difficult to create. There are, of course, some areas where this is feasible, such as in mathematical applications, but even here efficiency concerns may limit the use of generally applicable classes. Frameworks, on the other hand, can be focused to meet a more limited set of needs very efficiently.

Regardless of which approach will prove the most valuable, both approaches can be used simultaneously. Together, or even separately, they have great potential in fulfilling the dream of software reusability. Most of this potential is yet unrealized on an industry-wide basis because of the lack of maturity of object-oriented products. However, a growing number of companies are creating toolkits and general object-oriented frameworks for specific applications that greatly increase user productivity. The numerous commercial math and container class libraries are examples of the former, and object-oriented database management systems (ODBMSs) are examples of the latter.

A headline in the March 1994 issue of *Byte Magazine* stated "Object-Oriented Has Failed." If you saw the headline, I hope you read the article since it did not support the headline. Object technology has succeeded. Apparently, *The National Enquirer* is not alone in selling magazines by using outrageous headlines. Success stories with the use of object technology abound but were ignored. Marie Lenzi, editor of *Object Magazine*, wrote a searing reply to the *Byte* article entitled "Irresponsible Journalism." Her parting shot in the article was, "The irresponsible press should be taken out and flogged!" (Lenzi, 1994).

It is premature to expect a new technology to have solved so vast a problem. However, as misleading as the Byte headline was, the actual article had a grain of truth in claiming that object technology has not solved the problem of the lack of code reuse. So far reuse is in its infancy from a global view. One reason no good national repository of the reusable software exists is that reuse is too much of a competitive advantage for companies to share. Some companies even hide the fact that they use OT because they prefer not to wake up their competition to the importance of OT. However, a global reuse industry will come, not from companies that compete in an application area, but from companies serving these competitors.

1.3.6 Decreased Time to Market

Shortening the time span from initiation to delivery of a project is a critical competitive advantage. Getting a product out that is equivalent to one a competitor gets out a year earlier is generally a losing proposition. For example, pharmaceutical companies with expiring patents have found they can capture the bulk of the generic market simply by getting their generic version out one to three months before the expiration date (when the competition can release their product). For most industries, including software development, it does not take much of an advantage in improved delivery time to constitute a major competitive advantage. This assumes that the product delivered is a quality product; rushing buggy software to market is not usually an advantage, although some companies seem to get by with it.

The preceding describes the conventional wisdom about the importance of being the first to market; however, a caveat is needed here. Being first to market is not always desirable and may be undesirable if the market is not ready for the product. Asthana describes this condition as when a product has no time lag between the technology S-curve and the marketing S-curve (Asthana, 1995). (The S-curve is typical of the slow initial development of a product or market acceptance of it, followed by a steep advancement in technology or market acceptance, later followed by a tailing off.)

One is not likely to decrease time to market on the first object-oriented project, but once significant reuse takes place on subsequent projects, the time span may be dramatically reduced. Of course, one can reduce the time to market in other ways, too, but as we have seen from Brook's law, additional personnel by itself may not be effective. Adding people can be effective if the project can be divided into smaller loosely interacting tasks. Object-oriented division of the application makes concurrent development more feasible and therefore can speed the time to market in this manner. But nothing speeds time to market as much as creating a new product by assembling existing parts.

Furthermore, for some products the time to market would be so long without using object technology that companies would not even consider creating the products. For example, Graham asserts that "most of the current GUIs just could not have been written without the use of object-oriented techniques" (Graham, 1994).

1.4 Summary: Productivity

If there is one word that summarizes the benefits of object technology, it is productivity. Most of the previously discussed benefits of OT translate into productivity gains.

Better customer communications helps productivity because errors detected during the analysis phase are one to two orders of magnitude less expensive to fix than ones discovered during implementation or during use by the customer. Since the object model describes the problem in terms of the customer's application, it results in better developer/client communications, making analysis errors due to misunderstandings less likely.

Various studies have indicated that the maintenance phase of the life cycle has traditionally consumed 50% or more of the total effort on projects. So the benefits of creating more extensible and maintainable software are obvious.

The smoother development process that the object-oriented approach makes possible also contributes to productivity. This improved process includes a smoother transition and improved traceability from analysis to design to programming.

The reliability of object-oriented code resulting from a better cognitive model and proper use of the inheritance capability of object-oriented languages reduces the time spent in correcting errors.

The reduced time-to-market made possible by OT is an effect of the various productivity improvements facilitated by OT.

The object oriented approach improves productivity most significantly through reuse; assembling reusable parts requires a small fraction of the time it takes to custom build each part of a program.

1.5 References

Asthana, P., (1995). Jumping the technology S-curve. *IEEE Spectrum.* 32(6):49–54.

Booch, G. (1991). *Object Oriented Design with Applications.* Redwood City, CA: Benjamin/Cummings.

Booch, G. (1993). Objectifying information technology. *Object Magazine.* 3(3):26.

Booch, G. (1994). *Object Oriented Design with Applications.* Redwood City, CA: Benjamin/Cummings.

Booch, G. and Rumbaugh, J. (1995). *Unified Method for Object-Oriented Development, Documentation Set, Version 0.8.* Santa Clara, CA: Rational Software Corporation.

Brooks, F. P. (1982). *The Mythical Mon-Month.* Reading, MA: Addison-Wesley.

Chen, P. P. S. (1976). The entity-relationship model — toward a unified view of data. ACM Transactions on Database Systems. 1(1).

Coad, P. and Yourdon, E. (1990). *Object-Oriented Analysis.* Englewood Cliffs, NJ: Prentice Hall.

Coad, P. and Yourdon, E. (1990). *Object-Oriented Design.* Englewood Cliffs, NJ: Prentice Hall.

Coleman D., Arnold, P., Bodoff, S., Dollin, C., Gilchrist, H., Hayes, F., Jeremaes, P. (1994). *Object-Oriented Development, The Fusion Method.* Englewood Cliffs, NJ: Prentice Hall.

Cox, B. (1986). *Object-Oriented Programs: An Evolutionary Approach.* Reading, MA: Addison-Wesley.

Cox, B. J. (1990). There is a silver bullet. *Byte.* 14(10):214.

Executive brief. (1995). *Object Magazine.* 4(9):8.

Goldberg, A. and Rubin, K. S. (1995). *Succeeding with Objects: Decision Frameworks for Project Management.* Reading, MA: Addison-Wesley.

Henderson-Sellers, B. (1995) Methodology — Convergence is in the air. *Object Magazine.* 5(7):61.

Henry, S. and Humphrey, M. (1993). O-O vs. procedural programming languages: effectiveness in program maintenance. *Journal of Object-Oriented Programming.* 6(3):41–49.

Jacobson, I., Christerson, M., Jonsson, P., Overgaard, G. (1992). *Object-Oriented Software Engineering.* Wokingham, UK: Addison-Wesley.

Jacobson, I. (1996). A large commercial success story based on objects. *Object Magazine.* 6(3):96,94–95.

Lato, K. and Parks, T. (1995). Automatic code generation at AT&T. *Object Magazine.* 5(7):71–75.

Lenzi, M. (1994). Irresponsible journalism. *Object Magazine.* 4(3):4–6.

Love, T. (1993). *Object Lessons.* New York: SIGS Publications.

Meyer, B. (1988). *Object-oriented Software Construction.* Englewood Cliffs, NJ: Prentice Hall.

Parnas, D. L. (1972). On the criteria to be used in decomposing systems into modules. *Communication of the ACM.* 15(12): 1053–1058.

Pinson, L. J. (1994). NEXTSTEP/486, Release 3.1 & 3.2. *Journal of Object-Oriented Programming.* 5(9):73.

Rentsch, T. (1982). Object-oriented Programming. *ACM SIGPLAN Notices* 17(9): 51–57.

Rumbaugh, J., Blaha, M. Premerlani, W., Eddy, E., Lorensen, W. (1991). *Object-Oriented Modeling and Design.* Englewood Cliffs, NJ: Prentice Hall.

Wirfs-Brock, R., Wilkerson, B., Wiener, L. (1990). *Designing Object-Oriented Software.* Englewood Cliffs, NJ: Prentice Hall.

Yourdon, E. (1992) *Decline and Fall of the American Programmer.* Englewood Cliffs, NJ: Yourdon Press.

Chapter 2

Committing to Object Technology

To go OO or not to go OO, that is the question. Managers can not avoid making the decision of whether or not to adopt object technology. The fact that you are reading this book indicates your willingness to make deliberate decisions rather than to make decisions by default by taking no action.

Committing to object technology involves more than convincing oneself that the technology is "good." It also requires ensuring that the project, organization, and personnel are compatible with the technology. This chapter examines these issues along with the questions of costs, benefits, and risks.

2.1 Is Object Technology Right for Your Project?

This is probably the easiest question in the series of questions in this chapter designed to help you decide if you should switch to object technology. If you are currently using structured analysis, a data-structured–oriented method, or information engineering, then some form of object technology could be a better solution to your software development problems. With few exceptions, object technology can do everything the structured techniques and information engineering can do and do it better. For small projects it is less likely that a transition to object technology is desirable. A transition from a fourth-generation language (4GL) that is satisfying a project's needs to an object-oriented language also may not be desirable. Nor is a conversion needed when using other specialized products that are currently working well. However, whenever one finds that the current technology is causing software maintenance problems, the development process is inefficient, or a large new project is to be undertaken, then a conversion to object technology should be considered.

From a technology point of view, object technology is a clear winner over traditional techniques for most applications. However, if object technology is so great, why are there failures? This is like asking someone who is trying to sell me a rifle, "If this rifle is so accurate, why can't I hit the target?" It's not the rifle's fault that I haven't trained myself how to use it. Insufficient training of analysts, designers, programmers, and managers is the most common cause of failure on object-oriented projects. Of course, when this occurs, this may not be the reason given for the failure. A person responsible for an unsuccessful project is more likely to blame the technology than accept responsibility for the failure.

Object technology does not do anything; people do. So the real questions about object technology are matters of organizations, personnel, scheduling, and conversion costs. An improved technology should make it easier to succeed, and once people are trained this is true of object technology. However, until people are as well trained in the new technology as they were in the old, efficiency is lower and the risk of error is increased.

2.2 Is Object Technology Right for Your Organization?

As every manager knows, there is more to success than just using the right technology, and there are prerequisites to even being capable of using the right technology. A major prerequisite to the use of object technology is that the organization be at a sufficiently high level of maturity in developing software.

The Software Engineering Institute's (SEI) model of the maturity of a software development organization is typical of several such

Table 2.1 *Maturity Model Source Table*

Topic	Reference	Comments
Brief description of SEI maturity model	(Booch, 1994)	Lists of level of process maturity; minimal discussion
SEI maturity model	(Humphrey, 1989)	Original source of SEI maturity model
Extended discussion of maturity models based on SEI model	(Yourdon, 1992)	Describes SEI model and its implications (e.g., "Esoteric new technology should be avoided at lower levels")

models. It describes levels from the primitive level 1 to the rarely attained level 5. Level 1 is ad hoc development. It is typified by a comment from an individual at a name-withheld organization who said, to an auditor (of all people), "Software quality assurance—we don't need that, we do scientific work." In level 2, a process exists, but it is not a documented, integral part of the way the organization operates. Level 3 is characterized by a disciplined adherence to documented development standards. Levels 4 and 5 involve measuring and optimizing the process. Table 2.1 provides sources of further information about organizational maturity models.

If one's organization is at level 3 or above, it is more difficult to switch to object technology. It is easiest to explain by analogy why minimal maturity levels are precarious take-off points for object technology. If we make a maturity model of youth soccer, then in level 1, the comet level, (Figure 2.1) everyone runs after the ball. In level 2, the kids play positions, and in level 3 players cooperate. Introducing the execution of planned plays at level 1 or 2 is extremely difficult. Unless the players are in habit of cooperating and passing to each other, planned plays aren't likely to work. Similarly, unless an organization has developed the habits of software discipline required by object technology, they probably are not going to make effective use of its potential. Therefore it is important when adopting object technology to also expend the effort to get

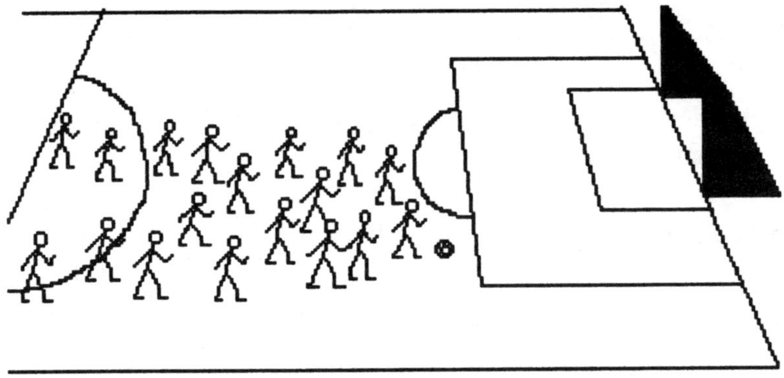

Figure 2.1 *A Level 1 Maturity Model*

the organization up to level 3. A conversion to object technology requires a certain mind set about how software development should be accomplished. For example, the practice of promising a customer fast results and planning to fix the code later is totally incompatible with the OO approach; if this method is to be the standard procedure, one should forget about adopting object technology.

2.3 Is Object Technology Right for Your Personnel?

Do your software engineers keep up with current changes in the industry? By now they should be straining at the reins for an opportunity to get into object technology. Do they look for innovative solutions to problems or just keep repeating old techniques even if they do not work very well? Who is pushing whom to change the existing system? If management is trying to force the software engineers to improve their quality assurance efforts, this is not a good sign of the readiness of the developers for technological change. If the software engineers are asking management for more time to be devoted to analysis, design, and running tests rather than more time for debugging coding, then this is a favorable indicator.

The easiest way to tell if software engineers are ready for object technology is to offer them a course in it. The ones who say they aren't interested will probably not make the transition well. Eagerness to learn is a prerequisite to the type of change that switching to object technology involves, but is not sufficient by itself. One must also have the ability to shed old ideas. John Kenneth Galbraith, the economist, wrote that the strongest of vested interests are those of the mind. To make progress in software development, we must overcome the vested interest in our minds that says, "I understand something, so anything that reduces the value of what I understand must be wrong."

The reason the conversion to object technology is difficult for many competent, experienced people is simply mental inertia. It is difficult to change one's way of thinking. This is why people with no previous software experience may internalize the object-oriented paradigm faster than the old hands. This does not imply that management should fire all their experienced software developers and replace them with people fresh out of school. Understanding the paradigm is only a small part of the entire body of software engineering knowledge. One can still teach the old dogs one new trick faster than one can teach the young dogs all the still-valuable old tricks.

2.4 Method of Transition

Some projects succeed and some fail using traditional technology. The same is true of object technology. The failures in both tend to be total; that is, the project is canceled prior to completion. The easiest way to avoid a major failure is to start off with a small pilot project and to proceed deliberately and cautiously. The ideal project for introducing object technology is less than a year in length, is important enough to place top-notch personnel on it, and has more funding than needed for a comparable non–object-oriented project so that training and other start-up costs are well covered.

The ideal project may or may not be one that will produce reusable software likely to benefit other projects later. The enterprise-wide, long-term costs and benefits need to be determined before the value of attempting to create reusable code during a pilot project can be resolved. If in doubt, simplify the pilot project by not attempting to create reusable software. Even though reuse is potentially the greatest benefit of object technology, there are many other reasons that it is worthwhile even without reuse.

If an organization has a pressing need to convert to object technology and must start on a major project, the risk of failure can be minimized if certain prerequisites are met. These prerequisites include those mentioned in the previous sections plus having a budget and schedule that accounts for the extra cost and time for training and consulting. Obtaining external consulting becomes critical if object technology is to be first applied on a major project, while with a sufficiently gradual approach the need for outside consultants might be eliminated entirely, although it would still be desirable to get as much help as possible.

Before making a firm commitment to object technology, select a methodology and understand the implications of using it. Since this book is organized by concept rather than by methodology, some of the information provided about methodologies is scattered throughout the book. Chapter 6 summarizes this information, and Chapter 7 provides assistance in choosing a methodology.

2.5 Considering the Costs

Estimating the cost of conversion to object technology is extremely difficult. The development of object-oriented metrics is in its infancy. Even estimating an enterprise-wide return on investment after completion of a project cannot be done accurately, since one cannot accurately determine the value to later projects of reusable software produced by the current project. Because of the primitive state of cost estimation in object technology, this section focuses on qualitative considerations for making cost estimates.

Provide ample funding for the pilot project; as the following sections discuss, there are many additional costs to cover compared to those for ongoing projects. Funding spent on additional training beyond what is needed for completion of the pilot project will probably provide cost savings on subsequent projects.

2.5.1 Tracking Costs

Use the pilot project to gather data for making cost estimates on subsequent projects. Document all different types of costs so one-time initial costs can be separated from costs that will recur on all projects. The cost of training, tools, and process changes will be quite high. Discount estimates of productivity made during the earlier stages of the pilot; future productivity should exceed that achieved near the end of the project. Estimating the cost of future projects is complicated by the need to determine the amount of reusable software that will be available.

2.5.2 Training Costs

The cost of training and using a methodology varies considerably according to many factors: (1) whether the methodology is proprietary, (2) how complex it is, (3) how much competition there is in providing training programs for a particular methodology, (4) the cost of CASE tools for the methodology, and (5) how much tailoring the methodology needs to fit one's application.

Once a year, The *Journal of Object-Oriented Programming* publishes a guide to object-oriented training organizations. Requesting course outlines and prices from about a dozen of these organizations should help you locate reasonably priced object-oriented training. If the organization provides several different types of training, ask each one what they consider their best course. To get the best quality in several areas such as object-oriented management training, object-oriented analysis and design, and language training, consider choosing the best course of several different organizations. Table 2.2 provides sources of information about education, training, and consulting.

2.5.3 Consulting Costs

The range of costs of consultants varies from almost unaffordable for anyone to free. It is easy to understand why some well-known consultants can charge very high rates, but what's this about free consulting? Some consultants who are experts in a particular area are willing to trade consulting in their area of expertise for experience in some area that they cannot get experience in without unusual software or hardware resources. For example, a consultant might be willing to trade time mentoring the design of project in exchange for time using an expensive ODBMS or certain hardware. The range of costs for consultants is too large to give any meaningful figures here.

2.5.4 Tool Costs

In general, the cost of CASE tools should be a small fraction of the total costs of converting to object technology. CASE tools that provide

Table 2.2 *Source Table for Education, Training, and Consulting*

Topic	Reference	Comments
Listing of Training and Consulting Companies	(see comment)	"JOOP Guide to Project Mentoring" is published each year in the March–April issue of the *Journal of Object-Oriented Programming*
The cost of object	(D'Souza, 1994)	Argues for value of expert training and education against do-it-yourself training; costs and benefits discussed
How to hire an outside consultant	(Lorenz, 1993)	Covers the why, where, what, how, when, and which of hiring a consultant
Selecting and using consultants	(Berard, 1993)	Compares cost and benefit of hiring a consultant

excellent diagramming capabilities and object dictionary services are available from $200 to $4000 per license. The tools at the low end of the range tend to be little more than good drawing tools. At the high end, they have numerous additional capabilities such as partial code generation. Consider postponing the purchase of more expensive integrated programming environment tools until after a pilot project, until a real need for them is demonstrated, until there is no doubt about the methodology to be used, and until personnel are sufficiently trained in object technology to be able to properly evaluate the tools. While the cost of a CASE tool is not a major consideration in the selection of a methodology, the existence of a CASE tool that will run on an organization's existing and future operating system is essential for large projects.

2.5.5 Invisible Costs

Besides the visible costs of training and tools, until everyone is up to speed there will be the invisible cost of slower progress. This is the most likely cost to be inadequately anticipated. Since it depends on the abilities of many individuals to learn how to think in a new way, it is also the most difficult one to estimate.

2.5.6 Process Change Costs

The impact of object technology on existing software management practices will vary greatly depending on the methodology selected and existing quality assurance (QA) procedures. Some methodologies assume a continuation of existing procedures and some can provide a complete replacement for existing procedures. Making a cost estimate requires first understanding how much effort will be required to modify the documentation governing the development, verification, validation, use, and maintenance of the software. Then one needs to compare the old and new procedures to determine whether there is a net gain or loss in the amount of time required by the new procedures.

There are several reasons why the new object-oriented procedures may reduce the amount of effort required by the QA procedures; however, some initial conversion cost is unavoidable and may be quite large compared to the other costs of a pilot project. To be able to make any reasonable cost estimates in this area, a deeper understanding of the differences between object-oriented and conventional projects is needed. This book should advance this understanding, but only an extensive examination of the interaction between the selected methodology and an existing software development environment will allow generation of reasonable estimates.

Table 2.3 shows the effect of object technology on the cost of creating software development documents. The effects and comments in the table apply to the costs once the organization has had experience with the technology; short-term costs may be different while personnel are still learning the technology. Note that the relative costs for the analysis and design specification are dependent on the how analysis and design are defined. A different definition than the one assumed might reverse the relative costs of analysis and design. The definition used for

Table 2.3 *Comparative Costs of Project Components*

Quality Assurance Element	Effect of Object Orientation on Costs	Comments
Software requirements specification	Major cost increase	The object-oriented approach places more emphasis on the requirements phase of the life cycle.
Software design specification	Cost decrease	The requirements phase of an object-oriented project provides most of the architectural design, so that the design phase is more of a refinement of work done during analysis. The savings apply to conceptual design; implementation design is not affected. (See qualifying comments in text.)
Programming	Major cost decrease	The implementation phase of an object-oriented project tends to require less coding through the use of reusable libraries and by use of inheritance. However, the biggest saving is due to reduced maintenance.
Verification and validation	Cost decrease	Verification is simplified by the improved traceability that the object-oriented approach provides and by building on previously well checked out code.

Table 2.3 *Continued*

Quality Assurance Element	Effect of Object Orientation on Costs	Comments
User documentation	Cost decrease	The object-oriented approach reduces the need to document differently for the user and for the software developer.
Reviews and audits	Cost decrease	The continuity in representation of the system through all life cycle phases simplifies review work.
Software configuration management	Little effect	The cost of software configuration management will depend more on the CASE tools selected than on the paradigm used.

the table assumes that a description of the problem structure is included as part of analysis. Chapter 4 discusses how different methodologies define analysis and design differently.

2.5.7 Cost of Reuse

The benefits of reuse must exceed the costs of reuse; otherwise, one should not attempt to create reusable software. The cost of reuse includes the cost of determining what future software needs will be, determining which parts of the software are candidates for reuse, coordinating the reuse effort, performing accounting to allocate the development costs, generalizing the software, creating and managing a reuse library, and locating the reusable software. There will undoubtedly also be the cost of some wasted effort in generalizing software for anticipated needs that do not materialize.

The number of different costs shows that investing in reuse is best approached as a long-term enterprise-wide effort, if it is to prove cost effective. Don't expect a lot of reuse on the first project because there is nothing from previous projects to reuse. A first project usually achieves a small amount of reuse because the use of inheritance precludes the need for repetitive coding. This is a form of reuse, but it is not generally what is referred to by the term *reuse*; rather, reuse usually means transferring coding, design, or analysis from one project to another. Reuse of analysis and design, not just coding, is critical because the cost of creating the specifications normally exceeds the cost of writing the code. Achieving reuse will also probably require organizational changes; Chapter 11 discusses this topic.

2.5.8 Comparing Costs and Benefits

One must weigh the costs described in this chapter against the benefits described in Chapter 1, which are even harder to quantify than the costs. Short-term costs should be calculated for the first object-oriented project, but, unless the project is very large, the immediate benefits are unlikely to justify doing the project using object technology. Both the cost and benefits of the first project will be atypical.

The cost of the initial project is of interest mainly to gain experience in cost estimation on object-oriented projects. The important estimate to make is the long-term costs and benefits for the entire organization. Estimates depend greatly on the amount of reuse that can be achieved. The pilot project will not provide much of a clue to estimating this. A better approach would be to examine a similar industry that has been involved in object technology long enough to have mature reusable libraries; however, gaining access to their cost data may be a problem. Henderson-Sellers (1993) describes the problems with using traditional estimates on an object-oriented project and gives equations for costs and return-on-investment. Kain (1994) expands upon the measurement of return on investment.

2.6 Managing Risk

Since failure is always a possibility, plan to reduce the cost of not continuing into object technology. For example, avoid significant process changes that one would not want to make to the existing process. If feasible, simply continue using the existing life-cycle model and quality assurance procedures for the pilot project if the cost of conversion is great. One can add a second pilot project to phase in these changes if the first pilot is successful.

Managers can understand most of the risks of object technology without technical training. Such risks include resistance of developers to change, unavailability of the right kind of consultants (e.g., ones who understand the application domain), the hostility of higher management toward depending on technology they do not understand, and failure to predict all the development process changes needed.

Other risks require the manager to understand the technology in some detail or to depend on the quality of the technical personnel. For example, one of the worst problems that can occur with object technology is for the analyst-designers to create bad inheritance structures. Bad inheritance structures are worse than not using inheritance at all. An inheritance structure that grossly violates the intent of the concepts of classification can make it extremely difficult and costly to change code and can greatly increase the amount of testing that is needed. Of course, good inheritance structures do exactly the opposite. Hiring an independent expert to check inheritance structures to ensure that one's analyst-designers are proficient in this area is one of the most important tasks for object-oriented consultants.

Managing risks involves understanding potential pitfalls, such as the following. A common error is hiring C++ "experts" who are really just C programmers who have been using a C++ compiler for a long time, but who have little understanding of the object-oriented paradigm. Do not assume that even a knowledgeable C++ programmer understands object-oriented analysis and design. Evaluating consultants is also quite difficult. Consider hiring an object-oriented consultant for the sole purpose of evaluating candidate consultants for the project. Choosing the wrong methodology for the project can be a major mistake; the cost of hiring a consultant to avoid this should be quite cost effective. Not allowing enough time for the transition and training time can doom all projects until such training takes place. Make sure that everyone is committed to the technology and don't just depend on a few leaders to take the blame if anything goes wrong. Domain experts frequently belong to a different organization than the one creating the product. Make sure that the project management has some control over the priorities of the domain experts. A much longer list of potential problems that may be encountered in object-oriented projects (82 of them) can be found in *Pitfalls of Object-Oriented Development* (Webster, 1995).

2.7 The Cost of Trying

For various reasons, an organization may abandon the conversion to object technology. The results of the pilot project may discourage an organization from continuing with object technology. In addition, any of the reasons that large traditional projects have a high failure rate may cause the pilot to fail or not meet expectations. If the pilot project completes but management simply considers the change too risky, the conversion may be abandoned. The organization-wide conversion may be abandoned because the key analyst-designers leave for better jobs after getting some experience in object technology.

It is unlikely that a conversion to object technology will be abandoned after a pilot project is begun if the prerequisites discussed in Chapter 1 were satisfied. However, if it is, the pilot project will still have great value to the organization. Object technology represents some of the most advanced thinking in software engineering, and many of the lessons learned from the pilot project can be used with traditional methods. Two of the most significant of these are modern life-cycle models and Jacobson's use-case concept. The strong emphasis on encapsulating the data and functionality of real-world entities can also be applied to structured analysis, design, and programming. Achieving encapsulation using this route will be more difficult than with an object-oriented approach, but it will still have significant benefits.

2.8 The Cost of the Status Quo

Adopting a new technology involves risk, but not adopting it does not guarantee a continuation of the status quo. As General Motors and other large companies have discovered, profitability can erode by steadfastly holding on to an old technology or management style. Maintaining the status quo makes results more predictable, but it does not improve the process or account for the effects of competition. If the competition is capable of succeeding using better technology, the choice may be not between guaranteed mediocrity versus uncertain excellence, but rather between extinction and survival (Figure 2.2).

2.9 Summary

The prerequisites for an organization to experience success with object technology include the following:

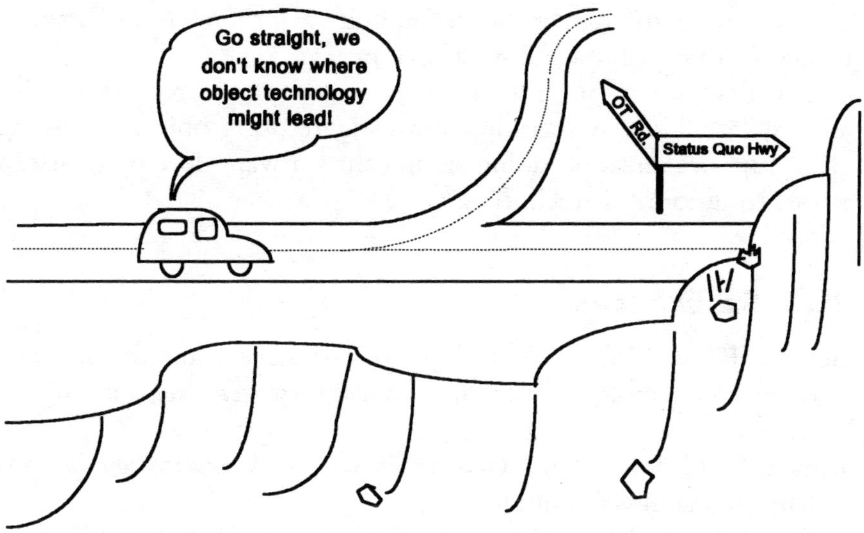

Figure 2.2 *The status quo has risks, too.*

- A relatively high degree of sophistication in applying software engineering prior to switching to object technology
- Developers who are eager to learn new techniques
- Managers who understand of the implications of the technology
- Adequate budget and schedule for training

Meeting these prerequisites does not ensure success, but it does eliminate many of the causes of failure.

While it is quite difficult to estimate the cost of one's first object-oriented project, the attempt should be made. Comparing anticipated costs with actual costs will help create more accurate estimates for subsequent projects.

Even if object technology is not pursued past the pilot project, the project experience will expose software developers to the best ideas software engineering has yet produced, and many of the ideas are transferable to non–object-oriented projects. Warning: object technology is like honey; once developers lay their hands on it, it tends to stick to them. It may be difficult to get them to work again on projects done in the traditional manner.

The decision of whether or not to use object technology is not always clear, but the decision to investigate using object technology is clear. Any organization doing significant software development cannot afford to ignore this technology.

2.10 References

Berard, E. V. (1993). Selecting and using consultants for object-oriented technology. *Journal of Object-Oriented Programming.* 6(5): 48–53.

Booch, G. (1994). *Object-Oriented design with applications.* Redwood City: Benjamin/Cummings.

D'Souza, D. F. (1994). The cost of object education. *Journal of Object-Oriented Programming.* 7(3): 62–64.

Henderson-Sellers, B. (1993). The economics of reusing library classes. *Journal of Object-Oriented Programming.* 6(4):43–50.

Humphrey, W. (1989). *Managing the software process.* Reading, MA: Addison-Wesley.

The JOOP guide to project mentoring. *Journal of Object-Oriented Programming.* 8(1): 60–74.

Kain, J. Bradford. (1994). Measuring the ROI of reuse. *Object Magazine.* 4(3):49–54.

Lorenz, M. (1993). A return on your consulting investment: How to hire an outside consultant. *Journal of Object-Oriented Programming.* 6(5): 43–47.

Yourdon, E. (1992). *Decline and fall of the American programmer.* Englewood Cliffs: Yourdon Press.

Webster, B. F. (1995). *Pitfalls of object-oriented development.* M&T Books: New York.

Chapter 3

Object-Oriented Concepts

The purpose of this chapter is to give the reader an intuitive feeling for what *object-orientation* means and to provide a formal definition without getting overly technical. First, we examine some important concepts that laid the groundwork for object technology.

It is obvious that object-oriented concepts affect the everyday decisions that software developers must make about the analysis, design, and implementation of software. What is less obvious is that the concepts also have a profound effect on management decisions. This is because the concepts affect the development process, which in turn affects not only the management of individual projects but the manner in which software should be developed for an entire enterprise. This will be shown in later chapters that discuss reuse as an enterprise-wide effort for improving productivity.

3.1 Underpinnings of Object Technology

Object technology owes its existence to the principles established by structured methods. This section describes some of the basic principles that helped pave the way for object technology.

3.1.1 Low Coupling and High Cohesion

The quality of a design can be measured in terms of the degree of coupling and cohesion of the programming units. These affect the degree of modularization of the program. *Coupling* refers to the amount of information shared between two software components and the nature of the sharing mechanism. *Cohesion* is a measure of the degree to which a component has one specific purpose, that is, the degree to which the tasks within the component are functionally related. *Modularization* is the separation of components so that changes to one component have minimal impact on other components.

The desirability of achieving low coupling between program entities is a well-established principle of software engineering. Low coupling makes it easier to understand individual units of code because the needed information is localized. This also means that one can change the coding with less likelihood of creating errors in distance coding.

Achieving high cohesion within a program entity is another well-established principle of software engineering. It is as fundamental as the idea of sorting nails and screws and paper clips into different bins. Assuring that a programming unit performs only functions related to a common task makes it much easier to locate functionality within a program. It easier to understand programming that deals with a single topic rather than one that performs several unrelated functions. Without applying this principle, a module could have low coupling with other modules, but it could contain a hodgepodge of unrelated parts.

Low coupling and high cohesion work together to facilitate modularization. The word *module* is a general term that refers to a subroutine, procedure, object, or group of related programming units. The principle of minimizing module coupling applies to all software development, regardless of whether a structured or object-oriented approach is used.

The traditional separation of data and functionality has undermined adherence to these principles. The data and operations in a program module need to be closely related to each other. The union of data and function provided by objects adds meaning to data and makes it much simpler to turn the principles of low coupling and high cohesion from sought-after goals that are seldom achieved into common practice.

Reducing coupling has been a goal of software engineers for decades, but it has been difficult to achieve because of lack of language support. The object-oriented paradigm allows designing for reduced coupling. Object-oriented languages make the implementation of reduced coupling much easier by allowing the encapsulation of data and operations related to the data.

We can see the importance of linking data and functionality in everyday life. A person from a different culture than ours might think it strange for a man to use stiff bristles and a buzzing object (data) in a daily ritual without understanding the associated functionality (cleaning one's teeth and shaving). Similarly in software, data lacks meaning without knowing the functions that are intended to be applied to it.

The object-oriented paradigm has made strong cohesion a natural outcome of the design process. This is because the real-world objects that the object-oriented approach focuses on modeling are usually inherently cohesive (except for poorly designed physical systems and Rube Goldberg machines).

3.1.2 Entity Relationship Model

The entity relationship model is a key concept in the transition from the structured to the object-oriented approach. It models real-world entities, which made it easier for analysts and users to communicate about the problem, but it still maintains the separate representation of functionality and data.

Since most object-oriented methodologies use some form of the entity relationship (ER) model, it is important to understand ER diagrams. Figure 3.1 provides an example in which a relationship connects two entities. It is not a big step from these diagrams to assigning both attributes and methods to objects, but when Chen proposed his diagrams in 1976, object-oriented programming languages were still years away from becoming part of the software culture.

Figure 3.1 *Classic entity relationship diagram*

3.2 An Intuitive Approach to Understanding Object Orientation

Part of understanding object technology is understanding the concepts discussed in the last part of this chapter; however, truly understanding object technology involves thinking in terms of objects in addition to thinking in terms of the steps of a process. The object-oriented paradigm does not replace the old thinking skills, such as creating sequential procedures; it simply puts them in their place and adds a new way of thinking. Within an object-oriented model, procedural thinking belongs in the details; the new way of thinking in terms of objects instead of steps should dominate the conceptual representation of the model.

3.2.1 What's an Object?

Definitions of something as basic as the idea of an object are almost futile. A twentieth-century philosopher, when asked for a definition of his specialty, responded that if you've got to ask, you'll never know. The specialty in question was jazz and speaker was Louis Satchmo Armstrong.

Rumbaugh et al. (1991) define an object as "a concept, abstraction, or thing with crisp boundaries and meaning for the problem at hand." This tells us that an object may be tangible or intangible, but the problem is that any definition of object must use words that are less fundamental than the idea of an "object." With such a fundamental concept as an object, perhaps the best way to explain it is to point out numerous examples.

The most obvious objects are those that correspond to real-world objects. But as Rumbaugh's definition indicates, objects may also be concepts or abstractions. A refrigerator is an object and so is the cooling system of a refrigerator. A drawing is an object and so are a grid, a vanishing point, and a projection. An air traffic control system is an object and so are its components like radar, computers, and communication equipment. A matrix is an object, as are vectors, the inverse of a matrix, and the identity matrix. An economic theory, an accounting system, and a savings account are objects. As you can see, objects do not have to be concrete. An object can be something abstract or intangible that is purely a product of the human mind.

Understanding what is not an object can help one understand what an object is. Members of the set of nonobjects include nonobjectvalued properties like color, texture, and order, which have values like red, soft, and first. Nonobjects also include behaviors (which are components of objects) like move, get, and accelerate.

One's view of an object is different depending on whether one is dealing with analysis and design or with implementation. The explanation in this section mainly describes the former view of an object. The implementation view of an object is simpler because it is expressed in more concrete terms; namely, it is an area of computer memory that represents an analysis and design object.

3.2.2 Message-Passing Philosophy

Messages are the main way we communicate in the object-oriented paradigm. As an approximation to the idea of a message, one can think of it as being a subroutine or procedure call. A message has a name, may have arguments, may return a value to the sender of the message, and has a destination. The purpose of a message is to provide communication between objects by one object requesting another to perform an operation, which is called *invoking a method*.

How is a message any different from a subroutine call? Using messages for communication represents a significant difference in philosophy compared to using its traditional counterparts. A message normally has few arguments and usually does not allow them to change in value; rather, it receives a single object back as a returned value from the recipient of the message. A message does not tell the receiving object how to do something; rather, it expects the receiving object to have the intelligence to perform its intended function.

The philosophy behind a message is similar to the attitude of a busy supervisor who believes in delegating responsibility. It is, "Just do the job and don't bother me about how; come back when you have the answer."Relying on individual responsibility is an important trend in managing employees using the philosophy of empowerment because it's more efficient. It is also an efficient way to organize software.

While the message-passing philosophy is an essential part of the object-oriented paradigm, it is not the starting point for describing communication between objects. This would be much too fine a level of detail, so interobject communication is first described in terms of relationships similar to those of the entity-relationship diagram (Figure 3.1). Chapter 5 discusses the modeling of relationships.

3.2.3 Anthropomorphism

Anthropomorphism is not part of the definition of what object orientation means, but it is important to understand that object-oriented developers think in terms of objects exhibiting anthropomorphic characteristics. *Anthropomorphism* literally means in the form of a human being; it is the interpretation of what is not human in human terms. Object-oriented developers talk about a car finding a location and a street light deciding to come on because it is dark. This may not seem unusual, since we know there is the intelligence of person behind the car and a sensing device in the street light.

However, the object-oriented approach extends this way of thinking to all objects as having operations as if the objects themselves were controlling the operations with human-like intelligence. For example, a hurdle has a "fall over" operation that it executes when its center of gravity has been sufficiently displaced. A roof has a "collapse" operation when the load on it exceeds a certain limit. Developers talk as if the hurdle knows what it should do when someone bumps into it. A software program would send a message to a roof telling it that snow is falling continuously at the rate of one centimeter per minute, and they would expect the roof to know enough to collapse when it decides it should.

Just as putting oneself into the other person's shoes is a good way to gain an appreciation of why someone behaves the way they do, the anthropomorphic way of thinking about objects is a very effective way of realizing what functionality objects should have.

3.2.4 Polymorphism

Polymorphism is a critical element in the object-oriented approach. Literally, it means having many forms. "Many forms" refers to having many ways of responding to the same message—each object receives the message but responds to it differently.

An example of polymorphism occurs during a brown-out. With the object-oriented approach, every machine in a plant will receive the message that the voltage to it has fallen. Each machine will react in its own way: some machines will stop immediately, some types of electrical motors will burn out, heaters will still work but will put out less heat. In other words, the type of machine determines how an object responds to the message; the message does not provide instructions about *how* to respond.

The traditional approach to modeling these events would be for some high-level program unit to receive the brown-out message, look at the type of each machine in the plant, and determine which machines stop, which burn out, and which reduce their output. The procedural paradigm tends to put the intelligence of the system at a higher level in the program than does the object-oriented paradigm. With the object-oriented approach, the intelligence of the system resides in the objects themselves, not in the requester of the behavior. This allows a client object to tell a set of supplier objects what to do without worrying about how they do it.

Polymorphism is closely related to the idea of inheritance, which is discussed in Chapter 5.

3.3 Technically Speaking

While the ideas of using objects and communicating with messages are essential aspects of what it means to be object oriented, these ideas are also characteristics of object-based computing. There is only one concept that is new to object-oriented computing that was not present in the technology from which it evolved. This is the idea that generalization or specialization hierarchies can be implemented using inheritance and that polymorphism may be applied within these hierarchies. However, to form a complete definition of *object orientation* one needs to include all the earlier ideas upon which it depends. The following sections enumerate and describe these concepts.

3.3.1 A Simple Acronym

Technically, we can define *object orientation* as including the ideas of polymorphism, encapsulation, and abstraction. The easy to remember acronym for this is PEA. (Alternatively, one can use the acronym PIE for polymorphism, inheritance, and encapsulation.) For the set of ideas represented by PEA to illustrate the idea of being object oriented, additional ideas associated with these three must be included. Closely related to the idea of polymorphism are the ideas of inheritance and dynamic binding that allow its implementation. Encapsulation can be considered the implementation of the idea of information hiding, which is accomplished by use of objects. Abstractions are represented by use of classes of objects that are products of the process of classification. All nine of these concepts are discussed in more detail below, as are three other candidates that are sometimes associated with object-oriented computing: concurrency, persistence, and garbage collection.

3.3.2 Encapsulation, Information Hiding, and Objects

Encapsulation separates the aspects of a program unit that need to be externally visible from the aspects of the program that should be internal and not accessible externally. Information hiding and encapsulation are frequently considered to be the same concept, and no distinction will be made between the two in this book. Objects are the entities used to implement the concept of encapsulation.

3.3.2.1 Information Hiding (Encapsulation)

Information hiding establishes a visible interface that defines what an object does and what data structure, if any, is externally visible. It also consists of an invisible implementation that describes the program's internal behavior and data structure. The separation of the interface from the implementation is essential to the value of information hiding. It allows the implementation to be changed without affecting the users of the interface. Information hiding is most effective when it hides the data structure and makes only the behavior part of the interface.

It may seem a strange idea at first to want to hide information; shouldn't most data be open and visible? Actually, information hiding is not so much hiding information as controlling its visibility and access. We are not talking only about sensitive data that needs protected; we are talking about all data. Data does not need to be confidential to be worth protecting in a program; failure to protect data from inadvertent change or destruction is necessary to prevent the software from failing.

To understand why encapsulation is desirable and how objects assist in achieving encapsulation, we need to go beyond the definition of objects as being concepts or things to looking at the characteristics of an object. Booch (1994) provides a useful definition for this purpose: "An object has state, behavior, and identity; the structure and behavior of similar objects are defined in their common class. . . ."

The values of an object's attributes determine its state. For example, attributes such as the position of the on/off switch, the thermostat control setting, the heater coil resistance, and the fan speed determine the state of a heater. The behavior of the heater can be "idle" or "fan blowing air." A unique serial number may identify the fan.

Objects allow us to easily accomplish encapsulation and thus hide attributes, protecting the state of the object from unanticipated or unauthorized changes, while making specific behaviors available to other objects. For example, if the heater coil resistance is determined at the factory and cannot be changed, one would like to hide this attribute from other objects. If another object were able to change an attribute that the heater object depends upon being a constant, the integrity of the heater object would be violated.

The use of encapsulation with the object-oriented paradigm has been compared to a hard-boiled egg in that there is a distinct visible part on the outside and a hidden part on the inside. In contrast, functional decomposition leads to a program more like a scrambled egg, in which the interface cannot be separated from what is happening internally. The lack of a separate external interface makes it very dangerous to change anything in a object because any other object might be depending on the changed item.

Exactly what is it what we want to hide? We want to hide the details of the object that are not essential to its externally available functionality. In particular, we want to hide its data structure and the implementation of its methods. This allows us to freely change the inner structure and workings of the object (consistent with the declared interface) without having an impact upon any users of the object.

The definition of encapsulation does not make a distinction between how we access properties and behaviors. However, it is generally accepted that while some behaviors should be externally available and some hidden, all nonconstant properties should be hidden.

What is the effect of accessing the properties of an object directly rather than through a behavior? If we let other objects directly manipulate an object's properties, we can lose control of the integrity of the state of the object.

For example, suppose we have a property of social security number for a bank account. Applying encapsulation we would have methods *getSocSec()* and *setSocSec()*. If we do not apply encapsulation and dispense with these methods, any other object can directly get and set the social security number. This seems simpler and preferable at first glance. However, there is nothing to stop someone from entering a 15-digit social security number that might cause unpredictable adverse effects on the object that tries to use it. With encapsulation, we can add constraints to the *setSocSec()* method to ensure that the social security number is in range and in the proper format. Encapsulation allows us to know precisely what can be done to the object.

Without encapsulation, the integrity of the object is in constant danger of being violated. It would be like a person walking around with his bank account number and personal identification number printed on his shirt. It is just a matter of time before he "loses his shirt."

3.3.2.2 Features of an Object

Booch's definition of an object focuses on the nature of an object, which is that an object has a state, behavior, and an identity. Examination of the three characteristics of an object in his definition will help us further understand what objects are.

3.3.2.3 Identity

Every object can be distinguished from every other object; that is, every object has a unique identity. The sun is an object. The sun is not defined by its properties such as being made mostly of hydrogen and helium and being 93 million miles from the earth. It has an abstract identity that will survive changes in its properties. It will still be the sun when it becomes a red giant and has expanded beyond the earth's current orbit. It will still be the sun when it becomes a burned-out cinder. Software objects possess the same manner of constancy of identity that physical objects have.

The fact that an object has a unique identity has a very practical advantage. It means that it can be directly accessed by address rather than having to search through a column of values to locate it, as is typical of relational databases. This provides a great advantage in the efficiency of the program, but it also requires more knowledge in advance of how various objects interact.

3.3.2.4 State

A physical object has a state, such as being off or on, standing or moving, awake or asleep, black or white, having two legs or four, having a current of three amperes, having a temperature of 99°F, etc. Similarly, a software object has a corresponding state that is defined by all of its properties and the values of its properties. For example, if a tea kettle is abstracted as a thing with a color and a temperature, then the state of the tea kettle consists of the color property, its value, say black, and its temperature and the value of its temperature, say, 100° C.

To be useful, the objects in the program must be able to change their state to represent changes in the physical state of the object being modeled. While one can design software to change the state of an object by directly modifying the data values of the object's properties, it is not advisable. Permitting the state of an object to change only by defining a behavior that changes the state provides a needed layer of protection of the data—one can assure the data can be changed only in meaningful ways, for example.

3.3.2.5 Behavior

Behaviors associated with objects include the creation of the object, querying the state of an object, changing the state of an object, destroying the object, and generating an event. Behavior is what one observes about the effects of these types of activities. While some physical objects are of interest mainly for observation of their state, many objects would not be of much use if they could not change their states. For example, a car that could not change its state from standing to moving would not be of much use. If the software model of a car could not change its state, it would not be of much use, either. We couldn't even transport our nonfunctional vehicle from our driveway to the auto salvage yard because that would entail changing the location property of the car. The ability of most objects to change their states is critical to their utility.

3.3.3 Abstraction, Classification, and Classes

Classification is a tool that helps us create more useful abstractions. Classification is implemented using classes.

3.3.3.1 Abstraction

The idea of abstraction is fundamental to all thinking, not just object-oriented thinking. Abstraction is the recognition of the commonalty among a set of entities. An abstraction focuses on the characteristics that are most significant and ignores nonessential details.

I remember when my oldest son first understood the idea of abstraction. We taught him that a tractor was a machine and a potato harvester was a machine. From then on, he would point out hay bailers, backhoes, and all manner of farm machinery and gleefully shout " 'chine!" Even at the age of two, it was a tremendous thrill for him to be able to apply the idea of abstraction.

In software development we create abstractions to satisfy our modeling needs. What is significant versus what is nonessential in defining the abstraction depends on the creator and purpose of the abstraction. Grady Booch gives a great example of this idea in his book with a cartoon that depicts the view of a cat by an elderly lady and by a veterinarian. The owner thinks of the cat as a purring ball of fur, and the vet thinks of it as a collection of bones and organs. Both views are valid abstractions depending on the purpose of the model. Both deal with what is essential to the viewer and ignore what is not of interest. If the perspective of the viewer did not determine the abstraction, we might define the difference between a cat and a dog in terms of DNA.

3.3.3.2 Classification

Classification is a software concept by which we create usable abstractions. The broad meaning of *classification* is any kind of grouping of similar things into sets or hierarchies. The classification process is an inherent part of the object-oriented approach, and it is a natural way for people and even animals to think. The deer in the woods see you, classify you as having two legs and therefore dangerous, and runs off. (Of course, that is what deer used to do. Now, if you try scare them out of your garden they just look at you as if to say, "You can't mean me; I know these strawberry plants were put here for me eat.")

Classification is the process of grouping similar things into categories called *types*. Classification is used in everyday life and in software analysis to improve our comprehension of abstractions. For example, suppose I tell you I want you show you my new car. You immediately start thinking about the abstraction "car" based on its classification. Based on this single word, you expect to see tires, headlights, an engine, and so on. A classification can convey a huge amount of information very simply, which is why it is so important.

We use the properties and behavior of objects to determine their classification. For example, if we see a blue animal, a green animal, and a red animal that all have three legs and are doing midair somersaults, we would create a classification based on the properties and behavior of all three animals. Of course, we wouldn't dare tell anyone about it, or they would probably give us a certain medical classification.

A dictionary definition of classification refers to the systematic arrangement of items into categories. Therefore, it is reasonable to extend the meaning of classification, as Coad and Yourdon do, to include arranging the groups, called types, into hierarchies that represent generalizations and specializations of other types. With this definition, *classification* refers not only to the relationship between an object and a type but to the relationship between types and subtypes. Anyone who has studied biology is quite familiar with this manner of classification. The elaborate decomposition of the animal kingdom all the way down to genus and species may be an extreme case of classification, but it is an extremely useful example. Classification of types of objects in software analysis is also a powerful tool in understanding an application.

Abstraction is needed because it is not necessarily easy to understand an object by just looking at a list of its characteristics independent of a classification hierarchy. For example, if I told you all of the characteristics of a lurkitt and you had never heard of one, you might have a hard time getting the picture unless I use classification. If I told you that it has two legs, eats meat, has excellent eyesight, is black in color, is good at grasping things, etc., I could be describing a human being or numerous other possibilities, so far. However, if I tell you it is an animal, a bird, and a member of the hawk family, then you get the picture quite quickly. (The lurkitt is fictitious, I didn't want to pick an animal anyone already knew about.)

The software meaning of classification includes grouping objects that have similar attributes and behavior together into types, creating generalization/specialization hierarchies, and creating aggregation hierarchies. Chapter 5 describes these concepts.

3.3.3.3 Classes

Note that I referred to grouping objects into types rather than classes. The words *type* and *class* have slightly different meanings. *Type* is a word used more often in analysis, and *class* is used more often during design and implementation. However, for most purposes, the difference between the two is minor, and many authors use the word *class* exclusively. I will also use *class* in preference to *type* when the difference is not important. For those interested in the technical difference, note that classifying objects by type allows a compiler to check for consistency in the use of typed variables. Classes are language constructs that implement types.

A class must meet many responsibilities to allow it to implement a type. It must provide the ability to create objects based on the template that the class provides. It must provide each object with attributes that can be assigned values that determine the state of the objects. It must provide operations that change the values of its attributes and thus allow the object to change its state. It must enforce any constraints needed to assure the integrity of its objects. For example, it could assure that a space ship object does not accept a command to open the inner airlock door if the value of the outer airlock door attribute is open. It must provide the information needed to link objects with other objects so that they can send or receive messages. It must have the ability to destroy the objects it creates. Object-oriented languages automatically provide the ability to create classes with these capabilities.

While most explanations of how object technology helps reuse focus on the ability to reuse classes by extending their capabilities using inheritance, the class by itself is an important vehicle of reuse. Each class created during compilation is reused during execution to produce an unlimited number of objects with possibly different initial states. A class is an object factory and certainly qualifies as a reusable tool.

3.3.4 Polymorphism, Inheritance, and Dynamic Binding

The concept of object orientation is characterized by the difference between thinking in terms of procedures versus thinking in terms of objects. However, from a more technical viewpoint, polymorphism is the main innovative concept of object technology and the concept that most distinguishes it from other paradigms.

As an example, polymorphism occurs in the conducting of an orchestra. Each player receives the same message from the conductor, most importantly the speed at which to play, but each player responds in his or her own way. Polymorphism improves the extensibility of the software by allowing the same message to invoke different responses from different classes that receive the message.

Polymorphism works within a generalization/specialization hierarchy, in which one type is a kind of another type. This term will normally be shortened to either *specialization hierarchy* or *generalization hierarchy*. In our orchestra example, the message conveyed by the baton to the musical instrument is understood by each violin object (through the members of the orchestra). The type violin is a specialization of the type musical instrument. Outside this hierarchy, the message is not recognized; the curtains do not open and shut in response to the baton. The idea of a specialization hierarchy is implemented in source code by the inheritance capability that is a feature unique to object-oriented languages.

Dynamic binding makes polymorphism useful by allowing the decision of which operation to use to be made at execution time instead of compile time. In our orchestra example, without dynamic binding, the members of the orchestra would have to decide how they will respond to every motion of the baton before starting to play. With dynamic binding, the conductor could change her interpretation, and the orchestra would respond to her revised movements.

3.3.5 Concurrency, Persistence, and Garbage Collection

A few methodologists add some additional characteristics to their definition of what object orientation means. These include concurrency, persistence, and garbage collection.

Concurrency refers to two or more tasks occurring simultaneously. If this were a requirement for object orientation, then many object-oriented languages would not be object oriented. *Persistence* refers to objects being able to be stored from one execution of the program to the next. Again, object-oriented languages do not generally handle this; object-oriented database management systems provide this extension to the languages. Garbage collection is a characteristic of some object-oriented languages like Eiffel, Smalltalk, and Java, but it is not built into the C++ language. While it is an extremely useful capability, there is no obvious reason why it should be part of the definition of object orientation.

3.4 Example

To accomplish information hiding, it is important to consider data and the operations applied to the data as a unit rather than two different entities. To explain what it means to encapsulate data structure and operations on the data, consider the following example, which compares the nature of the programming for moving a couple of robots.

Suppose a programmer has two robots named C3PO and R2D2, and is required to write a program to move the two robots from point A to point B. Suppose there is a ditch that is a foot across and a yard wide between the robots and their destination. A procedural program would approach the problem as outlined in Figure 3.2.

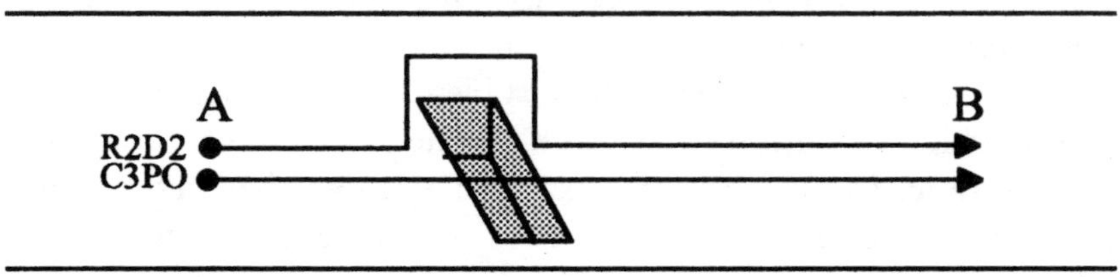

Figure 3.2 *Robots' task*

The central program reads its data about C3PO and determines that the robot's mechanics allow it to step across a foot-wide gap. The main program tells C3PO to go to the target by stepping across the hole and then continuing on to the target. The central program reads its data about R2D2 and determines the robot's mechanics do not allow it to step across a foot-wide gap. The main program tells R2D2 to go to the target by maneuvering around the obstacle with a series of four turns (see Figure 3.2). Notice that the central program processes the data that describes the robots and makes decisions about them. Consider how complicated the main program would be if it were to control 100 robots.

An object-oriented program approaches the problem in a different manner. The central program instructs C3PO to move to the target. C3PO checks its data and determines that it can step across the gap and does so as it proceeds to the target. The central program instructs R2D2 to move to the target. R2D2 checks its data and determines that it cannot step across the gap, so it maneuvers around the obstacle with four turns and continues on to the target.

Notice that in the procedural program, the robot does not contain operations that represent the behavior of robots. The robots are not objects; instead, they are just places where data about robots is stored. In the object-oriented program, the robots are objects. That is, the information they contain within the programming unit corresponds to the information that would be in a real-world robot along with the capability of implementing its own behaviors. The procedural program does not encapsulate the movement behavior with the capability data; the object-oriented program does encapsulate them.

Behaviors in an object are expressed through a set of methods that operate on an object's properties. R2D2 expresses behavior when it moves. For the robot to turn left when it encounters the obstacle, a method must operate on its "direction" property. For example, a method would have to change the direction property from "east" to "north." For each turn necessary to avoid the obstacle, a method would need to change the direction property for the robot to reach its destination.

Centralization versus Decentralization

The encapsulation example also illustrates the difference between the centralized and the decentralized approaches to program control. The centralized structure is characteristic of the procedural approach which tends to structure the code octopus-like with central control directing many activities. The object-oriented approach structures the code in a tree structure with the base of the tree controlling only the major branches and those branches controlling other branches. The centralized structure puts the intelligence of the program at a high level and makes use of "dumb" objects. It is typical of the structures resulting from functional decomposition. The decentralized model requires a more even distribution of intelligence among the types.

While the decentralized structure is normally the best approach, it is simply because most systems work that way. The system should have a structure that reflects the nature of the objects involved. A centralized structure is appropriate in some situations. For example, if you are modeling the decision-making process in a company in which the president insists on making all decisions himself, it will be appropriate. However, most systems are more appropriately modeled using delegation (which is also a more appropriate way to run an organization).

The decentralized method is consistent with many object-oriented experts' advice to distribute the intelligence of the system relatively evenly instead of centralizing it. This provides information hiding and allows manipulation of significant entities instead of details. It is usually easier to change the order of things in the decentralized case. Each type can keep track of the order of its own processes easily because it knows the details of its own nature. A master controller would have to know or find out the details of all of the lower-level types to know how to change the order.

Let's look at the centralization issue one more way. You are the master controller for your computer. Using the decentralized method, you can start your computer, open your word processor, get a document, open your accounting program, record your phone bill, switch back to your word processor, and print your document. Imagine what would be involved if you had to do all the work that the various tools are doing for you by controlling each step of the process, because each of the steps you took involves many steps within each process. The problem with the centralized structure is that the controlling type has to know a lot about the controlled types, necessitating high coupling between them.

3.5 Terminology

Anyone reading this book undoubtedly wishes to be able to discuss object technology intelligently. However, the lack of standard terminology makes it difficult for anyone to sound intelligent to someone else who is interpreting object-oriented terms differently. Thus it is important to understand the common meanings and frequently used alternative meanings of the most confusing object-oriented terms: type, class, object, relationship, and association.

The following establishes the most important definitions used in this book and, for some words, describes a common alternative definition. Appendix A extends this discussion to a greater depth and more terms.

A *type* is a set of logically similar properties and behaviors that a compiler can use to enforce some consistency in usage. For example, a programming language might have a type integer and a type character, and the compiler could ensure that an integer is not added to a character. In object-oriented computing, not only do built-in types exist, but we may create arbitrarily complex types that model real-world or conceptual entities. For example, we could create types like electric drill, ground transportation system, ball bearing, and matrix. The compiler could prevent us from adding a drill to matrix, but could allow us to change the size and position of a drill bit object. A type is also frequently referred to as a "class." As indicated in the following definition of class, the meanings are actually different, but the difference is not important for the purposes of this book.

A *class* is a software design and coding counterpart to a type; that is, it implements a type. In our coding we would define a class like *electricDrill.*

An *instance* of a type is one particular item of the group of items represented by the type. For example, *drill_for_part_ax-13_on_assem-*

bly_line_3 might be an instance of the electrical drill type.

An *object* is the same as an instance. Unfortunately, the most overused word in object technology is the word *object*, which sometimes is used to mean an instance of a type, sometimes a type, and sometimes either a type or an instance. If you really want to be clear, particularly if you are talking to someone who uses a different methodology, use the term *instance* or *object instance* instead of *object*. Like many authors, I will sometimes use the word *object* to mean either instance or type [illegible] eaking in general terms where either word applies.

A *relationshi* [illegible] nection between types or classes, where the [illegible] is not specified. In the Unified Met [illegible] lization and association. An *associati* [illegible] p that indicates the relationship is [illegible] *gation* is a tightly coupled form of a [illegible] class are composite parts of those of [illegible]

A *li* [illegible] ion between two objects (as oppos [illegible]

Th [illegible] be aggregate parts of an object. A li [illegible] r character) further describes the nat [illegible]

[illegible]

The b [illegible] psulated objects include reduced coupling, localiz [illegible] tion.

Reduced Coupling

By creating objects using encapsulation, the coupling between various parts of a program may be reduced. Reducing coupling makes it more feasible to reuse coding and to reduce program maintenance. Encapsulation reduces coupling by limiting the number of functions and characteristics that are allowed to communicate externally.

Localization

Encapsulation allows localization of machine and operating system dependencies, so that if one does have to change an implementation when porting, at least the change will be local. Since all of the hidden parts of an encapsulated object are localized, any error in them is much easier to locate. Thus, it localizes errors, making debugging easier and enhancing reliability.

Protection

Encapsulation has the effect of creating an abstraction of a complex entity. By hiding the details, it allows one to concentrate on the important aspects of the entity that are represented in the visible interface with external entities. In addition to protecting the developer from complexity, it also protects the state of objects from corruption by the user and from some types of programming errors. Because functions are used to modify the state of objects instead of directly modifying the object's properties, the functions can also contain checking procedures to further ensure state integrity.

3.7 Summary

Many of the principles of software development are decades old, including the concepts of reducing coupling and increasing cohesion among software modules. Reducing coupling makes it more feasible to reuse coding and to reduce program maintenance. High cohesion within a program unit makes it easier to understand and manage the functionality of the software. It used to be quite difficult to achieve the concepts in practice. What is new is that object technology makes it easier to implement these concepts.

The ideas of abstraction, encapsulation, and classification are interrelated. Classification of objects form a basis for creating abstractions. Abstractions exhibit information hiding in that they have a public interface consisting of those behaviors and properties that objects of other types may access. They have a private interface consisting of those behaviors and properties that objects of other types may not access.

The use of these concepts is now supported by object-oriented theory and languages. The support of inheritance and polymorphism in languages allows a more natural modeling of real-world objects. Thus the new ways of thinking about software development and new language capabilities have made it possible to implement the basic principles in a more rigorous manner and with less effort than in the past.

However, simply explaining the individual object-oriented concepts in this chapter fails to describe the combined effect of applying the new concepts plus the old ones to the total development task. For example, by adding the new object-oriented concepts to the old idea of using scenarios (which is discussed later), we now have a better way to solve the following long-standing problem.

All too often in software development projects, the customer presents the development group with a statement of the problem that needs to be solved, and this is the last thing he understands about anything that happens until he sees output from the program. Software developers immediately translate the problem statement into an esoteric representation of how a computer will understand and solve it. Since the form of the development documentation is comprehensible only to the initiated, the customer can only hope that the product that is being produced is the product that he really wants.

The key to solving communications problems between the customer and the developers lies in keeping the representation of the problem and its solution in the domain that is familiar to the customer. Object-oriented abstraction and classification contribute to the solution by describing the problem in terms of objects that the customer can relate to and that the analyst, designer, and programmer can model and implement. The real-world abstraction and the software abstraction can now be described in the same manner. This facilitates customer-developer communications and helps avoid the creation of products that do not fulfill the customer's requirements.

In the remainder of the book we will see ways in which these object-oriented concepts combine to solve other long-standing software development problems. In addition to everyday modeling problems, these include problems with the execution time of database operations and the ability to distribute certain types of information over networks.

3.8 References

Booch, G. (1994). *Object-Oriented Design with Applications.* Redwood City, CA: Benjamin/Cummings.

Rumbaugh, J., Blaha, M. Premerlani, W., Eddy, E., Lorensen, W. (1991). *Object-Oriented Modeling and Design.* Englewood Cliffs, NJ: Prentice Hall.

Chapter 4

The Development Process

The adoption of an object-oriented methodology can have either a profound or moderate impact on an existing software development process. Before selecting a methodology, one needs to understand this impact. If the existing process is deficient, a transition to a new process is desirable. If the existing process is already adequate, one must determine whether changes to the existing process are necessary.

This chapter discusses traditional life-cycle models and describes the impact of the object-oriented paradigm on life-cycle modeling, particularly with respect to analysis and design. A prototype life-cycle model is presented to describe current modeling trends and to allow for comparison of methodology life cycles. The decision on the type of life-cycle model to be used can have a significant impact on the efficiency of the development process.

4.1 The Traditional Software Life-cycle

A software life-cycle consists of a series of steps or phases used to organize a development effort and produce a software product. A representation of a software life-cycle is called a *life-cycle model.* The phases of the software life cycle typically include planning, analysis, design, implementation, testing, maintenance, and enhancement. We will first look at two general life-cycle models, the waterfall model and the spiral model, before examining more methodology-specific models.

4.1.1 The Phases of the Traditional Life-cycle

Each phase of the traditional software development process has an input and output. In the planning phase, the customer, project management, domain experts, analysts, and various software specialists input their ideas. The output of the planning phase includes a problem statement, budget, training schedule, procurement plan, work breakdown schedules, a quality assurance plan, and associated documents such as a software configuration management plan. Depending on the particular software standards used, such as ANSI/IEEE (Software Engineering Standards, 1993), DOD-STD-2167A (1988), or "homegrown," the documents from the planning stage may have different names than those mentioned here.

The problem statement provides the input to the analysis phase. It should be refined by the customer, domain experts, and analyst into something that we could reasonably refer to as a statement of requirements. The output of the analysis phase is the requirements specification. This specification is a formalization of the statement of requirements that completely and unambiguously describes the problem. The requirements specification feeds the design phase that outputs the architecture, also known as the design specification. This specification formally describes a structure and method for solving the problem. The design specification provides input to the implementation phase and produces source code in the programming phase.

The testing phase includes both verification (making sure the design and coding were done correctly) and validation (making sure that the requirements were actually satisfied). Testing is not a phase that follows completion of the implementation; rather, the verification part of testing is an ongoing process during analysis, design, and implementation. As a common example of these terms, consider baking a cake. Verification can be accomplished by having another person remeasure the ingredients and checking the procedure against the recipe; validation to assure the requirement that it meets culinary standards can be accomplished by having people taste the cake. Maintenance includes both error correction (very difficult with a cake) and enhancement, which is extension of the original requirements. Enhancement requires returning to the analysis phase to update the requirements specification. Error correction may also require reverting to the analysis phase if the error was in the requirements rather than the implementation.

The foregoing provides a brief background only. The intent of this book is to point out changes to the traditional approach entailed by object technology, not to duplicate what can be found in various texts and standards documents. Fortunately, most of what applies to the management of traditional software development applies equally well when applying object technology. However, object technology definitely requires a few important changes to how management needs to conduct a software development effort. Chapter 11 discusses these issues.

4.1.2 The Waterfall Model

When computer codes were small and life was simple, programmers used the code-and-fix method of development. When it became apparent that even for moderate-sized programs the code-and-fix method resulted in poorly planned code structures that made additional modifications and fixes difficult, life-cycle models were developed to control the process.

The waterfall model was developed to provide a well-defined sequence of steps in the development process. Depending on the particular version of the waterfall model used, either no feedback or minimal feedback to the previous step was allowed. The original Department of Defense (DOD) standard that dictated the use of the waterfall model, DOD-STD-2167, was particularly rigid by allowing no feedback. Even for versions allowing some feedback, the feedback from one step to the previous was limited. Each phase was to be completed, reviewed, and signed off on before the next phase could begin. This approach very effectively attacked the "hacking" mentality of the code-and-fix approach.

However, rigid adherence to the waterfall method worked poorly in many situations, particularly when it was difficult to determine the requirements without experimenting with the product. Such a situation is typified by the comment of a Supreme Court justice who indicated that he couldn't define pornography but he knew it when he saw it. If you wish to create a graphical user interface for a customer, the customer is unlikely to be able to tell you just what he wants, but after you finish he will be able to tell you whether or not he likes it. In this situation, presenting the customer with a series of prototypes is an effective means of assuring his satisfaction. The waterfall model assumes that one can create a specification document that precisely defines the product in advance and is, therefore, not compatible with prototyping.

A fundamental problem with the waterfall model is that it takes too long before anyone knows if the project is going to work out okay. No test results exist until all previous stages have been completed. After years of work, the customer might see the results of the testing and say that obviously the developers didn't understand the requirements.

Furthermore, a political problem compounds the technical one. If the customer sees money going only to create documents he has no interest in and if no product exists to demonstrate progress, he may decide to cut his losses and terminate the project. The cancellation of large projects is a very real problem. Yourdon (1992) quotes the statistic that "25% of large system development projects are canceled before completion."

Summarizing the sins of the waterfall model, we find that it:

- Is very dependent on the requirements being correct
- Does not respond well to changes in the requirements since there is little feedback
- Delays the detection of errors until the end, even though the later in the life-cycle that these errors are detected, the greater the cost of correction
- Does not encourage reuse or prototyping
- Can be paper-heavy

4.1.3 The Spiral Model

The problems of the waterfall model stimulated the creation of models with a more flexible life-cycle model. One of the best known is the spiral model, proposed by Barry Boehm (1988).

The spiral model made two significant contributions. It provided for alternative process models within the spiral model, including the waterfall model, a prototype-oriented model, and others. It also provided a risk analysis method for determining the best process model to use and evaluating general risk each cycle of the spiral. Interestingly, what is spiraling out from the center in the spiral model is the cost. Boehm's discussion of risk management is well worth reading regardless of the life-cycle method one uses. Boehm's spiral model also allows the inclusion of concurrent development, the topic of the following section.

4.1.4 Concurrent Development

The root of the problem with the waterfall model is that, on a large project, it takes a very long time for each phase to complete. However, if we were to apply the model on a project that took a week each for analysis, design, and implementation, the magnitude of the problems would be greatly diminished. Concurrent development addresses this problem with the waterfall model.

Concurrent development is implemented by separating the project into a series of tasks that can be conducted in parallel. This is particularly valuable in large, complex projects. The system is partitioned and the analysis and design for one partition overlaps with the analysis and design of other partitions. Concurrent development also makes scheduling human resources much easier, and it greatly reduces the problem of implementors sitting around waiting for the analysts and designers to finish. The trick, of course, is being able to perform this partitioning.

If we can accomplish the partitioning, we can create a series of mini-waterfall models or mini-spiral models for each task. This get results faster and reduces the impact of errors in the requirements. However, accomplishing this partitioning has been difficult in the past. The most common form of partitioning, functional decomposition, is a form of hierarchical decomposition in which major system functions are separated into subfunctions recursively until the entire system is represented by simple functions. This tends to scatter the functionality of the program among many separate programming units, making it difficult to assemble disjoint tasks that can be independently developed. Even when such a decomposition is achieved, minor changes to the requirements can destroy the original partitioning.

Because the object-oriented approach does makes it easier to create a stable partitioning of the system, it encourages the use of concurrent development. The partitioning is easier because the object-oriented approach maintains a near one-to-one correspondence between the real-world representation of the problem and the analysis, design, and programming objects. Since real-world objects are more stable than the steps in processes applied to them, their software counterparts reflect this stability.

Overlapping portions of the analysis, design, and implementation for a single task has a limited effect on total time to completion. However, overlapping many concurrent tasks can have a major impact on delivery time. For example, if 30 tasks of equal duration can be overlapped, the time for the three phases can theoretically be reduced by a factor of 30. Of course, such an ideal overlap is unlikely; when tasks are of unequal duration, the length of the longest task dominates. One also has to consider the time involved in coordinating the tasks.

4.1.5 Traditional Analysis and Design

So far we have treated the software life-cycle as if it had cut and dried divisions into analysis, design, and implementation and as if everyone agreed upon what these entail. Things are never so simple. While the definition of other phases of the life-cycle are well defined, the question of how to distinguish analysis from design generates considerable debate among the experts. The difference may be well defined for a particular methodology, but it is certainly not clear for methodologies in general.

Let's first look at the traditional meanings of analysis and design. Later in this chapter, we will see how object technology has inadvertently complicated the picture by blurring the distinction between the two in some people's minds.

4.1.6 The Nature of Analysis

The simplest way to differentiate between analysis and design is to say that analysis deals with *what* the problem is and design deals with *how* the problem is to be solved. Although in practice people will argue extensively about what is *what* and what is *how*. Consider this alternative rule: if the customer says he wants it, it is a *what*, that is, a matter for analysis.

Analysis focuses on understanding and describing the problem. Describing the problem is by no means a trivial task, and you can expect it to require over 20% of the total project time. If less than 10% of a project is devoted to analysis, one has good reason to be concerned about the cost of maintenance and enhancement.

The output of the analysis phase is a specification of the software requirements. The exact nature of this specification may differ according to both the software paradigm and methodology used. The software analyst is responsible for creating the specification but is quite dependent for success upon the cooperation of both the customer and domain experts.

A *domain expert* is anyone who understands the concepts of the application space. The domain expert is essential to the creation of the analysis specification. To create specifications it takes a customer who knows the result he wants, domain experts who know how the application should work, and analysts who understand the software development process. In addition, it takes effective communications among all three to create good specifications.

During analysis we need not be concerned about implementation methods. For example, the analysis may specify that we sort people's names alphabetically. Not until design should we worry about what type of a container class we need to store the names or what type of sorting algorithm to use.

4.1.7 The Nature of Design

Once the analysis specification has precisely described what the problem is, the design specification is needed to describe the structure and details of the software solution to the problem.

Design can be subdivided into conceptual design and implementation design. Conceptual design describes the structure of the solution using problem domain entities and design constructs. The problem domain entities use the terminology of the customer and domain experts to describe problem space objects or concepts. The design constructs do not have to have real-world counterparts but can be added to facilitate the solution of the problem. Conceptual design is generally independent of implementation considerations. Implementation design describes the part of the solution that depends on the means of implementation, such as the language or hardware used.

Sometimes design is divided into preliminary design and detailed design or into system design and local design. Here, the intent is to assure that the overall design structure is established before time is spent on the details. The difference between these methods and the previous ones is not great, since preliminary or system design corresponds roughly to conceptual design, and detailed or local design includes implementation design.

4.1.7.1 Conceptual Design

Conceptual design defines the structure of the problem and considers issues of how to create quality programming. During design, it is usually necessary to invent classes and objects with no counterpart in the real and conceptual world of the application. These are solution-oriented classes and objects that provide a particular functionality or form needed for the solution. For example, a sorting class can be created to improve the efficiency of locating information. A matrix class can be created to simplify the solution of linear equations. The idea of a matrix may not appear anywhere in the problem statement, so we invent it as part of conceptual design.

4.1.7.2 Implementation Design

Implementation design is the part of design that adapts to different languages, operating systems, and hardware. For example, suppose the analysis and conceptual design express a relationship in terms of multiple inheritance, and one is using Smalltalk (which does not have a built-in multiple inheritance capability). Implementation design would describe how to accomplish the implementation, such as by using delegation, which is a technique for allowing one object to perform requests directed at another object.

If the design is done well, implementation should be a fairly mechanical process. In fact, CASE tools are being developed to generate implementation code from the design specifications; creation of declarative code by CASE tools is already commonplace. If the design is not done well, the implementation becomes a combination of design and implementation, which is very undesirable if the design affects anything outside of the implementation of individual classes.

The reason we want to keep the implementation design separate from the analysis is that we don't want the implementation to drive the analysis. It is by no means unheard of for people to write the code and then write the specifications to reflect how they did the coding. Normally, even when such coding does solve the immediate problem,it is difficult to extend. (Occasionally this practice is justified, such as when a prototype is required to determine whether it is possible to satisfy a performance requirement.)

4.1.8 Analysis or Design?

This section discusses a few issues in the controversy about the appropriate content of analysis and design.

To what degree should the analysis anticipate the design? For example, one might see three different ways to specify part of the analysis. If one looked at the options from a design point of view and picked the best way, one could make the analysis structure consistent with the design structure. Iteration on the analysis and design phases accomplishes the same result but with more effort. Therefore, there are cases in which it might be desirable for the analysis to anticipate the design. This will certainly improve the traceability from analysis to design. However, this is usually a dangerous practice because it may distract the focus of the analysis away from discovering what the problem is. It also may cause an unnatural structuring of the analysis that does not reflect the nature of the problem but starts to describe the problem in terms of how a computer works. Furthermore, if the requirements change during the analysis process, the time spent worrying about design issues may be wasted.

Some people distinguish between analysis and design by saying that analysis is independent of the implementation and that design describes only that which is dependent on the implementation environment. In this case they are usually considering design as detailed design only and do not include conceptual design.

Even knowledge of implementation issues can feed back into analysis. For example, suppose a prototype indicates that it will be impossible to meet run-time requirements with a particular code structure. Then one might be justified in letting the implementation affect the analysis. The danger here is that the analyst may not understand what is possible and what is not. For example, Ellis (1994) points out that with existing 8-bit microprocessors it was inconceivable to build a full-digital helicopter automated flight control system. However, had the analysts assumed the impossibility of the task, the completion of the task using the new technology of 16-bit microprocessors would not have been accomplished.

One should give some consideration to how the implementation might affect even the conceptual design. One reason is that one may have a reusable library available that can be used for one design but not for another design. However, one should be very cautious about doing this sort of thing to avoid overlooking a good design solution by jumping to the conclusion that it would be great to be able to reuse something.

One might be tempted to adapt the design to the nature of the programming language to be used. For example, if one were going to use Smalltalk, which does not have multiple inheritance, one might not use the equivalent analysis construct, multiple classification, during analysis. However, if multiple classification is the most straightforward way to describe the nature of the problem space, then by all means use it. There are standard ways of implementing multiple inheritance in languages than do not have the built-in construct. There really is no need here to allow the implementation tail wag the analysis dog.

All advice given here should be taken as guidelines, not rules. Every situation is different and no one can anticipate every complexity. Rules are no substitute for judgment, and one can generally find exceptions to the rules. Judgment based on the entire situation should take precedence over whatever nice, simple rules experts advocate. We all draw conclusions based on the applications with which we have had experience, and we cannot anticipate all other legitimate arguments based on different experiences. Nevertheless, knowing some guidelines may help avoid common errors, and one needs to understand the basic issues before one has the judgment to apply to new situations.

4.2 Object-Oriented Life Cycles

The title of this section may be misleading, because generally speaking, there is no such thing as an object-oriented life-cycle model. Some methodologies do not provide a life-cycle model but assume the continuation of an existing one. Many object-oriented methodologies specify the process quite precisely, but each methodology does this somewhat differently.

Most object-oriented methods advocate their own iterative, recursive, and incremental extension of the concept of the spiral model. *Iterative* means that the same process is repeated with the same goal in mind until the developer is satisfied that the goal has been reached. *Recursive* means that we increase the amount of detail already achieved on a product. For example, a high-level description is expanded to a mid-level description of detail by adding elaboration or new subparts, as in hierarchical decomposition. *Incremental* means that we repeat the same process with the goal of creating a product with capabilities beyond that already achieved. The recursive process is usually part of the incremental process.

This section provides a method for comparing object-oriented methodologies with respect to their life-cycle models. The method consists of a prototype model that describes the essential steps in the object-oriented life cycle. First we consider how object-oriented and traditional life-cycle models differ.

4.2.1 Differences between Object-Oriented and Traditional Life-Cycle Models

Object-oriented life cycles differ from traditional life-cycle models both with respect to the process and the contents of the steps of the process. The analysis and design steps differ more in content than the other steps in the life cycle. There are two fundamental differences between the traditional approach to analysis and design and the object-oriented approach:

- In the structured approach, the representation of the requirements specification is in terms of computer-implementation entities, such as data stores and data flows. With the object-oriented approach, it is in terms of problem entities to which customers and domain experts can relate.
- A chasm exists in the structured approach between the analysis representation and the design representation. A transformation is required between analysis and design. With the object-oriented approach the chasm is reduced to a gully; a refinement of the analysis is needed to create the design.

Earlier paradigms did not encourage similarities between the analysis structure and the design structure; however, with the object-oriented paradigm, the structure of the problem and the structure of the solution are naturally similar, because both are rooted in the nature of real-world objects. In the structured approach the division between analysis and design was made clear because a representational transformation was needed between the two phases. In the object-oriented approach, the representation, at least of the object model, not only requires no transformation, it may require minimal changes in going from analysis to design.

4.2.2 A Prototype Life-Cycle Model

To provide a basis for comparison of how various object-oriented methodologies model the software life cycle, this section describes the steps needed in the process with emphasis on the analysis and design phases. I will refer to this model as the *prototype life-cycle model.*

If one considers the simplest meanings of *analysis* and *design,* it would appear that there should be little controversy about the topics. Analysis describes what the problem is, and design describes how to solve it. However, as soon as we start to be a little more specific in our definition, differences of opinion surface.

Some definitions of analysis concentrate on describing the functional nature of the problem. This can be done by partitioning a system into parts (e.g., functions or objects) and describing how the parts relate to the each other and the system as a whole. Alternatively, it can be done by describing the system independently of the structure of the system and concentrating solely on what the inputs and outputs of the system are. Or it can be done by describing not only the inputs and outputs of the system but the intermediate behavior that occurs within the system.

The primary difference in the definitions of analysis is the extent to which the structure of the application is used and described during analysis. Many experts feel strongly that considering the structure of the application space should not be part of analysis. However, historically, analysis has partitioned systems in some way related to the structure, so other experts feel that the traditional meaning of analysis should be preserved and that structure should be used to describe what the problem is.

The definition of design is greatly affected by the definition of analysis; essentially, design becomes everything that was not accomplished during analysis but which is required to provide a sufficient specification for proceeding with implementation.

The approach taken here is to avoid the debate on the meaning of the words, since the meaning of words is essentially an arbitrary decision. The important question is what steps should be performed in the combined analysis and design process. There is actually a lot more agreement on this than there is on the meaning of the words. Therefore, the steps listed below describe the combined analysis and design process. Later, we will examine how various methodologies assign the steps to analysis or design.

The steps given below are an attempt to describe the emerging consensus of object-oriented experts and are similar to the processes of Jacobson, Booch, and Rumbaugh, although not identical to any of them. A primary purpose of describing the steps is to be able to succinctly explain the life-cycle processes of various methodologies by comparing them to a prototype. Therefore, the steps are kept fairly general without a lot of specifics that might not carry over well to some of the methodologies. The steps may be applied to an entire system or any partition of one. The planning step is omitted since it is not of interest in the comparison.

These steps should help create a requirements specification that has the following characteristics:

- It is easy for the user, the domain expert, and software engineer to understand and thus describes the functionality of the system based first and foremost on objects and types.
- It efficiently and unambiguously describes the requirements using the natural mechanism of human thought, including the concepts of classification, generalization and specialization, and aggregation.

Step 1 Creation of the Problem Statement

The first step in the analysis and design process is the generation of a problem statement, usually by the customer. This problem statement is virtually always incomplete and ambiguous. It should be developed further by customer, the domain experts, and the analyst until it is at least complete and unambiguous with respect to the concept of what is to be done. However, it will still be quite deficient as a specification at any lower level of inquiry.

Step 2 Initial Entity and Relationship Identification

To provide a framework for the customer-oriented behavior specification that follows, initial identification of types, objects, and the relationships between them is needed. This step does involve describing the structure of the problem, but the model may be relatively crude and need not be a permanent document. This step is also a good time to create much of the object dictionary, the development of which will continue throughout all of the remaining steps.

The purpose of software is to model behavior, not objects. Just modeling objects does not do anything. Why, then, do virtually all methods start out by identifying objects and types, at least to some extent, rather than identifying behavior as structured analysis did? The reason is that one needs a relatively stable foundation to which the specification of behavior can be attached. Some methods devote considerable effort initially to determining types and their relationships; in others this effort is more cursory and is expanded later after behavior is identified. Regardless of which approach is used, initial entity and relationship identification is needed to prevent the object-oriented approach from degenerating into a functional-decomposition approach.

Step 3 Creation of a Customer-Oriented Behavioral Specification

Historically, the structure of the system was used early in the process to define the problem. Not only did this approach require detailed definition of the problem structure, but frequently the structure used reflected the nature of the solution (as in functional decomposition), not the nature of the application. This made the specification relatively unintelligible to the customer.

An alternative to using the structure of the system to describe the behavior of the system is to use scenarios to describe it. However, this was seldom done comprehensively in practice. If used at all, scenarios usually provided a few examples of usage. The primary reason was the difficulty in providing a complete specification by enumerating what was usually a "barely finite" number of possible scenarios.

The publication of Jacobson's description of a new form of scenario is changing this. Jacobson applied the object-oriented paradigm to the scenario concept to formalize the generation of comprehensive sets of scenarios, which he calls *use cases*. By using the same concepts of classes, objects, inheritance, aggregation, and other elements of object-oriented analysis and design, Jacobson made it feasible to describe numerous scenarios in a concise, manageable manner.

This, in turn, made it feasible to describe the behavior of a problem without first defining the structure of its solution or even being particularly concerned about describing the structure of the application. Creating a rough description of the structure of the application (as in step 2) is useful in the process of creating scenarios, but it need not become part of the specification. Rather, it can be discarded or more efficiently used as a starting point for the later formal description of the structure of the system. The focus in steps 2 and 3 is on the behavior of the system, and any consideration of structure is in the way of aiding that process, not in the way of specification. The structure need only be considered at the level of identifying objects in the problem space and their responsibilities to each other. Details of the structure are not needed at this stage.

Step 4 Creation of a Software-Oriented Requirements Specification

Once we have specified what behavior is required in terms of application-space objects and types, we need to describe it in terms of corresponding software entities. Here we are still not interested in how the problem will be solved but simply in creating a software structure that corresponds to the real-world objects and concepts. We create a near one-to-one correspondence between real-world and software entities without introducing the complications of design objects not present in the problem space. By relating the types and objects described in the scenario to software counterparts in the software-oriented requirements specification, traceability between these documents is straightforward.

Step 5 Creation of the Conceptual System-Level Software Architecture

By the beginning of step 5, we have completed specifying what the problem is both in terms independent of the software and in terms described by the structure of the software that reflects the structure of the problem space. We now shift the focus of our attention from concentrating on the problem to concentrating on the solution of the problem. While the intent of Step 4 was to describe the problem space, not the structure of the software, the nature of the object-oriented paradigm makes the requirements specification a very close approximation to the architecture that we seek to specify in this step. Therefore, to create the software architecture, we start with the software-oriented requirements specification, refine it, add types and objects that were not present in the problem space but are needed for the solution. We keep this at a high level to avoid spending time with details before an overall framework is established. High-level considerations such as partitioning the problem into subsystems are included in this step.

Step 6 Creation of the Conceptual Detailed Level Software Architecture

Once the overall architecture is determined, we fill out the details of the software architecture. These include low-level considerations such as individual class design. This step describes the structure of the solution of the problem still independent of any implementation considerations, giving us great flexibility to change the implementation without impacting the previous five steps.

Step 7 Creation of the Implementation Architecture

Implementation considerations are now added, including the effect of the programming language to be used, specifics of how data is to be stored, and what input and output devices will be used. By the end of this step a specification document is complete for the task or system.

Step 8 Implementation

The implementation step should be straightforward. The main point of interest here is that the classes and objects in the implementation will have a close correspondence to the previous steps all the way back to the behavioral scenarios with respect to names, semantics, and functionality. When concurrent development is used, implementation includes the integration of tasks.

Step 9 Testing

The testing mechanism is already in place at the beginning of this step. In fact, the testing criteria for the functional requirements was established in step 3 by the scenarios. The verification portion of testing is a continuing process. The validation portion of the testing step consists of executing the scenarios, comparing results, providing feedback to earlier steps, and documenting results. Nonfunctional requirements, such as performance requirements, must also be tested here.

Step 10 Evolution

Maintenance and enhancement are conducted by returning to an appropriate previous step in the process. The entire process is iterative and incremental, so all or some of the preceding steps may be performed on the entire system, on only one task within one version of a prototype, or on anything in between.

4.2.3 Keeping the Process Flexible

Once one has a crude idea of what the problem is, it is essential to define the problem in a reasonably complete and unambiguous manner without becoming bogged down in the process. However, at some point one should describe how the problem is to be solved or prototypes should be written, even if the entire problem is not yet precisely defined. It only needs to be defined well enough that further refinement will not significantly impact later phases of the life cycle. As soon as the necessary insight is gained from the later phases about what needs to be accomplished, this detailed information can be inserted into the behavioral specification (provided the proper reviews are performed and authorization is granted).

4.3 Analysis and Design Goals

The analysis and design phases have similar goals with respect to achieving quality. The analysis describes the level and nature of the quality standards and the design implements them. The goals related to quality are also known as *quality factors*. From the number of quality factors discussed in the following it is obvious that achieving quality is a difficult task.

4.3.1 Correctness

Correctness is the degree to which a life-cycle phase implements the requirements specified by the previous phase. In particular, the design must exactly implement the requirements specification and the implementation must exactly implement the design. Correctness is more important than any other quality factor. After all, the fact that code is efficient, reusable, ease to use, and portable is of no value if the code is not correct.

In fact, it would be better if an incorrect code were not reusable and portable so that the errors are not propagated among many programs.

Correctness is generally assumed to be a requirement without further elaboration; however, how one is to verify the correctness requires considerable thought and must be specified in the requirements. The idea of correctness presupposes the existence of specifications. One can't tell if something is correct unless one has a specification that spells out precisely what must be done. Even then, determining correctness is quite difficult. The object-oriented approach has made it a bit easier to achieve consistency between the requirements specification and the design by making the design a refinement of the analysis rather than a transformation of it into a new form. The near one-to-one correspondence from analysis types to implementation classes made possible by the object-oriented paradigm helps enormously in tracing requirements from analysis through design. Being able to trace the requirements is a prerequisite to determining correctness.

There may be innumerable different designs that satisfy correctness of the requirements. Nevertheless, absolute proof of correctness of any solution is, as a practical matter, usually not possible. A code may very well be correct, but unless the user can have confidence in its correctness, use of the results may be precluded by the risk of acting on results of unknown quality. Fortunately, there are techniques that greatly increase the probability that a solution will be correct. Application of testing methods can give the user some confidence, although not absolute certainty, that the results are worth using.

4.3.2 Testability

Testability is a measure of the ease with which the correctness of a specification can be determined. Testability applies to both of the traditional components of testing, verification and validation.

Verification questions whether the system is being built correctly. In other words, verification is the process of checking to assure that we did what we did correctly (as described in the specifications). For example, one way to verify coding is to have a line-by-line walkthrough in which the coder presents the code to a group of reviewers and the coding is compared to the design specification to insure that the implementation reflects the design. The analysis needs to describe the nature of the effort to insure that the code will be verifiable. Verifiability means that the code needs to be easy to test and that any errors discovered can be traced to their source, and it means that correctness can be estimated quantitatively. Verifiability requirements may affect the nature of the design. For example, if the requirements state that the hydraulic model will be separately testable from the heat transfer model, then the design must assure sufficient decoupling of the modules to make this possible.

Validation questions whether the correct system was built. In other words, validation is the process of checking to assure that what was done met the needs of the customer. In particular, were the specifications adequate to solve the user's problem? For example, if one is modeling a traffic light system, validation might include running the code and making sure that, regardless of the inputs or passage of time, the green lights are not on for both opposing directions at the same time. Failure to describe this condition in the specifications would not satisfy the customer's intend and would only generate work for lawyers if not caught.

Most of the methods for verifying a code have little to do with the object-oriented paradigm. For example, quality assurance procedures must be rigorously applied throughout any development process; traceability from requirements through implementation and back is essential regardless of the paradigm used.

As an example of a method of improving testability with respect to validation, suppose that one is calculating a complex physical phenomenon in which a code can only approximate reality, such as the effect of a piece of hail impacting on the wing of a plane. One could improve the testability with respect to validation by adding the requirement that the program be able to calculate results for problems with analytic solutions (known solutions that can be calculated mathematically). For example, one could require that it also model the effect of a perfect sphere bouncing off an idealized curved surface. If providing this capability is a minor addition and exercises most of the same coding, it can validate major portions of a code.

Verifiability is needed not only to insure correctness but also to insure robustness.

4.3.3 Robustness

Robustness is the ability of software to handle conditions not described in the specifications. A robust code can withstand unusual stress. A code can be partially stress-tested by supplying it with bad input. However, other abnormal conditions related to hardware may also stress the code. For example, a C++ program that does not check for a zero return value or an exception following a *new* statement used to create objects will probably not be a robust program. Under normal conditions the program may be correct and run perfectly. However, the program may fail mysteriously if a computer with less memory compared to the one the program was tested on is used. While a properly written program will still fail if memory is insufficient, the program can still be considered robust if it informs the user of the reason for failures that are unavoidable, such as lack of sufficient resources or erroneous user-provided input.

4.3.3 Extensibility

Extensibility is the ease with which the analysis, design, or implementation can be modified. Extensibility is important only if the requirements change, which they almost always do. Creating extensible specifications and code is one of the opportunities facilitated by the object-oriented approach, and is one of its greatest challenges. Inheritance and polymorphism make extensibility easier but add the difficulty of figuring out how to make profitable use of these constructs. They also have the potential to aggravate extensibility problems when misused.

4.3.4 Reusability

Software reuse is one of the shining lights of object technology, but it is one that it can take the patience of a Thomas Edison to achieve. Reusability is a measure of how successful one has been in creating software components that can be reused for different applications or within an application. A software component refers to either an analysis or design specification or code. It also applies to any other product of the software life cycle, such as test cases. Reusability can apply to analysis, design, or implementation.

While some definitions of reusability refer only to reuse in other projects or applications, object technology should get credit for reuse within a large application as well. Some applications are so large that parts of them may greatly exceed the size of other individual projects. Achieving reuse on projects that are sufficiently large that individuals on one part of the project have little communication with individuals working on other parts can be as challenging as achieving reuse in separate projects.

4.3.5 Portability

The need for portability, the ability for a software component to be easy transferred among various software and hardware environments, is a direct result of the lack of standards in both areas. How one achieves portability is specific to particular application needs, methodologies, programming languages, software, and hardware. It is generally outside the scope of this book, except for the discussion of standards in other chapters.

4.3.6 Ease of Use

Ease of use is a goal of extreme interest all users of software. Object technology has greatly contributed to the ease of use of computer software by its contribution to the development of graphical user interfaces.

4.3.7 Reliability

Reliability can be defined as correctness plus robustness (Meyer, 1988).

4.3.8 Efficiency

Efficiency of software is usually thought of first in terms of execution speed and then in terms of the efficient use of resources such as memory. However, one should not lose sight of the need for efficiency in the development process. One must weigh the cost of improving the efficiency of execution against the cost of the efficiency improvements on increasing future costs in code maintenance. Many times there is no additional cost with improving execution time; in other cases, it can have a great impact on the maintainability and extensibility of the software.

4.3.9 Trade-offs

While all of these goals are desirable, time and funding place limits on the degree to which they can be achieved. Even with unlimited resources not all of the quality factors can be implemented to the maximum degree because there are some inherent trade-offs among them. The fact that the quality factors are closely interrelated means that some may contribute to each other and some may conflict with each other. For example, increasing the number of ways an object can be reused increases problems with testability. Improving efficiency may hurt portability. Increasing ease of use may jeopardize reliability.

The requirements specification needs to provide guidance to the designers by stating the relative importance of the quality factors and how conflicts between the various goals should be resolved at a philosophical level.

4.4 Requirements Elicitation

Now that we have established the goals of analysis and design, we need to examine how one goes about achieving these goals. After the initial planning of the project is completed, the next step in the process is requirements elicitation, the process of precisely determining the customer's requirements. This process spans the first three steps of the prototype life-cycle model. This section discusses requirements elicitation in general. Later, Chapter 6 examines Jacobson's use case, which supplements the techniques discussed in this section in addition to contributing to the rest of the development process.

4.4.1 The Requirements Elicitation Process

Requirements elicitation is the process of discovering what the problem is. When the customer provides a statement of what he wants done, he is providing a description of the problem that is, in a sense, the product requirements. Since the product of analysis is a description of the problem, the analysis is done, right? Hardly! Even in the extremely unlikely event that the problem statement is an accurate representation of what customer wants, the level of detail is totally inadequate to base a design upon. Requirements elicitation requires many sources of information and may involve using many techniques.

4.4.1.1 Raising the Quality Factor Issue

The analyst should raise quality factor issues discussed in the previous section with the customer. The software quality factors like reusability, extensibility, and testability involve increased short-term costs with possibly more than compensating long-term benefits. The analyst and customer need to discuss these trade-offs and incorporate decisions concerning them into the requirements specification. Otherwise, cost estimations may be faulty and the customer may be disappointed with the product quality. Explicitly describing the degree to which the product will contain reusable components, will be extensible, and will be testable will forestall later recriminations. At a minimum, the nature of the effort to achieve these goals needs to be described.

4.4.1.2 Domain Experts

If the problem is at all complex, the analyst may need to consult many domain experts just to understand the true nature of the problem. Domain experts are people who understand the business process, scientific application, or technical or operational area related to the problem. They understand the existing process because they created it, use it, manage it, model it, or observe it.

Because of the limited expertise of the software developers, making full use of domain experts is critical to the success of any complex project. Even the best analyst with an excellent technical background in the domain has a biased view of the problem and needs the input of other experts. For example, even if someone knew all there was to know about how automobiles work, that person would not likely also be an expert in the ability of individuals to respond to emergency driving conditions, the effect of body contours on the potential customer, and the effect of world market conditions on the cost and availability of materials.

4.4.1.3 Requirements Elicitation Pitfalls

Requirements elicitation is a skill that is essential to the analysis process but which is by no means an easy task. Unfortunately, as far as I know, universities seldom teach how do to requirements elicitation. A journalism course might help because good interviewing techniques are critical. Regardless, it takes experience or training to develop the skill.

The first complication is that just because someone wants you to do something for them, it doesn't mean that the requester knows what that something is. In some ways it is like a patient going to a doctor and saying, "I want to be cured." The doctor first has to figure out what the problem is, and that is often the biggest part of the job.

Frequently, software is used to model or control part of a larger system. In this case part of requirements elicitation is determining where the system boundary is for the software product. What does the software control, and what is controlling it? It is easy for hardware experts and software analysts to become confused because the hardware experts usually talk about how actual physical devices should work and analysts talk about how the software models the device. The analyst must ensure that every part of the system is explicitly designated to be within or outside of the responsibility of the software. For example, a problem statement may say that a valve is turned off. One must determine whether it is an external event that signals the software to take some action or whether this is an action that the software is supposed to initiate. The analyst and the domain experts need to establish a common terminology. This should be done by having the domain experts name the types used in the object model in conjunction with the code architect, who may wish to coordinate the development of some kind of taxonomy.

Having many experts with whom to consult may be a problem itself. One must make sure that the various domain experts agree on how their parts of the domain should interact with the parts of the other domain experts. Ideally, the domain experts should communicate with one another, but it is ultimately the analyst's responsibility to ensure that their contributions are compatible. This cannot be done by overriding the advise of an expert but only by getting the experts to agree with each other. Yes, the job of an analyst is challenging.

For example, if you are an analyst modeling a thermal-hydraulic system, you will be talking to an expert in fluid flow and also to an expert in heat transfer. If the fluid flow expert is assuming that the wall temperature means the interior surface temperature of the pipe and the heat transfer expert is assuming that it means the average temperature of the pipe, the analyst must catch it.

One good technique is to repeat back to the domain expert your understanding of what she told you. The analyst also has keep the domain expert focused on the essential aspects of the problem, not the details of what she is currently interested in. You have to extract from her what the key objects and classes are and how they depend on each other.

The more information you can get in writing from the domain expert, the better. When you get information from the expert, put it into writing for her to review. If acceptable to the expert, start organizing the various concepts into a coherent whole, using the methods we will be talking about later.

Another pitfall in requirements elicitation is to attempt to do it without first determining a documentation method. A documentation structure is required to organize the information into a useful form.

Jacobson's use case provides a framework that not only organizes the information, but provides a useful tool for other phases of the software development life cycle.

Analysts must also look beyond the immediate problem and elicit future requirements. Creating reusable analysis, design, and coding is a major objective of requirements elicitation. Without knowing the customer's future plans, one is unlikely to create a product that is easily extensible and contains reusable modules.

4.4.2 Domain of the Sample Problem: Windows Programming

A sample problem is introduced here to illustrate the application of requirements elicitation. An example of windows programming is used as the sample problem in this section for several reasons. First, windows programming has become so popular that most customers insist that their programs provide a windows interface. Second, because there are a large number of places a mouse may click on a display screen with different actions expected in different areas of the screen, even a simple windows capability can illustrate the complexities of requirements elicitation. Third, windows programming is event-driven programming, and it is important to understand how this is different than traditional sequential programming. Finally, windows programming uses many external events (e.g., mouse clicks and keystrokes) that lend themselves to the use of Jacobson's formalized scenarios, which can play a vital role in requirements elicitation and specification.

Because of the huge success of Microsoft's Windows operating system and the popularity of numerous applications based on it, the word *windows* is synonymous in many PC users' minds with Microsoft Windows. However, Microsoft is neither the only platform for developing windows programs, nor was it the first out with the concept. Apple Computer first popularized the windows concept with its Macintosh operating system. UNIX users think of the X- Window System, a standard created at MIT, when the idea of windows is mentioned. Each of these systems provide a more user-friendly environment for users than traditional text-based operating systems and programs.

Windows applications are the dominant subset of the set of graphical user interface (GUI) applications. The GUI for windows is based on the manipulation of rectangular shapes called windows that contain other graphically represented conveniences such as various types of pull-down menus, dialog boxes, icons, and scroll bars.

Windows applications are popular because of the relative uniformity of how they are used and because they are easy to learn to use. This contrasts with text-based applications, such as the famous or infamous (depending your point of view) UNIX utility, the vi editor. The vi editor is a marvel of efficiency in minimizing the number of keystrokes required for modifying text. However, beginners almost always detest it because it is so difficult to learn. The many windows applications for text editing are a breeze to learn by comparison, because all the user needs to do is move a cursor around with a mouse and click on icons and commands. However, moving a mouse around is a relatively slow process for most operations compared to doing most operations with the keyboard. Windows applications make up for this by providing equivalent keyboard commands, but, again, training time is required to make effective use of them.

4.4.2.1 Event-Driven Programs

The sample problem in this chapter involves a windows dialog box that is based on event-driven design. To understand the problem and how a program can solve the problem, one needs to understand the basic differences between traditional sequential programming and event-driven programming.

In traditional programming, a program executes a preplanned sequence of statements. While the user may respond to options provided by the program and thus influence the logic path through the program somewhat, the program generally greatly limits the user's options and particularly limits the order in which the options are available. The user must stay in lockstep with the program. If a user wishes to change a value, she must wait until the program offers the opportunity. The program drives the behavior of the user.

In the event-driven programming used in windows applications, the windows software automatically provides the polling of the mouse and keyboard input instead of leaving the problem to the application. This gives the user great flexibility in creating her own sequence of events instead of having to conform to the dictates of the application program. In windows applications, the user can click the mouse to access numerous options, quickly switch to an entirely different application, and have access to multiple applications simultaneously. If a user wishes to change a value, she enters the commands needed to access that capability. The user drives the behavior of the program.

Event-driven programming and the object-oriented approach are an excellent match. Both use a message-passing philosophy. Events in a windows program, such as mouse clicks or keystrokes, result in messages being sent to the windows program, which constantly polls for all hardware events. Therefore, the user is less restricted in the type of event that the program will process at a given moment than in a non-windows program in which the application itself is responsible for polling for events. Event-driven programming is designed to interact flexibly with the external environment, which includes actions by users as well as hardware devices other than those controlled by the user.

4.4.2.2 Dialog Boxes

Specialized types of windows are used to perform specific types of tasks in a windows program. The specialized type of primary interest in the sample problem of this section is the dialog box. Figure 4.1 shows a simple dialog box, which is a type of window that is typically used to input additional information needed to complete another command. This one consists primarily of two dialog control boxes, namely, a list box and an edit control box.

The list box contains an optional scroll bar that allows access to information not currently shown in the list. The object is considered to include the rectangle and everything in it including the scroll bar. The area excluding the scroll bar will be referred to as the list area. The edit control box allows textual information to be edited. A dialog box frequently contains button objects that allow the execution of a command (e.g., using a pushbutton) or selection of alternatives (e.g., using a radio button or check box).

4.4.3 Requirements Elicitation Example

This section demonstrates how to apply general logical skills toward specifying the requirements of a sample problem.

4.4.3.1 Problem Statement

The following problem statement provided for the dialog box example is described at a level that is typical of customer-created problem statements. The customer has a general idea of what he wants but does not understand all of the potential ramifications and the multitude of choices that must be made for the specification of the problem to be complete. Part of the analyst's job is to deal with the vagueness of

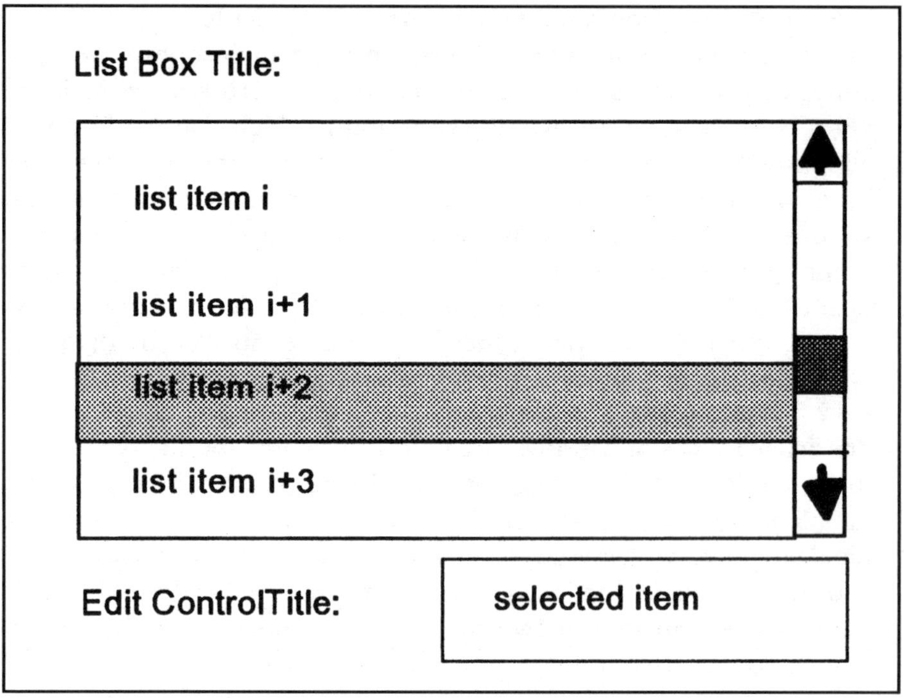

Figure 4.1 *Simple Dialog Box*

problem statements and to make sure the customer gets what he wants, not just what he says he wants.

Problem Statement

Create a part of a program to allow easy selection of data from a list. A capability to enter data must be provided in case the required data is not in the list. For example, the list might contain file names or people's addresses. The program is a windows program and therefore a dialog box should be used to access and display the options.

The analyst will need to question both the customer and domain experts (in this case, the people who will be using the dialog box). The customer's input is needed to explain anything that isn't clear in the problem statement about the intent of the task. The domain experts are needed to describe how they wish to use the product and exactly what they expect of it. In this particular case, the analyst is a windows user and therefore a domain expert himself; however, he should still seek out the views of the people who will actually be using the system.

4.4.3.2 The Analyst's Questions

Requirements elicitation is the art of asking the right questions. An analyst presented with the above problem statement must ensure that his questions and their answers are comprehensive. This is quite difficult by just trying to think of everything without using a framework to organize the possible uses of a system. First we attack the obvious questions without the use of such a framework. In Chapter 6 we will see a technique (Jacobson's) that organizes the process to help insure that all cases are covered. While the first method is quick and of considerable value initially, the Jacobson's method reveals much that would otherwise probably be overlooked. Discovering all of the requirements at this stage is much more economical than waiting until after the code is executed and fails because someone tries to do an unanticipated operation.

Early in the informal elicitation of requirements an analyst needs to ask, "What are the entities in the problem and what are the relationships between them?" For this example this is a fairly easy question that is most usefully answered using some form of class diagram. Rather than use the notation of a specific methodology at this point, the answer is shown in Figure 4.2 in terms of the familiar entity-relationship diagram. Jacobson uses a similar diagram he calls a "domain object model" at this stage in the process. The important point here is that the analyst seeks to create an intuitive picture of how the entities in the system are related; the diagram need not be detailed and, in fact, may give a clearer picture without the details. This figure and the dialog box figure form a convenient basis for visualizing what questions need to be asked about the problem.

Next, the analyst needs to ask which of the entities are part of the system to be modeled and which are entities outside the system that act on the system. Jacobson calls these external influences "actors." The process of making this determination is called defining the system boundaries. The actors are not shown in the entity relationship diagram in the figure; however, they would be in Jacobson's equivalent, the object domain model. The actors here are the keyboard and the mouse. Since they are more or less equivalent (one can program the keyboard to perform mouse operations), they can be treated as a single actor with

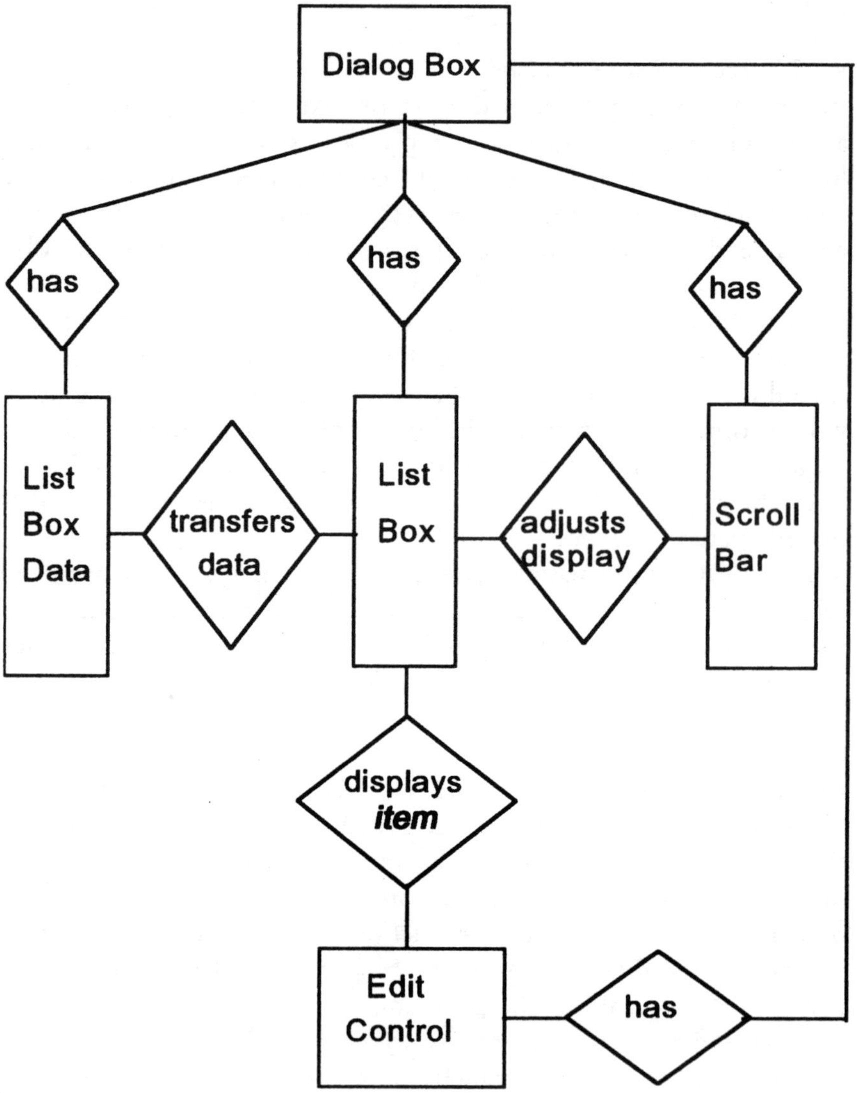

Figure 4.2 *Dialog box entity relationship diagram.*

respect to the logical nature of the input. While determining all of the objects in the problem domain is not necessary at this stage, it is essential to identify all the actors that interact with the system.

The analyst must anticipate needs that the customer did not think of. For example, a user who brings up the dialog box may change his mind and wish to do nothing. Therefore the analyst suggests adding a **Cancel** button and also recommends adding an **OK** button to allow selecting whatever appears in the edit control box by using the mouse.

Some issues are matters of analysis if the customer cares about them but become a matters of design if the customer does not care. For example, the analyst should ask the customer whether he cares what happens what if mouse clicks come faster than the program can display results. If the customer cares, some requirement may be added that, for example, causes a beep to sound if this occurs. Otherwise, the designer must decide whether to ignore some clicks (undesirable), display a warning, or allow a fixed or unlimited (except by memory) number of messages to accumulate and eventually be displayed. Generally, issues that affect how the users interface with the program should be fully specified in the requirements. Purely program-internal matters are more appropriate to be left to design.

The analyst will want to know whether keyboard commands should be provided as alternatives to mouse clicks. For example, hitting the **Esc** key is usually allowed in place of clicking on the **Cancel** button. If the program is being implemented in an environment that automatically provides capabilities like this at no extra cost, then the customer will undoubtedly not be upset if such extra features are considered design issues and do not show up in the requirements. Nevertheless, all inputs must included in the requirements specification, or one has no basis for determining exactly what behavior is required of the system. Therefore, it would be unclear as to what tests need to be exercised to verify that the program meets the requirements. Placing all user interactions in the requirements has the additional advantage that the information in the requirements document transforms with little effort into the user's manual.

Since our dialog window is rather primitive, the analyst would naturally have many more questions about whether additional features might be needed. However, to keep the problem from consuming the book, the problem is limited to some simple features.

The analyst should go looking for trouble. This includes considering extreme cases. For example, he should consider what happens if the list is extremely long, so that it would take a long time to find anything in it by scrolling. If he ascertains that the list may be very long, he may propose adding a search capability to the requirements. Then the user could enter the first letter or letters of the list item being searched for and the program would automatically scroll to the part of the list that starts with the typed letter(s). Of course, the list needs to be sorted alphabetically for the display for this to work.

Another question the analyst should ask is whether a user should be allowed to leave the dialog box, go to another window, and return to the dialog box later. If he wishes to require the user to immediately complete the current dialog box, then he creates what is known as a *modal dialog box*. If he wishes to allow the user to wander elsewhere, then he creates a *modeless dialog box*.

The advantage of the modal approach is that it prevents the user from forgetting what he was doing and returning to the parent window of the dialog box without making a decision that might be important to the parent window. Modal dialog boxes are also easier to program, so most dialog boxes are modal. However, most high-level windows are modeless to allow the user to switch from application to application as desired. The difference between the two approaches internally is that in the modal method uses its own message loop instead of a global loop provided by the windows library.

The answers to questions like these are the start of the analysis process. The analyst and customer should jointly rewrite the problem statement to reflect the discoveries made during requirements elicitation. However, this is only the beginning of requirements elicitation because many details of the requirements have yet to be uncovered. A mechanism like the use case is needed to discover these hidden requirements before the analyst can complete the customer-oriented requirements specification.

4.4.3.3 Revised Problem Statement

The following revised problem statement shows the results of the analyst's initial efforts, in conjunction with the customer, at more precisely defining the problem. Note that capabilities that the product will not have are mentioned whenever one might normally expect the capabilities to be included. This prevents recriminations later after the customer has forgotten which capabilities he agreed to omit. Figure 4.3 shows the **OK** and **Cancel** buttons added during the initial requirements elicitation process and shows some typical data that might be present in a dialog box.

Revised Problem Statement

Create a part of a program to allow easy selection of data from a list. A capability to enter data must be provided in case the required data is not in the list. For example, the list might contain file names or people's addresses. The program is a windows program and therefore a dialog box shall be used to access and display the options. The dialog box must satisfy the following specific requirements.

The dialog box will contain a list box and an edit control box that will show the currently selected item in the list box window, as shown in the Figure 4.3. The list box shall show either all or a portion of some external list of items, depending on the size of the list. If not all of the items can be shown, the scroll bar can be used to display other parts of the list. An item in the list may be highlighted by a single mouse click in its area or may be selected by a double mouse click in the area.

The length of the list will be assumed to be of reasonable length so that no alphabetic search capability will be needed. The keyboard will be used only to enter text in the edit control box; all other functions will be controlled by mouse input. If mouse clicks are made more rapidly than the display can respond, the click events will be stored until the display can respond to each event. The number of messages that can me stored may be determined by the limitations in the windows class library used.

The edit control box shall show the currently selected item. One must to be able to edit the data in the edit control box or enter new data that may be selected instead of data from the provided list. A double click in the edit control box will select the data in it and return it to the parent window.

The scroll bar of the list box must have a position marker (called a *thumb*) in the scroll bar area between the arrows to reflect the relative position of the displayed part of the list. The user must be able to drag and release the thumb and have the window display show the list items that correspond to the marker's position. A single

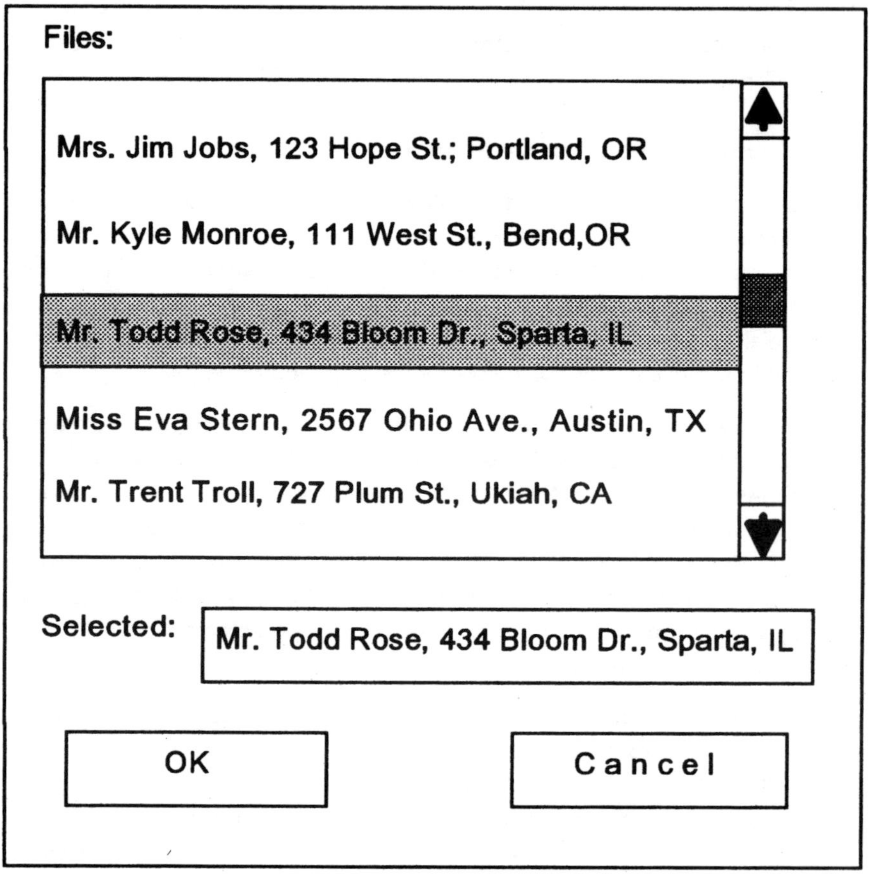

Figure 4.3 *Revised dialog box*

click on an arrow must move the scroll by one item in the appropriate direction.

A single click in the scroll area of the scroll bar must cause the display of the list of items to scroll one display width up or down corresponding to the location of the mouse click above or below the position marker.

An **OK** button will terminate the dialog box and return the currently selected item to the parent window. A **Cancel** button will terminate the dialog box and cause nothing to be changed in the parent window.

The dialog box will initialize the highlighted area and the edit control box text area to the first item in the list. The dialog box must be terminated before another window can be accessed (the dialog box is modal).

It is important that the above steps in the requirements elicitation process be performed before launching into the detailed specification of the requirements. Time spent in improving the initial statement of the problem will avoid a great deal of confusion later.

4.5 Summary

A life-cycle model is needed to ensure that all steps needed to create and maintain a software product are fully addressed. While some debate exists about what constitutes analysis and what constitutes design, there is closer agreement about the content required for the combined analysis and design steps. The prototype life-cycle model outlined in this chapter provides a relatively methodology-independent list of the essential steps in the object-oriented development process.

It is somewhat ironic that object technology is giving the waterfall model a new lease on life. The root of the problem with the waterfall model is that for a large project each phase of the life-cycle typically requires many months or years to complete. The combination of object technology with concurrent development can greatly reduce the duration of each phase of each task. Concurrent development partitions a project into many mini-projects and allows application of a life-cycle method to many small tasks instead of one large task. The object-oriented approach makes the decomposition of large projects into many smaller tasks much easier to accomplish. Reducing the length of each cycle to a few months alleviates the problems with the waterfall model. Of course, other life-cycle models may also be used with concurrent engineering. Therefore, the main advantage of sticking with the waterfall model, instead of switching to a more flexible life-cycle model like the spiral model, is simply to avoid transition trauma.

The goals of the development process include achieving correctness, testability, robustness, extensibility, reusability, ease of use, portability, and efficiency. Some trade-offs are necessary. Therefore, it is essential that the customer be involved in specifying the degree to which each goal is to be met whenever achieving the goals will affect budget or schedule.

A major portion of this chapter was devoted to requirements elicitation because the process is difficult and frequently inadequately addressed. Failure to property accomplish the task can result in the wrong product being produced. It is not the customer's responsibility to take the initiative to ensure that the problem is well defined; the analyst must take the responsibility for requirements elicitation and create unambiguous and complete specifications.

4.6 References

Boehm, B. W. (1988). A spiral model of software development and enhancement. *Computer.* 21(5):61_72.

DOD-STD-2167A. (1988). Defense System Software Development. Washington, DC. U.S. Department of Defense.

Ellis, J. R. (1994). *Objectifying Real-Time Systems.* New York: SIGS Books.

Meyer, B. (1988). *Object-Oriented Software Construction.* New York: Prentice Hall.

Software Engineering Standards. (1993). 3rd ed., New York: Institute of Electrical and Electronics Engineers.

Yourdon, E. (1992). *Decline and Fall of the American Programmer.* Englewood Cliffs, NJ: Yourdon Press.

Chapter 5

Object-Oriented Specifications

The development process requires documentation of each step in the life cycle. Specifications record decisions made and dictate the framework for further decisions. This chapter examines the two specification documents that are most affected by a switch to object technology, the analysis and design specifications. Specifications for major projects are extremely complex and detailed documents; therefore, the manner in which they are organized is of considerable importance.

First, we will examine the traditional methods of using partitioning and layering to reduce the complexity of the representation. We will then examine how object-oriented specifications are developed using multiple modeling views and how they are represented graphically.

5.1 Specifications

A requirements specification is needed to provide the requirements for the design phase, and a design specification is needed to provide the requirements for the implementation phase. The general content of specifications is covered well elsewhere, such as in Thayer and Dorfmann

(1990), ANSI/IEEE Standards (1993), and DOD standards (DD-STD-2167A, 1988). These references describe why a specification needs to be complete, unambiguous, verifiable, traceable, and consistent. Specification goals are unchanged with a transition to object technology; however, the content changes considerably in some areas. The areas in which the content changes are the main focus of this chapter.

5.2 Managing Complexity

Because it is mind-boggling to attempt to simultaneously conceptualize all aspects of a complex problem, techniques are needed to help organize the system specifications into comprehensible parts. Two important techniques for accomplishing this are layering and partitioning views that decompose the system by levels of detail and by subject matter, and modeling views that represent the system as orthogonal views that concentrate on one particular aspect of a system, such as data, control, or functionality.

All methodologies capable of managing complexity use some form of partitioning and layering. Figure 5.1 shows the relationship between layers and partitions.

5.2.1 Layering

Layering of the information provides a range of detail from a high level to a low level. For any particular abstraction it allows the expansion or contraction of the amount of detail displayed for the abstraction. This allows the developer to concentrate on high-level interfaces, intermediate levels of complexity, or implementation details.

Expanding all layers within an abstraction forms a tree structure with the base of the tree showing an overview of the entire abstraction and branches showing increasing detail. The components of the base layer can be expanded to view the details of each part, and each of these parts can be expanded until a level of detail is reached that completely specifies the abstraction.

5.2.2 Partitioning

While layer divides the system by level of detail, partitions are obtained by separating the system into components according to subject matter.

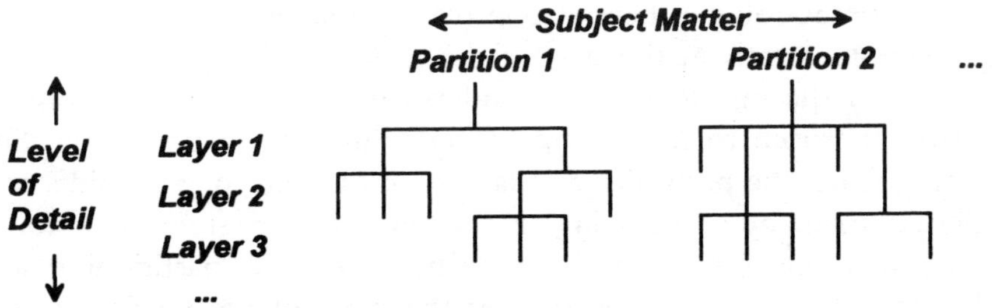

Figure 5.1 *Layers and partitions*

Partitioning allows a group to concentrate on smaller, more manageable tasks at one time and allows different groups to overlap their efforts. Frequently encountered terms used to describe partitions include *cluster, module, domain, class category, composite object, subject,* and *subsystem.*

Structured analysis addressed in considerable detail the need to partition the problem; however, early object-oriented methodologies did not address partitioning techniques very well. Perhaps this is because they were well documented in traditional methodologies, and object-oriented authorities preferred to concentrate on new ideas. Exceptions are Shlaer/Mellor (1992) and Firesmith (1993) who have paid particular attention to decomposition techniques. Rumbaugh has addressed the question well subsequent to his original book (1994).

Object-oriented methodologies need to address the issue because there are inherent differences in the partitioning techniques needed for the structured and the object-oriented approaches. Traditionally, the basis for the partitioning was functional decomposition or data decomposition for structured techniques and for information engineering. Object-oriented partitioning is typically based on classes and collections of classes of a similar nature.

The use of partitions in analysis and design needs to provide a level of abstraction appropriate to all steps of the development process. Unfortunately, the use of partitions for implementation has been limited by the lack of high-level class-like language constructs to implement the concept of encapsulation at a higher level of granularity than the class level.

5.2.2.1 When to Partition

Some methodologies have strong biases in favor of constructing partitions immediately at the start of the project; others advocate delaying this until the problem is well understood. Others take a more pragmatic approach to the timing of performing the partitioning. Sometimes, when the partitions and layers are obvious, one should start the development by partitioning the system. If the system does not have natural or apparent parts that may be decoupled, partitioning should be done later in the process after the parts of the system are better understood.

5.2.2.2 How to Assign Classes to Partitions

Partitioning may result in a decomposition of the system; however, this does not necessarily imply that the process is one of decomposition. It could be a process of composition from smaller parts or some combination of the methods. A common method for partitioning a system is to iteratively decompose and then reconstruct the system. This alternating between top-down and bottom-up design keeps the big picture in perspective as the details are filled out.

The key issue involved in the partitioning is how to determine which classes belong with each other. One approach to partitioning is centered around the nature of the problem objects. This works well when classes are related by aggregation (a whole-to-part relationship) or have naturally low coupling between sets of classes. However, often there are many communicating classes that are related mainly by the fact that they send messages to one another rather than having any inherent relationship. Here, Jacobson's use case matrix (1995) may be of use in isolating classes that relate mainly to the same set of use cases. Such subsets are candidates for partitioning.

The quality of the partitioning and layering is important; an arbitrary partitioning will result in difficult to understand and maintain code. A methodology should facilitate this process by providing one or more kinds of partitions designed to meet the above needs. Layering and partitioning provide a general philosophy of how to simplify the representation of a system, but they do not describe the specifics of how this may be accomplished. The modeling views described in the next section implement this general philosophy.

5.3 Object-Oriented Modeling Views

Traditionally, specifications have been represented using three modeling views: a data view, a state view, and a process view. The data view deals with the static structure and interrelationships of the entities used to represent the system. The state view deals with the control aspects of the system. The process view represents the functionality of the system. Each of these is explained in more detail later in this section. A methodology that uses these three views is referred to as a *ternary methodology*.

Because the object-oriented approach encapsulates data and operations on that data into classes, this creates an opportunity to use a single view that describes classes, their external interactions, and their internal behavior and dispense with the more complicated three-view approach. Two of the earliest object-oriented methodologies, by Wirfs-Brock and by Coad and Yourdon adopted this unary approach. Other methodologies, such as Rumbaugh's OMT, adopted the traditional ternary approach.

Both approaches had deficiencies caused by the fact that it is difficult to be early out with a methodology and be very complete and mature at the same time. While the unary methods worked well for some applications, they were obviously deficient for applications that require a state model. While OMT was complete, it had two problems. First, it lacked a detailed description of how to reconcile the three different views. Second, the process model was essentially a copy of the traditional methods and did not fit well with the object-oriented approach. These methodologies have made progress since their original versions in resolving these problems.

The data model view is central to object technology; that is, objects provide the focal point in the object-oriented approach. However, the process view has also changed significantly with the advent of object technology. The state model view has evolved the least of the three views, and traditional techniques still dominate this model. Sections 5.5, 5.6, and 5.7 describe these models. Chapter 6 discusses the views used by various methodologies.

The traditional terms used to describe the views are not the most commonly used ones in object technology. In the case of the data model, the term does not describe the specific nature of the object-oriented view.

Therefore, when discussing this view, the term *object model* is usually used to refer to the view relating to the static structure of the system. Since the term *object* is frequently used to refer to either class or instance, the ambiguity of this usage is descriptive of the model—the object model may contain diagrams describing either classes or object instances. The data model describes data structure; the object-oriented counterpart, the object model, describes classes, objects, and relationships.

Rumbaugh uses the term *dynamic model* instead of state model. This is a good choice because this model deals with more than just the state of objects; it also deals with events and does not depend exclusively on state diagrams to describe the control aspects of the model.

While I see no compelling reason to use one term instead of another for the third model, which is referred to as the process model or functional model, I will use the term *functional model* henceforth and thus be consistent with Rumbaugh's terminology.

To say that the views are orthogonal is an exaggeration; there are interdependencies among the views that must eventually be reconciled. Effectively reconciling them is one of the challenges that object-oriented modeling has addressed only recently.

5.4 Representation of Views

Effective software modeling requires the efficient representation of information. Part of this task involves categorizing information using object-oriented constructs that concisely model how we think about the physical and conceptual aspects of the problem. Another part of the task involves the visualization of entities and the relationships between them. Graphical representation is virtually indispensable in visualizing some situations. This section provides a sample of the type of graphical representation used by object-oriented methodologies.

Graphical Representation of Views

Most representations are graphically based and supplemented with textual descriptions. This chapter focuses on what needs to be specified, not the form in which it should be specified. Graphical representations vary widely from methodology to methodology, so only samples are given of how specifications may be represented. What those representations should contain is relatively independent of the methodology chosen.

Object technology is a reasonably mature technology if measured by the amount of information available about it and the number of major successful projects completed using it. However, it does not look very mature with respect to the development of standards. The lack of standards for graphical notation may appear to be a major obstacle for beginners. However, once one understands the concepts that one needs to model, it is usually not difficult to understand the graphics of the various methodologies. One can usually examine a sample graph of any methodology and deduce what most of the symbols mean. For example, suppose one is not familiar with Coad and Yourdon's graphics; let us see what can be deduced from the sample in Figure 5.2.

It should be immediately apparent that the rounded rectangles in Figure 5.2 represent classes and that the names of the classes, *slug* and *hurdle*, appear in the top section. Since *speed* and *position* are apparently attributes of the class, we can deduce that Coad and Yourdon place attributes in the middle section. Since *jump*, *fall over*, and *sneak under* show behavior, they must be methods, so we deduce that the bottom section contains methods (called *services* in Coad/Yourdon). The line with crow's feet connecting the two classes obviously represents some kind of relationship between the classes. We know that the cardinality of a relationship (the number of individual objects involved) needs to be specified. Since we would expect more than one slug to participate in the race and since we expect many hurdles will need to be navigated somehow, we can conclude that the crow's feet represent "many" in a many-to-many relationship. Other graphical representations can usually

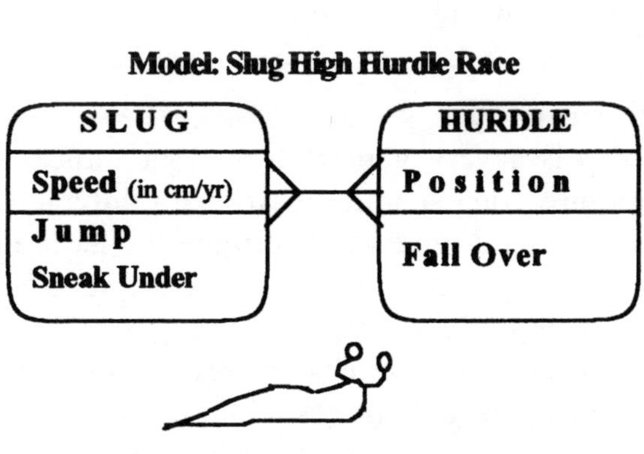

Figure 5.2 *Example of Coad/Yourdon notation*

be figured out similarly without a key, although it may take more than one example.

Figure 5.3 describes the scope of information that exists in the object diagram and shows differences among various methodologies. We shall not dwell on these differences.

5.4.1 Textual Representation of Views

Graphical notation is ideal for visualizing network type of information; however, it has no advantage in describing purely sequential information, and it is at disadvantage in representing complex decision making processes needed to determine the sequence of events. Rumbaugh (1995) recommends text (including equations, pseudocode, or natural language) rather than graphics to represent iterations, conditionals, and other forms of control. Because graphical notation is more difficult to generate and maintain than textual information, one should use it only when it is more enlightening than text.

5.5 The Object Model

A methodology needs to be able to represent at least the following constructs: classes/objects, attributes, behavior/operations/methods, constraints, relationships, cardinality, roles, and specific kinds of relationships including aggregation and inheritance. The items in this list that are most closely related to classes and objects were discussed in Chapter 3. This section discusses the remaining items that constitute the "glue" between the objects.

5.5.1 Relationships

A *relationship* is a very general term that indicates that the entities involved require some communication or interaction. A relationship becomes more useful once we determine the nature of the relationship and apply a more specific term to describe it. The aggregation relationship, the using relationship, and the generalization relationship are important kinds of relationships and are discussed in the following.

Model developers are interested in relationships because isolated objects are not very interesting. Without any association between them, the objects water, a wheel, an axle, and a cylindrical stone do not model a system. Only by relating the objects and describing how

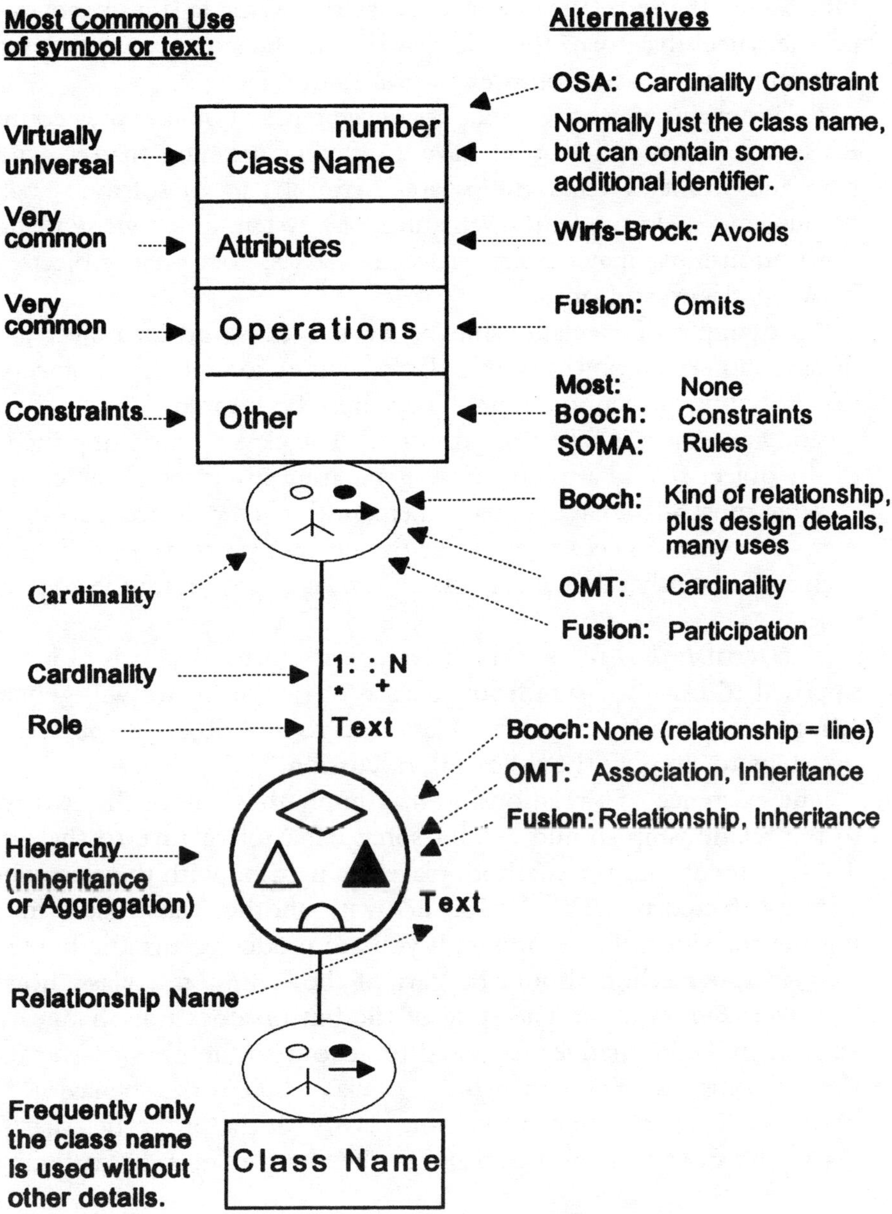

Figure 5.3 *Object model class diagram essential notation*

they communicate or interact can we turn the objects into a meaningful system. If the relationships are that the water falls and moves the paddle wheel that turns the axle that rotates the stone, we can describe a system that uses hydropower to grind flour.

Relationships affect the semantics of the types of objects they connect. An isolated man and woman have a different meaning than a married man and woman. Relationships are a critical part of software analysis because they help model the semantics of a system in a concise manner.

Relationships may exist between classes, between objects, or between classes and objects.

An example of a relationship between a class and an object is the instantiation of an object. While classes exist at compile time, objects do not exist until execution time. They must be created. The process of creating an object is called *instantiation*. The class representing the type of the object acts as a template for generating instances of the class.

What must a language do to implement this? First, it needs to allocate memory. Next, it needs to initialize the object's properties. If the object is an aggregate that contains other objects, it has to create the contained objects.

The term *link* is used to refer to a relationship between objects, as opposed to classes. Aside from the use of this term, we will generally ignore the distinction between class-to-class and object-to-object relationships to simplify the following discussion.

The existence of a relationship may imply that one of the two types in the relationship should exhibit some behavior relative to the other. To implement this as a method, place the method with the class whose state is affected by the behavior, not with another class that is initiating the transition. For example, if you are modeling a traffic light, the *changeColor* method should be part of the *trafficLight* class, not the *pedestrianButton* class. The state of the button does not change. The state of the light changes from red to yellow, so the *changeColor* function belongs with the *trafficLight* class. Keep the behavior that changes a state together in the same class with the properties that represent the state. Only in this way can the encapsulation be maintained.

5.5.2 Aggregation

An aggregation is the simple and fundamental concept of the whole/part relationship. In a whole/part relationship one object can be considered to be in a "has a" relationship with another object. Aggregation is also known as *composition*.

Aggregation is an important conceptual tool in analysis because it occurs frequently and is a natural mechanism for information hiding. It is a great conceptual simplifier because it allows one to deal with the interaction of large units interacting with other large units without having to deal with their parts. For example, if we describe how fast a person can run, we normally wish to avoid also having to describe how fast his arms, legs, and head are going.

An airplane is an aggregate object. Booch (1994) quotes J. Gall as describing an airplane as "a collection of parts having an inherent tendency to fall to earth, and requiring constant effort and supervision to stave off that outcome." This emphasizes that the many parts have to collaborate to perform the function of an airplane. The aggregate parts of an airplane include the wings, the body, the tail, the cockpit, and the landing gear. However, if one is interested in other aspects of the airplane, the aggregate parts could be the structural parts, moveable parts, the electrical system, and the hydraulic system. One decomposes a complex type depending on the nature of the problem to be solved. Booch suggests using aggregation when one wants to hide the parts within the whole and not to use it if one needs a looser coupling in which other objects need to be able to directly access the object.

5.5.3 The Using Relationship

A *using* (also called "uses") *relationship* means that messages can pass between the objects. The purpose of a using relationship is to allow one object to request services from another object. The objects in a using relationship can have two roles, client or server. Since an object may have client relationship with one object and a server relationship with a different object, a third role is needed to cover this case. Booch (1994) uses the word *agent* for this third role. An agent is "An object that can both operate upon other objects and be operated upon by other objects. . . ."

A client/server relationship is asymmetrical. The client requests and the server provides. In a peer-to-peer relationship one object is sometimes making a request that the other object satisfies and other times the roles are reversed. A series of using relationships generally creates a top-down hierarchy from client to agent to agent (for as many agents as needed) and then to server. Having a series of classes in using relationships can simplify the structure of the code since it can result in a simple tree structure of message passing. It is possible for two objects to send messages to each other in a peer-to-peer relationship, but it makes for a much more complicated structure.

Agents are very useful in applications such as locating information on the Internet. Agents are designed to take instructions from a client, such as a request to find the best price on a particular mountain bike. Here the agent is acting as a server. Then the agent can wander around the network asking for prices on mountain bikes and returning the information on the best price. Here the agent is acting as a client for accessing the vendor's services.

5.5.3.1 Contracts

There are two basic philosophies about representing a using relationship. In the Rumbaugh, Booch, and Coad/Yourdon methods, using relationships are generalities that describe conceptually how the types are related. In the Meyer, Wirfs-Brock, and Ptech methods, relationships are represented as contracts that are decomposed into specific behaviors. Contracts are a functionally related set of abstract using relationships that are denoted by a contract name.

5.5.4 Generalization and Specialization

A generalization and specialization relationship is a bidirectional relationship that allows one type (the specialization) to share the properties and behavior of another type (the generalization). A generalization is a unidirectional relationship from a type to a supertype; a specialization is a unidirectional relationship from a subtype to a type.

The analysis concept of generalization and specialization is usually implemented in object-oriented languages using an inheritance capability built into the language. Therefore, the structure specified by a specialization hierarchy is frequently simply described as an inheritance hierarchy. However, inheritance is just one way of implementing a specialization relationship, and its implementation in programming languages is not an exact model of the relationship.

Many different terms are used to show a specialization hierarchy, as shown in Figure 5.4. Each term in the rectangle is more or less equivalent, although in some cases there are slightly different meanings. The

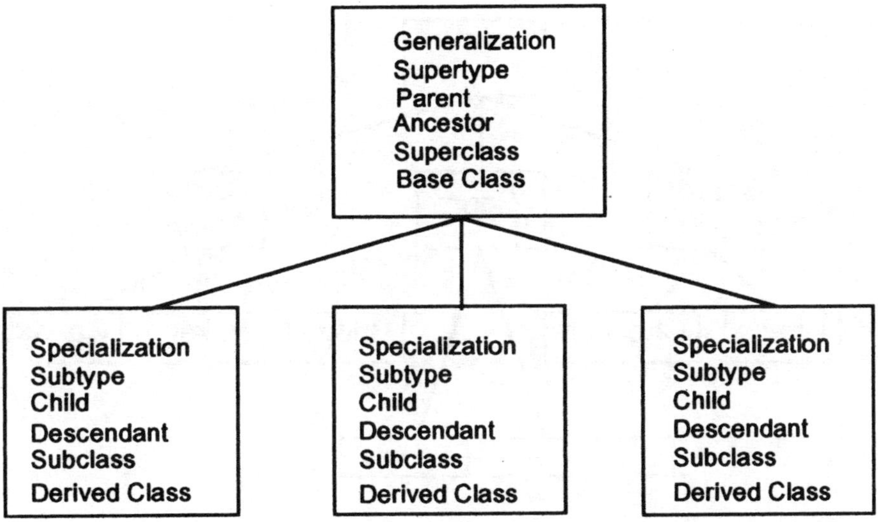

Figure 5.4 *Alternate names for parts of a generalization/specialization relationship*

terms *ancestor* and *descendant* usually refer to types that may be any number of levels above or below the type in question. The words *parent* and *child* are usually reserved for an immediate ancestor or descendant class, but the other terms are sometimes used for more distantly related ancestors or descendants. In C++ terminology, Ellis and Stroustrup (1990) use *base class* and *indirect base class* for the immediate and distant ancestor classes, respectively.

5.5.4.1 Example

It is easiest to understand specialization relationships by way of example. The All-Games Company makes games and supplies for games and sports of all kinds. They need to keep track of different kinds of games and associated products and parts in an efficient manner. The specialization hierarchy in Figure 5.5 shows a sample of the games that the company needs to track.

The base type of the hierarchy, *Game*, is a generalization of all of the subtypes beneath it. The specialization relationship can be described by the words *is a kind of.* A *Board Game* (the specialization) is a kind of

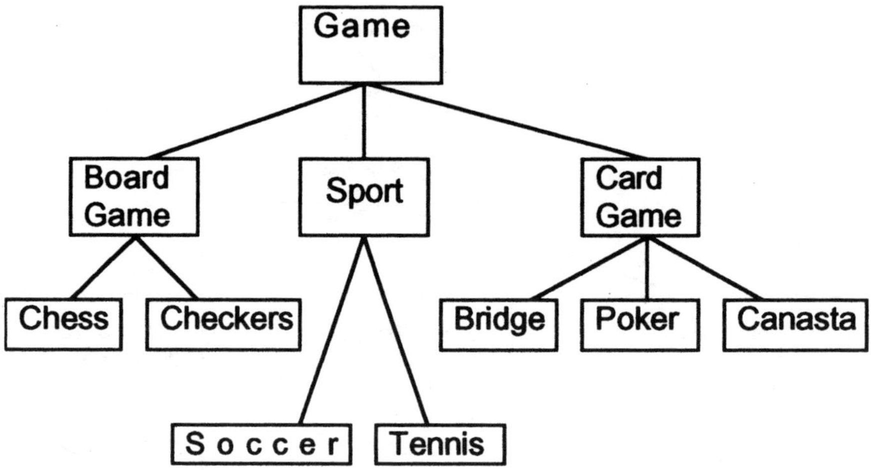

Figure 5.5 *Sample specialization hierarchy for games*

Game (the generalization). *Chess* (the specialization) is a kind of *Board Game* (this time, the generalization) . That is, each subtype is a kind of a *Game*, and each subtype should have all of the characteristics that a *Game* has. Everything that is true of a *Game* in general should be true of *Board Games* and of *Chess.* A specialization may have additional properties and behavior that the generalization does not have.

For example, if a *Game* is something that has a number of players associated with it, then *Chess* must have a number of players associated with it (e.g., two). If a *Game* has a behavior associated with it, such as the ability to get a list of associated products, then *Chess* must have products associated with it (e.g., a board and chess pieces). The reverse is not necessarily true. The fact that a chess game has a checkered board of 64 squares does not imply that all games have the same type of board or even a board at all.

Each instance of the subtype is an instance of the supertype. For example, this means that if the instance *IvorySet* is a member of the *Chess* type, then *IvorySet* is also an instance of *BoardGame* and of *Game*. Therefore, if a behavior of some type exists that is expecting to operate on an instance of the *Game* type, we can pass it the *IvorySet* instance and expect it to work.

5.5.4.2 Benefits

A primary benefit of using specialization relationships in analysis is to improve the clarity of the model. Placing types into natural or reasonably derived hierarchies of related kinds of things makes it easy to see their relationships. It also allows one to easily refer to common properties of many types without enumerating them each time.

One obvious advantage of creating a supertype is that it avoids duplication that would otherwise be required in the subtypes. It also allows use of the supertype in the program to represent uses of the subtypes and be able to later add additional subtypes without affecting any of the properties or behavior of the supertype. This makes specialization relationships a major contributor to the reuse of analysis modeling.

5.5.5 Features of Relationships

To fully specify a relationship, many features of the relationship need to be specified. These should at least include the following: direction, roles, constraints, and cardinality.

5.5.5.1 Direction

In the earliest stages of analysis, it is appropriate simply to draw a line connecting two types to indicate that there is an association between them. Eventually the direction of the relationship needs to be specified because the direction of the relationship can affect the semantics. For example, consider the relationship in which person A and dog B are in a biting relationship. While this fact is of interest, the semantics of the relationship are quite dependent on the direction of the relationship. If the direction of the relationship is the inverse of the dog is biting the person, it puts an entirely different perspective on the situation.

5.5.5.2 Roles

If someone tells you that John and Joe are in an employment relationship, you are still missing a vital aspect of the relationship—who's the boss? Even though the relationship is bidirectional, since in one direction the relationship is "supervises" and the other is "is supervised by," some means in needed to distinguish between the two cases. Specifying a direction is one way. A more explicit way is to specify a role that each type plays in the relationship. A *role* describes the purpose of the objects in a relationship.

5.5.5.3 Constraints

A *constraint* is a kind of restriction. Constraints may be placed on either types or relationships. A constraint on a type is used to more precisely define the nature of type and to ensure the integrity of its state. For example, a bicycle type might have the constraint that one can't pedal the bicycle backwards. This becomes part of the definition of the state of the bicycle.

Similarly, a *constraint* on a relationship is a condition that further defines the relationship. For example, a constraint placed on most marriages in the U.S. is that they consist of exactly two people. The specification of the relationship between a marriage type and a people type that did not provide this cardinality constraint would be incomplete. When possible (when the language provides the capability), constraints should be declared so that compiler guarantees their enforcement. Otherwise, the programmer must code run-time checks to assure conformance. Embley (1992) describes constraints in detail. Only the most commonly specified type of constraint on a relationship, cardinality, is discussed here.

5.5.5.4 Cardinality

Cardinality, also called multiplicity, describes the number of instances that participate in a relationship. When applied to a type it describes how many instances a type can have.

Specifying cardinality during analysis is critical to design. As an example, if the specification says there is a one-to-one relationship between a driver's license and a driver, a much simpler design is possible than if we do not specify this. The general case of one driver being allowed to have many driver licenses and for people to be able to share driver's licenses is a much more complex problem to design for. Therefore, it is important to get this specified during analysis, or the designer will not know what was intended and will have to plan for the most complicated case.

5.6 The Dynamic Model

The concepts we have been discussing so far relate to static objects and relationships that are independent of time. However, objects may change in many ways with time; so temporal relationships are needed to document how the objects are allowed to change and what causes them to change. The dynamic model describes the time-dependent, control-related nature of object behavior in terms of the following items:

- The state of objects
- The properties that define the state of the objects
- Events that cause their states to change
- Behaviors that the objects exhibit that cause their states to change
- Behaviors that the objects initiate to change of states of other objects
- Conditions that determine whether the state may be changed

5.6.1 States

Knowing the existing state of a physical object is important if one is going to change the state of the object. For example, suppose on the weekend that daylight savings time begins, you set your alarm clock from 7 a.m. to 8 a. m., but don't realize that it was really in the set alarm state. Therefore, the time did not get switched to daylight savings time, but the alarm got reset to eight. So the time is an hour behind and the alarm is an hour ahead, and you end up two hours late. Knowing the state of software objects is similarly important because the state of the object determines future states and its response to input events.

An object's state is defined as all properties of the object that are useful in describing the time-dependent behavior of the object, including those properties that describe the communication of the object with other objects (links). The idea of state applies only to objects; classes are templates for creating objects and cannot have a state themselves. Nevertheless, state diagrams deal with classes rather than individual objects. State diagrams can represent all possible states of any objects of the class by representing the pattern of changes in state; but they do not specify specific states of any of the objects.

If a *state* is represented by all of an object's properties, how does this square with common usage of the word? For example, we refer to the state of a car as being moving or stationary, but the car has many other attributes that, by definition, define its state. The car may also be in first or second gear, for example. The stationary state of the car is really a substate that is referred to as a state. Substates may be formed by useful combinations of properties that form the complete state of the object.

A state or substate partitions objects into similar groups of values. Many different objects of a type can have the same state, but they don't have to have exactly the same values of their properties. For example, the "moving" state of a car is the same whether its speed attribute is 10 mph or 50 mph.

Because substates may be independent, an object can be in more than one substate at a time. Concurrency is the characteristic of multiple objects, operations, or events that overlap in time because they have no effect on each other. We expect the operation of an airplane's landing gear, radio communications, and reclining passenger seats to be concurrent, that is, to have no effect on each other. If you discover otherwise, switch airlines fast.

Physical objects are inherently designed to act independently of their internal operations. Therefore, aggregation can be used to simplify state modeling by decomposing large objects into aggregate objects. This reduces the number of possible states, and it works because aggregate parts are naturally concurrent. See Rumbaugh (1995) for a explanation of not only aggregation as applied to state modeling but state generalization in which a substate can inherit the state of its superstate.

5.6.2 Events

An event is something that happens in an amount of time that is negligible compared to the time span of activities of the model's objects. One can think of an event theoretically as taking place instantaneously. Of course, everything actually takes some time—nothing happens instantaneously, not even your teenager disappearing when you say that you did the dishes last. In practical terms, it simply means that nothing can interrupt an event.

5.6.3 Transitions

A change from one state to another is called a *transition*. Transitions are initiated by events. A trigger is the event plus the conditions that activate a state transition (Embley et al., 1992). When the event occurs and the conditions are satisfied, the transition is said to fire, causing a change in state. An event results in an action occurring, such as the invocation of an operation. A change of state in an object-oriented program is implemented by an operation belonging to an object changing the values of properties of the object. Changing a state can be an event that causes another change of state and so on, allowing arbitrary sequences of events and operations to be modeled.

To understand the cause and effect of an object's state being changed, one can examine the inputs and outputs to the state. Preconditions and postconditions are useful when considering changes in state. A precondition is a constraint that must be satisfied before an operation can be invoked. A postcondition is a constraint that is guaranteed to be satisfied after an operation has terminated.

A precondition can insure that an operation is not invoked when it should not be. For example, a precondition to a saw being forced though a piece of timber is that the saw is turned on. A postcondition can similarly ensure that an object's integrity is not violated.

The usual purpose of an invocation of behavior caused by an event is to cause the object to make a transition from one state to another. This is important to remember because if you have a behavior in an object that does not affect its state (or retrieve part of its state), then the behavior may not belong with that object.

5.6.4 The Dynamic Model Specification

The dynamic model needs to be documented in some formal manner. Some form of state diagram can be used to graphically represent a system's dynamic behavior by relating events and states. Two different types of state representations are commonly used, the traditional unstructured flat representations, such as the state-transition diagram, and structured layered ones, such as Harel's statecharts.

5.6.4.1 Harel Statecharts

Harel's statecharts (Harel, 1987) are a structured form of state-transition diagram. Traditional state-transition diagrams suffer from a combinatorial explosion of interactions that make their use impractical when many states are involved. Harel's statecharts combat this problem by providing structure to the diagram that allows hiding of

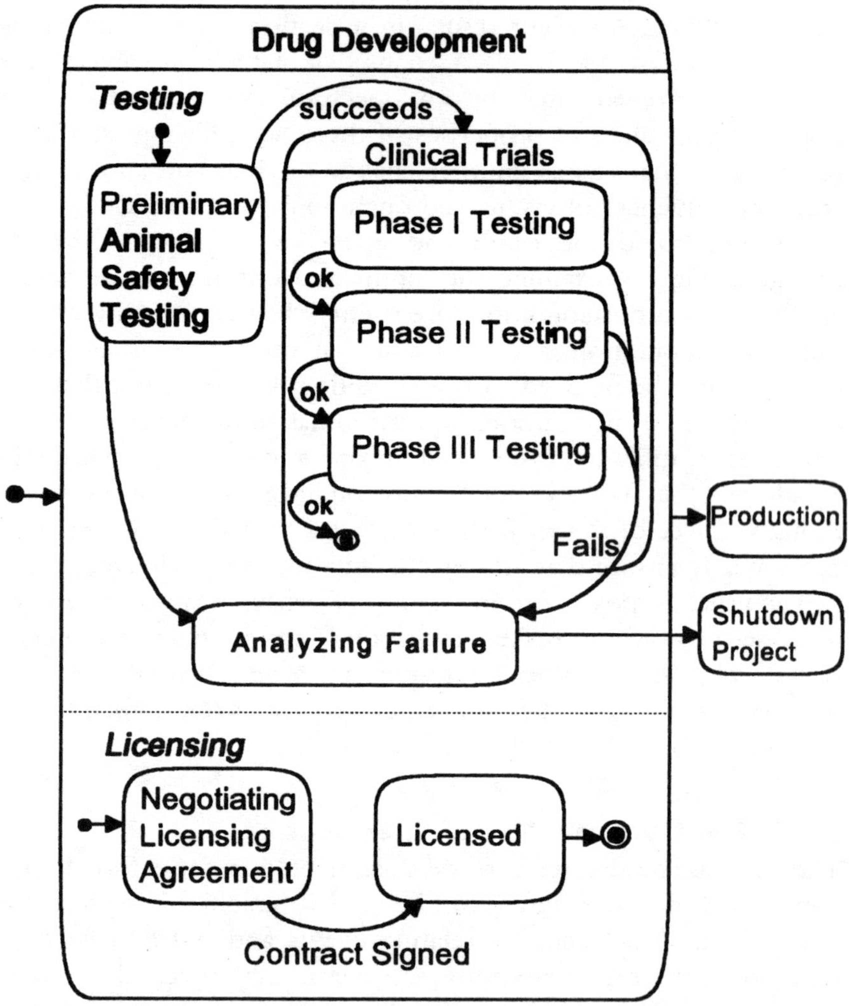

Key: Ovals are states. Dots are starting points. Targets terminate. Text on arcs are transition descriptions. Dash lines separate concurrent states. Encompassed ovals show nested substates.

Figure 5.6 *Statechart for the Development of a Pharmaceutical Product*

details so that the reader can more easily comprehend a complex system. The means for accomplishing this is to allow for the clustering of states and for concurrency of states. Clusters of states are encapsulated and layered by use of nested contours to show substates contained within other states. Concurrency provides the opportunity for simplification by further partitioning the states.

Let's look at a specific example of tracking the progress of the development of a pharmaceutical product, as illustrated in Figure 5.6. By creating a state diagram for the drug development class, we can track the state of a particular drug under development (i.e., a particular object) as events cause the state to change. To accomplish this, we identify states in which objects of the class might exist. The development may be in anyone of several stages of development, for example, in animal safety testing or phase III clinical trials. We next identify events that may precipitate a change in state. Here the events are simply the completion of each step.

Next we need to identify preconditions relative to the transitions occurring. In this example, the precondition is simply the success of the previous stage. For example, the animal safety studies must be successful before clinical trials are allowed. The clinical trials state shows the nesting of substates, which, alternatively, could have been shown on a separate diagram with details omitted from this top level diagram.

Simultaneous with the testing, efforts may be underway to negotiate with another company to buy a distribution license for the product. These concurrent processes are separated in the diagram by a dashed line. Concurrent processes do not have to be entirely independent; in this example, the negotiations are dependent on the success of the trials and both processes will be terminated upon failure of any test.

For more complex classes this process will need repeated with other events until all states, events, transitions, and conditions have been discovered. The example used here is too simple to illustrate the point, but "old-fashioned" state modeling is still an important tool in object technology when dynamic behavior needs to be specified.

5.6.4.2 Need for the Dynamic View

The dynamic view is needed for any application that has significant control behavior, that is, behavior that has a complex selection of the ordering of the invocation of operations. Generally, only those classes that have significant control behavior need a dynamic view. Therefore, some applications require no dynamic model at all. At least this is true for most methodologies—the Shlaer/Mellor method requires a state model for all classes because the methodology is based largely on state modeling. However, most methodologies let the developer decide, class by class, whether or not to use state model. Some applications require an extensive dynamic model because they are fundamentally time-dependent programs. For example, real-time embedded applications are of this nature.

5.6.4.3 Representation of State

The analyst must decide what type of state diagram to use. In most cases this will be determined by the methodology selected. OMT and Booch use statecharts; Shlaer and Mellor use state-transition diagrams. Fusion's use of state diagrams (Colman et al., 1994) is unusual; it develops life-cycle expressions during design that are text-based state models. These are translated into state diagrams during implementation as a preliminary step to coding. The main emphasis in design for Fusion is in describing sequences of messages.

In addition to using some form of state diagram, object-oriented methodologies may also use any of the following to represent the dynamic model: timing diagrams, event traces, scenarios, event hierarchies, and interaction diagrams.

5.7 The Functional Model

The dynamic model provides a nonfunctional view of behavior. It provides a general model for how behavior changes with time in response to any event, but it does not define how a change in state is to be accomplished. The state model is comprehensive but not specific.

For example, if state model indicates the event of igniting a rocket results in the location of the rocket being changed from the launch pad to an impact location, one still must decide exactly how the impact location is calculated. Does it involve monitoring the rocket until it disappears from radar view? Is it purely a theoretical calculation? Are changes in the density of the atmosphere with altitude included in the calculation? What formulas are to be used? In short, a simple change in state may involve extremely complex procedural calculations.

Even methodologies that are considered unary will have some representation of the functionality of a system, because every methodology needs to specify the operations that objects of a class may perform. For example, Wirfs-Brock's protocols that describe the operations for each class can be considered as representing the functional model.

Data-Flow Diagrams

The purpose of the functional model is to describe the transformation of data by processes, such as how the rocket trajectory calculations are performed. Data-flow diagrams have long been the standard representation of the functional model. Data, such as the initial angle of the rocket with the ground and the amount and type of fuel, are used as inputs to the process and are the outputs of the process, such as the landing location of the rocket. Of course, the process may be decomposed into multiple processes that provide a series of transformations of data.

Many object-oriented methodologies do not overtly use the functional model. One reason for this is that the first functional models used in object-oriented methodologies were simply copies of the structured analysis process model that used global data-flow diagrams. The process model is difficult to maintain because it is global in scope when global data flow diagrams are used. Furthermore, it has been my experience that people who have not strongly internalized object-oriented thinking are misled by the use of data-flow diagrams into creating an non–object-oriented structured programs. In addition, experience has indicated that the traditional model simply does not integrate well into the object-oriented approach. If global data-flow diagrams were the only option for use in the functional model, I would dispense with the entire model except for defining the operations.

However, alternative representations of the functional model have evolved that can be useful in obtaining a complete specification. These use local or low-level, rather than global, data-flow diagrams. The Shlaer-Mellor process model uses the term *action data-flow diagrams* to describe the use of data-flow diagrams to represent data flow within individual classes. This reduces the complexity of the diagrams and make them easier to maintain. However, it still tends to be overkill to use local data flow diagrams extensively at the class level; usually the information provided can be conveyed more simply, sometimes simply defining the operations being used is perfectly adequate.

The OMT process model originally used global data-flow diagrams but now uses object-oriented data flow diagrams (Rumbaugh, 1995) that describe a group of objects to represent the effects of an operation on the objects. These are intended to be prototypical not comprehensive. This use of object-oriented data-flow diagrams at a level between the local and global levels provides a description of local communications among classes, which is what is needed most to improve the understandability of the functionality of the operations. Again, the use of low-level data-flow diagrams should be limited to when there is an obvious need for them. The specification of operations for each class of objects is usually sufficient for most classes if one adopts the limited view of the functional model presented here.

While the processing view provides insight into the flow of data among client and server processes and provides a good description of the functionality of the program, it naturally tends to partition the solution space by functionality. This is in conflict with the goal of the object-oriented approach to partition the solution space according an object-oriented structure, and must be guarded against. The functional view must not be allowed to drive the design. Rather, it must work together with the other models to assure that behavior is represented in encapsulated objects.

Control-Flow Diagrams

A control flow can be thought of as a degenerate case of a data flow in which events input to and output from a data transformation have no data associated with them. As such, it appears reasonable to include representations of control flow as part of the functional model. Ward and Mellor added control flow to data flow diagrams because they were needed to properly model real-time systems (Pressman, 1987). Firesmith uses control flows as the more important item compared to data flows; he adds data flows selectively to object-oriented control flow diagrams. A trend exists to deemphasize but not ignore data flows and to merge data flows and control flows.

5.8 Reconciliation of Modeling Views

The issue of how the various modeling views may be reconciled and integrated is still a technical concern in object technology. The object-message diagram is a useful tool in the reconciliation task (Booch and Rumbaugh, 1995). Like some other of the latest developments in object technology, it does not fit naturally into the traditional ternary approach. The use case and the object message diagram might be considered part of an integrating view of the system.

5.9 Summary

Layering and partitioning are essential techniques for organizing the specification of complex systems. In addition, multiple views allow the developer to focus on one issue at a time. These views represent objects and their relationships, the dynamic behavior of the system, and the functionality of the system. Graphical representations are essential to effectively represent the views; however, textual representation is preferable for many parts of the specifications.

While documenting the behavior of the system is the starting point for the analysis, the classes, objects, and relationships of the object model are the building blocks that form the foundation for the modeling views. Therefore, objects are identified first so that behavior may be expressed in terms of objects. Actually, classes rather than objects dominate the object model; when objects are used they are prototypical in nature, that is, they provide specification for specific cases.

Relationships provide semantics for a system model that classes alone do not provide. Specific relationships such as aggregation, generalization, and the using relationship provide structure for groups of classes and define the communication path among objects.

The dynamic model is an architectural view that focuses on describing changes to objects with time in response to events. Object technology has borrowed heavily from existing technology to represent the dynamic model, but incremental improvements have been made. The dynamic model focuses on the states of classes and how they change by considering the values of the attributes of an object and the occurrence and effects of the events.

The dynamic model deals with the topics of states and events, which are inextricably linked. Neither is of much interest without the other, anymore than the concept of music makes sense without the concept of change. The state of an object is reached through a sequence of events that initiate changes that modify its state. A state is modified by changing the values of its properties. The intent of the object-oriented paradigm is for a state to have its own operations that are designed to change its state, rather than allowing objects of another class to change its state by modifying its attributes.

The functional model was the architectural view that was slowest to evolve. Global data flow diagrams have given way to more local representations of the behavior of the system.

5.10 References

Booch, G. (1994). *Object Oriented Design with Applications.* Redwood City: Benjamin/Cummings.

Booch, G. and J. Rumbaugh. (1995). *Unified Method for Object-Oriented Development, Metamodel Guide, Version 0.8.* Santa Clara: Rational Software Corporation.

Coleman D., P. Arnold, S. Bodoff, C. Dollin, H. Gilchrist, F. Hayes, P. Jeremaes. (1994). *Object-Oriented Development, The Fusion Method.* Englewood Cliffs, NJ: Prentice Hall.

DOD-STD-2167A. (1988). Defense System Software Development. Washington: U.S. Department of Defense.

Ellis, M. A., and B. Stroustrup. (1990). *The Annotated C++ Reference Manual.* Reading, MA: Addison-Wesley.

Embley, D. W., B. D. Kurtz, S. N. Woodfield. (1992). *Object-Oriented Systems Analysis, A Model-Driven Approach.* Englewood Cliffs, NJ: Prentice Hall.

Firesmith, D. G. (1993). *Object-Oriented Requirements Analysis and Logical Design.* New York: Wiley.

Harel D. (1987). Statecharts: A Visual formalism for complex systems. *Science of Computer Programming 8:* 231–274.

IEEE. (1993). *Software Engineering Standards,* 3rd ed., New York: Institute of Electrical and Electronics Engineers, Inc.

Jacobson, I. (1995). A growing consensus on use cases. *Journal of Object-Oriented Programming.* 8(1):15–19.

Pressman, R. S. (1987). *Software Engineering: A Practitioner's Approach.* (p. 394). New York: McGraw-Hill.

Rumbaugh, J. (1995). OMT: The functional model. *Journal of Object-Oriented Programming.* 8(1):11.

Rumbaugh, J. (1994). Building boxes: subsystems. *Journal of Object-Oriented Programming.* 7(6):16–21.

Shlaer, S. and S. J. Mellor. (1992). *Object Lifecycles, Modeling the World in States.* Englewood Cliffs, NJ: Prentice Hall.

Thayer, R. H., and M. Dorfman, eds. (1990). *System and Software Requirements Engineering.* Washington: IEEE Computer Society Press.

Chapter 6

Methodologies

The word "methodology" is used in this book to mean a unified set of methods aimed at achieving a common goal. This definition is used with some trepidation, because the noted English methodologist Ian Graham accepts only the *Oxford English Dictionary* definition that describes a methodology as the study of methods, and refers to its use otherwise as a "barbarism" (Graham, 1994). However, as the dictionary on my desk supports my definition, and since I find it quite useful, I will join numerous other barbaric American methodologies in considering a methodology to be a set of methods.

Various methodologies develop object-oriented specifications in significantly different ways. After examining why we need a methodology at all, we will select one methodology from each of several major types to illustrate the major approaches to specification development. This representative selection of methodologies can be considered prototypical of the differences among the early methodologies. Recently the methodologies have incorporated more of each other's ideas, so that these differences have diminished. Those interested in some of the less popular methodologies not covered here should see Graham (1994) for a description of a greater number of methodologies.

This chapter examines the following approaches:

- responsibility-driven design
- the evolutionary methodologies
- the use case approach

- the so-called second generation methodologies
- evolving methodologies

Managers and software engineers frequently learn only about a single methodology. This chapter supplements this approach by explaining some of the best ideas of various methodologies. Valuable insights are gained by pooling the experiences of different experts with different backgrounds. A considerable portion of this chapter is devoted to Jacobson's use-case concept because of its importance and its wide applicability to multiple methodologies.

This chapter provides the background needed to better understand Chapter 7, which provides criteria that can be used to assist in the process of selecting a methodology. Advantages and disadvantages of the approaches are deferred until Chapter 7, in which evaluation information is presented.

6.1 Why a Methodology Is Needed

Software methodologies are needed to create a pattern for software engineers to follow when developing software. They impose a discipline on the process and supply a common foundation so that separate individuals can understand each other's work and so that the individual pieces will fit together. A methodology also provides a common terminology to aid communications.

A methodology encourages a systematic way to "cover all the bases." Just as missing first base in baseball ruins subsequent effort, so too does failing to devote adequate effort to the first phase of the software life cycle. Failure to properly create the requirements specification before doing the second and third steps of design and implementation can waste all of the effort of the later stages.

A methodology should help ensure that the requirements are well understood and documented, that the design is directed toward implementing the requirements specification, and that the coding attempts to implement the design. It should encourage proper documentation of all phases in a consistent manner. It provides rules that allow not only current developers to communicate better, but also helps future maintainers to understand what was done.

The importance of using a formal methodology increases when a project is complex and involves many workers.

6.2 Responsibility-Driven Design

Wirfs-Brock's methodology is referred to as responsibility-driven design because it focuses on the responsibilities of objects rather than on their attributes. Although other methodologies focus on the relationships among classes in terms of concepts like multiplicity and roles, Wirfs-Brock describes association relationships in terms of contracts. Contracts are general statements of what one object class must do for another object class. Contracts are broken down into a set of responsibilities each of which is further broken down into a set of operations. Thus, although a contract is a general statement, it is precisely defined by the operations.

If we view classes as if they have responsibilities to meet, then we naturally ask, "How do they meet them?" They can either do the job themselves or they can ask another class to it for them, that is, they collaborate with other classes. Wirfs-Brock's term for a using relationship is collaboration, a "request from a client to a server in fulfillment of a client responsibility" (Wirfs-Brock, Wilkerson, Wiener, 1990, p. 90). Collaborations are unidirectional; they show the flow of both control and information, however, they do not show the time sequence of control actions.

This may look a lot like functional decomposition, but there is a major difference. In functional decomposition one functionally decomposes the entire system. In object-oriented responsibility-driven design, one first identifies classes, objects, and the collaborations between them; then for a given collaboration, decomposes it functionally. Therefore, the functional decomposition is done only at a local level, not globally. Wirfs-Brock recommends a relatively even distribution of the "intelligence" of the model throughout the classes representing the system. This should be a natural result of decomposing types into component types and associating objects with their behavior.

Wirfs-Brock's methodology makes use of the CRC (Class, Responsibility, and Collaborations) card technique and is frequently referred to as a CRC methodology, although the phrase responsibility-driven design is more descriptive of the concept behind it. Wirfs-Brock's use of CRC cards is actually a minor part of the methodology.

Wirfs-Brock's graphical representation consists of specialization diagrams and collaboration graphs. Contracts are shown as semicircles inside the boundary of the class icons; the semicircles contain an identifying number. Arrows are drawn from the client to the server's contract. Each class has a textual description of each contract, each responsibility within the contract, and each operation signature within the responsibility.

6.3 Evolutionary Approaches

Rumbaugh's object modeling technique (OMT)could be considered the original evolutionary object-oriented methodology; the evolutionary methodologies allow a gradual transition from the structured methodologies. Because OMT has been discussed in several earlier sections, however, I will pick another methodology, Shlaer-Mellor (1992), to illustrate the evolutionary approaches. It definitely qualifies as an evolutionary approach because it uses the three traditional modeling views and has obvious roots in the structured approach to the real-time system development of Ward and Mellor (1995). It also has roots in database theory, as evidenced by the terminology and explanation of concepts.

The Shlaer-Mellor methodology, called OOA for Object-Oriented Analysis, is characterized by their book's subtitle, *Modeling the World in States*—it is a very state-oriented object-oriented approach. It provides a comprehensive documentation system with multiple layers of detail and integrates a localized data-flow model into the development of the design.

Figure 6.1 describes part of the Shlaer-Mellor methodology by treating elements of the methodology as objects and applying the methodology's information model to show the multiplicity of pairs of related objects.

Shlaer-Mellor provides an exhaustive approach to analysis. The specification is intended to be sufficiently detailed that the design is a more or less mechanical transformation of the analysis. Because of this approach, the methodology is complete and it includes design mainly by having the analysis subsume it. The approach contrasts with Jacobson's approach, in which the analysis classes are represented in design as design blocks to emphasize that there need not be a direct correspondence between analysis and design classes; rather, the design blocks may be split or merged to form design classes. Shlaer's approach also contrasts with methodologies that do not include internal behavior as part of the requirements specifications.

Shlaer and Mellor's company, Project Technology, Inc., has a CASE tool called BridgePoint that automates the conversion of the Shlaer-

Mellor analysis models into code in several languages. Many CASE tools will generate header files (declarative code) from a graphical model, but BridgePoint also generates implementation code (but not necessarily all of it). Although this is impressive, one needs to realize that at the low level of describing code logic, graphics may be harder to create than the actual coding. Bridgepoint has an archetype language to deal with this problem so it can still have language independence at the source-code level. The approach has the major advantage of keeping the representation of the analysis and the coding consistent. It can also have a major effect on increasing code reliability; if the translation process is reliable then one only needs to assure that there are no errors in the analysis. Furthermore, automatic translation of language-independent analysis into code has considerable value if the source code needs to be produced in more than one language.

One problem with the approach is that to be able to translate the analysis into code, the analysis must be a software-oriented representation of the system, not a customer-oriented representation. I am unaware of any tool that can automate the transition from customer-oriented specifications (e.g., use cases) to software-oriented specifications. Fortunately, with the object-oriented approach, the difference between

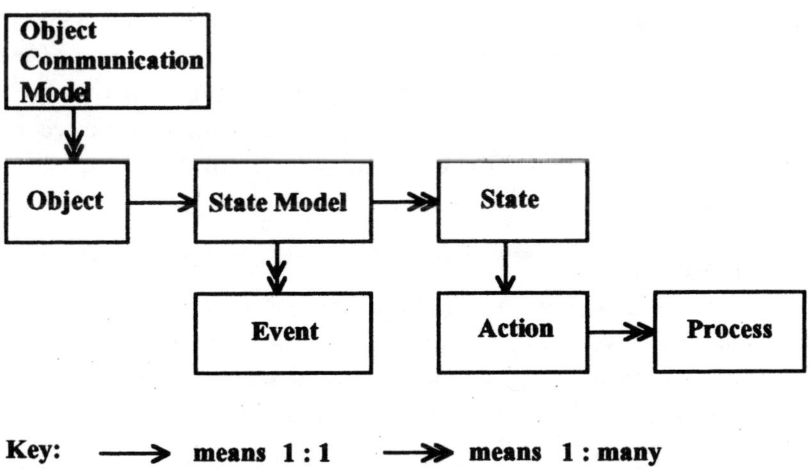

Figure 6.1 *The Shlaer-Mellor information model applied to its own methods. [From G. Singer (1993). An eclectic approach to developing an O-O methodology. Object Magazine, 3(4), page 40. Copyright © 1993 by SIGS Books, Inc. Reprinted with permission.]*

the two is not as great as it had been. Although this is the trend for the future, do not expect miracles from the technique in the present. The technology is still in its infancy; problems with automatic code generation abound in the areas of coverage, efficiency, and scalability.

6.4 The System-Behavior Approach

Objects provide one tool that contributes to making requirements specifications customer-friendly: they provide the language on which to base the requirements. In addition to objects, a method is needed to describe what is to be done in response to specific inputs to the system. The method also needs to describe the outputs of the system. Jacobson's use case meets these needs and is representative of what I call a system-behavior approach.

6.4.1 The Use Case

The idea of writing down a sequence of events to describe a behavior that a software product should model is about as old as programming itself. Nevertheless, this scenario concept remained in a primitive state of development until Ivar Jacobson extended and formalized the concept in his book, *Object-Oriented Software Engineering, A Use Case Driven Approach* (Jacobson, Christerson, Jonsson, & Overgaard, 1992).

Other methodologies have adopted the use-case concept for specifying requirements, but none bases its entire approach on the use case the way Jacobson does. It is important to differentiate between the use case itself and OOSE/Objectory, in which the use case is fully integrated and is the foundation of the methodology.

6.4.1.1 Scenarios

A *scenario* is used here as a general term that refers to a description of a sequence of events that is related to the behavior of a system. Scenarios include various representations called use cases, event traces, timeline diagrams, and object-interaction diagrams. These representations have different forms and purposes. Scenarios may be described graphically, by natural language text, using pseudocode, or using actual code.

In addition to describing interprocess communication among objects, scenarios can provide guidance to the developer as to how behaviors should be encapsulated. Classes are ideally designed for encapsulating information and behavior for objects; but they do not encapsulate the behavior of related objects. Some forms of scenarios allow us to identify and document a higher level of encapsulation, even though we may not be able to enforce this encapsulation during implementation as we can with class-level encapsulation.

6.4.1.2 Definition of the Use Case

Use cases are sets of usage scenarios in terms of events initiated from outside the system boundary. They assist in the development of requirements elicitation and specification, design specification, implementation, testing, and they help achieve full life-cycle traceability at the same time.

Because the use case has such broad implications, just defining it as one would define a scenario would be inadequate. A use case has many facets including: (1) it is a description of how a potential user will use the system from the user's perspective; (2) it is a sequence of events that are initiated by an outside entity and that constitute a complete flow in the system, and (3) it is the element of Jacobson's metamodel responsible for providing a unifying thread to the development process by maintaining a focus on user needs throughout the process.

In Jacobson's words,

> A use case is a specific way of using the system by using some part of the functionality. Each use case constitutes a complete course of events initiated by an actor and it specifies the interaction that takes place between an actor and the system. A use case is thus a special sequence of related transactions performed by an actor and the system in a dialogue. The collected use cases specify all the existing ways of using the system. (Jacobson et al., 1992, p. 154)

6.4.1.3 Description of the Use Case

The enormous number of possible logic paths through a typical program has made it difficult to completely describe a system using scenarios. When one thinks of all of the possible paths that can be taken through a complex system, it is difficult to imagine all of the scenarios that would have to be used. Because of this, scenarios usually have been used prototypically, that is, as examples of sequences than must be modeled.

Jacobson's use cases are intended to completely define a system, however, not just describe selected sequences of events. Jacobson's use of the object-oriented paradigm with the use-case concept constitutes a systematic approach to creating complete customer-oriented problem specification for complex applications. By using small building-block scenarios to create a structure and by classifying ones with similar behavior into use-case classes, a manageable set of use cases can describe concisely extremely complex behavior. Employing classes and objects, inheritance and aggregation, and use case "extend" and "uses" associations make it possible to be comprehensive instead of prototypical.

Jacobson's use case is both an extension and a specialization of a scenario. Use cases are a specialization because his use cases are rooted in actors (initiators of external events) that are outside of the software system and cause the system to perform some process. With traditional scenarios, these sequences of events can be any useful sequence, but in Jacobson's approach, all scenarios start with an external actor. The use case is an extension of the scenario because it extends the scenario with object-oriented techniques to create a metamodel of the application behavior. He defines both use-case classes and use-case objects; he allows aggregation hierarchies and inheritance-like "uses" associations of use cases. Because use cases exist in specialization hierarchies, one has both concrete and abstract use cases just as one has concrete and abstract classes. Furthermore, use cases can have "extend" associations that may be inserted into them.

What Jacobson has done is to make all of the power of the object-oriented paradigm available to the specification of user needs through this extremely sophisticated scenario model. Jacobson's methodology is actually a metamodel of the development process that describes a system, its environment, and the interactions between the system and its environment. The metamodel uses the object-oriented paradigm and terminology to describe the application of the use case to a system. In this terminology, a use case is a class whose instances (objects) represent the execution of a transaction belonging to the use-case class.

The use case became a prominent feature of many object-oriented approaches partly because of when it was published relative to the development of object technology. Although the use-case concept is not limited to use with object-oriented applications development, it has not become a staple of the structured approach because that is considered to be completed. On the other hand, object-oriented methodologies were trying to expand an initial object-oriented core of concepts and methods into a comprehensive approach to software development and found the use case filled a vital function.

6.4.1.4 Scenario-based Approaches in other Methodologies

Jacobson's book attracted great attention in the object community. Most major methodologists quickly adapted elements of Jacobson's use case into their own collection of methods. Although Jacobson builds his entire methodology around the use case, many other methodologies make more limited use of various forms of scenarios, including the use case. The primary appeal of Jacobson's use case to other methodologists is in the areas of requirements elicitation and definition, because early versions of object-oriented methodologies were deficient in these areas. The application of the use case to testing is another area that has particular appeal to other methodologists. Other applications of the use case for use in design were generally not incorporated into other methodologies, as Jacobson had envisioned, because other methodologies already had well-developed design methods.

6.4.2 Benefits of the Use Case

Because the use-case concept has so many benefits, it deserves its own section here so we can focus on the benefits and thus emphasize the importance of this technique when selecting a methodology. The value of the approach does depend on the extent to which the application is driven by external actions, however, as opposed to exhibiting complex internal calculations that depend on little input. The following assumes that the application is appropriate for the technique.

6.4.2.1 Communications Benefits

The use case provides a domain-oriented description of what needs to be done in an unambiguous manner that is natural to the code users and customers, because it describes the actual interactions of the software with the real-world environment. Although objects provide convenient building blocks for modeling complexity, objects as a whole deal only with the static aspects of specifying a problem. Another tool is needed to describe the dynamic aspects of the problem. The use case provides the dynamic dimension to the specification and, because it uses domain objects in its description, it provides a ready-made path to object identification.

The use case has considerable value in requirements elicitation. Because the use case employs the terminology of the customer to describe the problem as the customer sees the system, rather than describing it as a computer might model it, communication errors between the customer and the analyst are reduced.

6.4.2.2 Specification Benefits

A specification must be complete and unambiguous. The use-case approach provides a systematic way to completely describe the behavior of a system. It helps leads the analyst through an incremental exploration of the full functionality of the system. It encourages the analyst to look at the details; this makes previously unnoticed situations become more apparent and requires the analyst to deal with them. The creation of the use cases helps reveal any vagueness in the specifications early in the development process before such oversights become expensive to remedy. It avoids ambiguity because a customer will generally have no problem determining whether or not he wants the ability to perform a certain scenario.

Applying the use case to create a specification is not additional work that must be added to the development process. In order to thoroughly test the product and to describe to the user how the product interacts with the external environment (e.g., via a user's manual), the equivalent of the use case must be created in some form. Because the systematic generation of use cases is more efficient than the semirandom one that tends to occur late in the life cycle in most development efforts, the use case actually reduces the amount of work that needs to be done. Moreover, doing the work during the analysis phase avoids errors that would require redoing parts of the design, implementation, and testing.

6.4.2.3 Analysis and Design Benefits

Jacobson divides the analysis process into two parts, the creation of the requirements model and the creation of the analysis model. The requirements model is represented by a set of use cases that describe the functionality of the system. The analysis model describes the class/object structure that satisfies the functionality described by the use cases.

Each use case is implemented by mapping its functionally into the analysis model objects that correspond roughly to the objects in the description of the use case. Thus, the use case provides a basis for the selection of analysis objects and simultaneously provides the functionality that each object needs to provide. Use cases also help determine associations, because the descriptions provide information about what types communicate with each other. The application of the use case allows the requirements model to be well structured and relatively stable; the design step minimizes restructuring to those aspects of the problem that are implementation dependent. Therefore, the design model can contain blocks that bear a straightforward association with the analysis objects created in the analysis model.

If one role of the use-case model is to define a system's functional requirements, then how is this different than functional decomposition? The answer, in short, is that the use case is more firmly anchored in the subject matter of the application and to its external environment. Although functional decomposition may initially attack a description of a real-world entity, after many subdivisions of the process, the lower level processes lose their traceability to the objects in the problem domain.

To the extent that Jacobson's use-case approach does resemble functional decomposition, it has some of the disadvantages of functional decomposition. If use cases are created that involve numerous objects and each object satisfies the functionality of many use cases, then the transition between the use cases and the object model becomes difficult. The quality of the initial domain object model and the use cases themselves is critical in avoiding transition problems.

Potentially the use cases could be difficult to maintain, because processes are more volatile than objects. That is, real-world entities are more stable than their functionally. For example, a baseball bat is a fairly immutable object, but its function can quickly be changed from a ball-hitter to a lever. The use case is saved from the instability of the functional requirements in two ways. First, its building-block construction makes it easy to add, change, and remove functionality. Second, the object-oriented manner in which use cases are constructed provides the same advantages in maintaining the description of the functionality of the system that the object-oriented approach has in improving the maintainability of software. Furthermore, Jacobson protects against the tendency to decompose functionally by not allowing use cases to have associations between instances or to be related by aggregation (Jacobson & Christerson, 1995).

6.4.2.4 Testing Benefits

Jacobson's use cases are being widely accepted as a way of assuring that software requirements can be directly tested by running the code. The reason that use cases are so useful in testing the system is that they are designed to represent everything the system does, so that one has a comprehensive set of tests that the software must model exactly to be correct.

6.4.2.5 Traceability Benefits

The transition among the phases of the software life cycle using traditional methods requires a transformation of the analysis representation of the system to the design representation of the system. The analysis is typically represented as a processing network of data storage and data transformations, as described by a data-flow diagram. The design view has been represented hierarchically as structure charts that describe the actual program structure. Because of this representational mismatch, it requires considerable skill and effort to effect the transition. With the object-oriented approach, the diagrams for both the analysis and the design are based on objects. This constancy of representation changes the nature of the transition from analysis to design from a transformation to a refinement. The refinement of the object-oriented representation is more straightforward and requires less effort.

The use case further contributes to the simplification of achieving traceability. Scenarios can span the software life cycle from analysis through testing, providing a consistency to the methodology between life-cycle transitions. Such consistency is important to providing full life-cycle traceability without requiring excessive effort.

The following provides a greatly simplified conceptual description of how Jacobson achieves traceability. Sketches are made of the overall problem domain. Problem domain objects are identified and the relationships between them are diagrammed. The use cases are identified. The steps to this point are exploratory in nature. From the requirements statement (which is usually an imprecise description of what is required) and the use cases, a requirements model is created. The requirements model is then given structure, transforming it into the analysis model. During Jacobson's construction phase, which consists of design and implementation, the analysis objects are mapped into design blocks. Although this is not necessarily a one-to-one mapping, the mapping is kept simple. For example, changes from analysis to design that result in one analysis object becoming two design blocks still allow a straightforward tracing of the use cases through analysis into design. Traceability from design to implementation should be straightforward regardless of the paradigm used because design must precisely define the implementation. This chain creates a simple route from the required behavior represented by the uses cases to the coding that implements them.

Although normally we think of the requirements model as the start of traceability, here we already have an important type of traceability not usually available, that of the ability to trace from the requirements model back to an explicit representation of the user's actual needs in the user's natural vocabulary, as described by the use cases.

6.4.2.6 Development Process Benefits

One implication of the use case is that it becomes feasible for domain experts to create software specifications with training only in the application of the use case. The software analyst is no longer essential to this phase of software development. Therefore, the customer has the choice of training his domain experts in use-case development or training the software analysts in the application domain. Of course, the software analyst still needs an understanding of the domain, but to a lesser extent. This provides an opportunity to reduce costs, particularly if the application domain is very difficult for outsiders to understand.

The use of the use case approach is not limited to object technology. One can easily apply the use case to the creation of customer-friendly specification in traditional methodologies. Organizations that adopt this approach will have taken one step toward a transition to object technology. Applying the use case to later phases of the software life cycle outside of Jacobson's methodology is more of a problem. The development organization can choose the degree of integration of the method with the existing methodology; however, considerable effort will be required to extract the full capabilities of the use case that are tightly integrated into Jacobson's object-oriented methodology into other environments. Several object-oriented methodologies have already incorporated the use case, so for these no innovation is required for the integrated parts.

6.5 Integrated Methodologies

An integrated methodology is synonymous with a second generation object-oriented methodology, which is one that merges techniques from earlier first-generation object-oriented methodologies. There are several integrated methodologies that could be used to illustrate the category. Certainly Booch's methodology qualifies here, as Booch has been a leader in constantly integrating new ideas into his methodology. However, the Fusion methodology has some unique characteristics (Coleman et al., 1994); therefore, I will use it to illustrate the integrated methodology.

As shown in Figure 6.2, at the highest level Fusion consists of an object model and an interface model. The object model represents the entities and relationships involved in both the system, as represented by the system-object model, and its environment. The object model describes the static structure of the classes and relationships, as is usual for object models. The interface model describes the behavior of the system using two representations, the operation model and the life-cycle model.

The process starts with the identification of the objects and relationships involved in the problem domain needed to create the object model. Next, agents, system operations, and the system boundary are identified. *Agents* are entities that are capable of initiating or receiving events. The *system boundary* is the concept that separates the system, represented by the system object model, from its environment. *System operations* are inputs that cross the system boundary along with the effects caused by the operations; they are identified in conjunction with determining the system boundary. This identification process determines the system interface, which is the set of operations that allow the agents of the environment to communicate with the system.

It is best not to try to determine the system interface solely in terms of the abstractions previously described. Abstractions need to be rooted in concrete cases, so the interface is created by first developing scenarios that represent sequences of actions and events that drive the system. Fusion uses simple time-line diagrams. Because no script is used with the diagrams to specify decisions and iteration (in contrast to OOSE/Objectory and Booch), multiple time-line diagrams may be needed for each scenario.

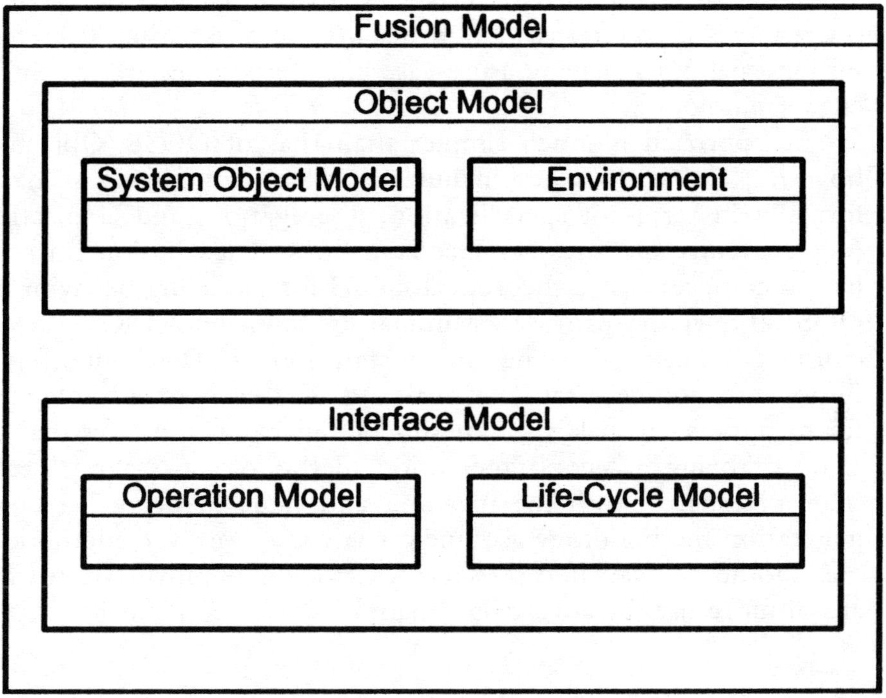

Figure 6.2 *The Fusion Models*

Once the system interface has been determined and scenarios exist, the interface model can be created. The life-cycle model combines and generalizes the scenarios using decision logic and iteration to represent the set of all ways in which the environment communicates with the system. The operation model describes the behavior of the system as a whole in response to external events; it does not describe, during analysis, the behavior and intermediate states needed to accomplish this. Therefore, Fusion delays specification of the behavior of individual classes until design. This is in keeping with the idea that analysis should deal only with requirements, and design should deal with how to meet the requirements.

Fusion is an integration and extension of earlier methodologies, but it does not borrow heavily from any of them. It does not adopt use cases by name but uses a parallel approach to the specification of external behaviors in a declarative manner. Note that system operations are a counterpart to a use-case class and that a schema for a system operation is a counterpart of an instance of a use case. Therefore, Fusion qualifies as having a use-case like method despite the different terminology.

The approach is much simpler than that of OOSE/Objectory, however, and it does not include the idea of modeling scenarios formally in terms of specialization, aggregation, and associations (e.g., extends and uses) as Jacobson does. Thus Fusion does not have a comprehensive theoretical model for modeling behavior like OOSE/Objectory provides. Minimal use is made of CRC (e.g., no contracts). Fusion does not use a state model. The limitations of Fusion are not necessarily critical and may even be advantageous for beginners—it makes the method simpler, but indicates that the claim of being a second-generation methodology is a bit weaker than advertised. Both the meaning and value of being a second-generation methodology are unclear anyway, however; methodologies should be evaluated on specifics, not on employing terms that are of more use for advertising than for enlightenment.

6.6 Evolving Methodologies

As this book is being written, major mergers are underway that will result in domination of the methods market by very few companies (Bowles, 1996). The companies that are surviving and profiting are those that have been most open to incorporating the ideas of other methodologists, that have been cooperating during the evolution of object technology into mature industry, and that are pooling their efforts toward the creation of industry standards. There is justice in this.

The most notable of the evolving methodologies is Rational Software Corporation's Unified Method. Because it combines two of the most popular methodologies, OMT and Booch, it was necessary for its authors to identify commonalities between the two methodologies. This resulted in the creation of a metamodel (Booch & Rumbaugh, 1995) that encompasses both and that can be used to compare the degree to which any methodology covers object-oriented analysis-and-design concepts.

6.7 Summary

Although it may be obvious to some that a methodology is desirable, this topic was discussed because of the widespread use of RAD (Rapid Application Development), in which methodology is more or less dispensed with. The reasons given for using a methodology are valid for large projects, regardless of the utility of rapid prototyping in small projects. The use of RAD without an encompassing methodology is risky for projects that may continue to grow beyond the limits of the RAD technique.

Five types of methodologies were discussed here to show the differences in approaches to the technology. The responsibility-driven approach represents a major shift in the manner of expressing the information in a specification compared to the traditional ternary approach. The evolutionary methodologies maintained the traditional three-view approach; however, they have evolved to contain radically different content than their structured analysis-and-design counterparts. The use case is both traditional and evolutionary with respect to its use of the scenario to represent system behavior, but it is radical in the comprehensive manner in which it is applied to object-oriented specification.

Considerable emphasis was placed on the value of Jacobson's use-case concept. The intent here is not to recommend his OOSE/Objectory methodology above the others, but to recommend that for most applications it is desirable to select a methodology that incorporates the concept of the use case.

As the technology developed, the various methodologies have trended toward comprehensive approaches that incorporate the best ideas of the other approaches. Fusion was one of the first to do this. At the same time, the original methodologies were becoming more comprehensive by adopting each other's ideas. Fortunately, this trend has resulted in a movement toward a degree of standardization in the industry. The currently evolving methodology that warrants the most attention is Rational's Unified Method.

Understanding the basic object-oriented approaches is necessary before one can intelligently select a methodology. The following chapter contains advice on one procedure that can be used in making the selection of a methodology.

6.8 References

Booch, G. & Rumbaugh, J. (1995). *Unified method for object-oriented development, metamodel guide, version 0.8*. Santa Clara, CA: Rational Software Corporation.

Bowles, A. (1996). Object technology markets in review. *Object Magazine, 5*(8), 12,14.

Coleman D., Arnold, P., Bodoff, S., Dollin, C., Gilchrist, H., Hayes, F., & Jeremaes, P. (1994). *Object-oriented development, the fusion method*. Englewood Cliffs, NJ: Prentice Hall.

Graham, I. (1994). *Object oriented methods*. (p. xiv). Wokingham, MA: Addison-Wesley.

Jacobson, I. & Christerson, M. (1995). A growing consensus on use cases. *Journal of Object-Oriented Programming*. 9(1),18.

Jacobson, I., Christerson, M., Jonsson, P., & Overgaard, G. (1992). *Object-oriented software engineering*. Wokingham, MA: Addison-Wesley.

Shlaer, S. & Mellor, S. J. (1992). *Object lifecycles, modeling the world in states*. Englewood Cliffs, NJ: Prentice Hall.

Ward, P. W. & Mellor, S. J. (1995). *Structured development for real-time systems*. (Vols. 1–3).

Wirfs-Brock, R., Wilkerson, B., & Wiener, L. (1990). *Designing object-oriented software*. Englewood Cliffs, NJ: Prentice Hall.

Chapter 7

Understanding and Selecting a Methodology

When we buy a car, we enjoy having wide a variety of models to choose from. We appreciate the choice since we can take one look at a car and know whether its appearance suits us. Furthermore, it is a relatively simple process of elimination to make a choice based on price, performance, and other personal preferences. However, a similar variety of choices in object-oriented methodologies is not as appealing. A glance does not reveal whether a methodology is suitable for one's project, and the cost and benefits of using a particular methodology are anything but obvious.

Selecting a methodology is one of the biggest decisions to be made when switching to object technology. Understanding how methodologies differ is a prerequisite to making an intelligent selection. Even when a methodology has been selected by fiat, going through an evaluation process before beginning a project is important. Evaluating a methodology provides a good overview of exactly what the methodology consists of and what its strong and weak points are. Knowing these, one is better prepared to use the methodology and to deal with any deficiencies in it.

For those who have not yet selected a methodology, the procedure described here will help in the selection. Performing the evaluation will have two additional benefits. First, evaluating multiple methodologies gives one a broader understanding of the technology compared to focusing on a single methodology. Second, knowledge of a broad spectrum of methodologies assists in extending one's selected methodology for special needs.

This chapter provides a technique that adds some objectivity to the selection process. It also supplies some information to support the reader in making the selection. Furthermore, it provides an understanding of the different varieties of methodologies and their evolution.

Many methodologists briefly describe other methodologies along with their own. Not surprisingly, the other methodologies never fare very well by comparison. The best sources of unbiased evaluations of methodologies are those who have no vested interest in promoting a particular methodology. Unfortunately, all evaluators have some vested interest in promoting those methodologies with which they are familiar over those they know nothing about, so it is best to find evaluators who are equality familiar with many methodologies.

7.1 Methodologies Galore

Table 7.1 provides a snapshot of some popular methodologies according to a single differentiating characteristic of the methodology. Do not attach too much significance to the differences listed in Table 7.1, because its only purpose is to look for a distinguishing characteristic, not to evaluate it. Furthermore, a feature that distinguishes one methodology from the others may be a relatively minor aspect of the methodology.

The following paragraphs elaborate on the material presented in the table.

Booch first published a book on his methodology in 1991, followed by a second edition in 1994 (Booch, 1994). His second edition is a second-generation method, meaning that it includes methods from other first-generation methodologies. Booch's approach is like Hinduism, in which all useful gods are welcome. Booch's methodology incorporates the best ideas of other methods, effectively keeping the method comprehensive, mainstream, and current.

Table 7.1 *Differentiating Characteristics of Object-Oriented Methodologies*

Object-Oriented Methodology	Primary Authors	Primary Differentiating Characteristic
Booch	Booch	Comprehensive and inclusive methods with round-trip gestalt design
Coad/Yourdon	Coad/Yourdon	Balanced emphasis on attributes and operations
CRC	Beck/ Cunningham	Class-Responsibility-Collaboration method—not a methodology
ADM	Firesmith	Strong support for concurrency based on Ada background
Fusion	Coleman	Inclusive methods with dynamic behavior postponed to design
Lorenz	Lorenz	Process definition added to responsibility-driven approach
Ptech	Edward/Martin/ Odell	Continuation of information engineering approach
OMT	Rumbaugh	Comprehensive evolutionary approach
OOSE/Objectory	Jacobson	The use case (formal object-oriented generalization of the scenario)
OSA	Embley/Kurtz/ Woodfield	Model-driven approach
RTOOSA	Ellis	Evolutionary approach to real-time systems

(continued on next page)

Table 7.1. *Continued*

Object-Oriented Methodology	Primary Authors	Primary Differentiating Characteristic
Shlaer/Mellor	Shlaer/Mellor	State modeling approach
SOMA	Graham	Merger of ideas from object technology and artificial intelligence
Unified Method	Booch/ Rumbaugh	Merger of two major methodologies
Wirfs-Brock	Wirfs-Brock	Responsibility-driven approach

Coad and Yourdon were early at the gate with an object-oriented analysis (OOA) book in 1990 and an object-oriented design (OOD) book in 1991. An object-oriented programming (OOP) book by Coad and Nicola in 1993 completed the series (Coad and Nicola, 1993). The methodology is straightforward, easy to use, and not distinguished by any strong philosophical predilections.

Class-Responsibility-Collaboration (CRC) is a method rather than methodology; it is really a useful technique for getting started describing the relationships between classes using index cards. This contribution of Ward Cunningham and Kent Beck can be a valuable tool for use in many complete methodologies.

Firesmith's ADM methodology is an object-oriented extension of his object-based experience in Ada and consistent with the Ada background is strong in modeling concurrency (Firesmith, 1993). It also has a very thorough discussion of the identification of classes and objects. The methodology will be referred to as "Firesmith" rather than "ADM" since the author's name is probably recognized by more people than his methodology.

The Fusion methodology of Coleman, Arnold, Bodoff, Dollin, Gilchrist, Hayes, and Jeremaes appeared in 1994 as a second-generation methodology that incorporated ideas from OMT, CRC, Booch, and formal methods (Coleman et al., 1994). It emphasizes a disciplined stepwise process. It postpones consideration of specialization hierarchies and dynamic behavior until later than most other methodologies. Fusion is also referred to as "HP Fusion" since it was developed by a group at Hewlett-Packard.

The Lorenz methodology is an elaboration of Wirfs-Brock's work with emphasis on the development process (Lorenz, 1993).

Edwards, Martin, and Odell's object-oriented methodology, Ptech, will interest anyone currently using the information engineering approach to software development.

Rumbaugh's 1991 publication of his Object Modeling Technique (OMT) was an eagerly read and well-received book for an audience of object-oriented analysis and design (OOAD) pioneers who had been trying to piece together a complete methodology from disparate sources. OMT was the first comprehensive evolutionary methodology to provide a road map for a transition to object technology for practitioners of structured analysis. Rumbaugh has continued to develop his methodology as described in a series of articles in the Journal of Object-Oriented Programming (JOOP). While at the time of this writing he has not yet published a second edition of his book, his original book plus the articles can be considered to constitute a second-generation methodology. I use the abbreviation OMT-2 in this book to indicate the improved version.

Just when it looked as if all the major ideas associated with object technology had been developed and that new publications would be minor refinements of these basic ideas, the OOSE/Objectory (object oriented software engineering) methodology of Jacobson, Christerson, Jonsson, and Overgaard (1992) proved this idea wrong. Jacobson applied object-oriented concepts to the development process itself and presented the world with the use case, a formalization and extension of the idea of a scenario. Chapter 6 discussed the significance of this innovative concept in more detail.

Object-oriented systems analysis (OSA) by Embley, Kurtz, and Woodfield is a methodology more noteworthy for its quality than its popularity (Embley et al., 1992). It has suffered from lack of CASE tool support, so its main value may be as a reference to state modeling.

The Real-Time Object-Oriented Structured Analysis (RTOOSA) methodology of Ellis (1994) provides a transition from structured real-time analysis into the world of objects. It has strong appeal for those with real-time applications who would rather wade than dive into the object-oriented ocean.

The Shlaer-Mellor methodology has one of the longest histories in the development of object-oriented methodologies. While their first book in 1988 on modeling the world with objects is not particularly noteworthy now, their second book on modeling the world in states (Shlaer and Mellor, 1992) provides the foundation of their rather elaborate methodology that emphasizes state modeling and what they call recursive design.

Rational's Unified Method is noteworthy for many reasons. First, by combining two of the most popular methodologies, OMT and Booch, it has a market base of appropriately half of the users of object-oriented methodologies. This fact alone should be a significant force toward the methodology gaining even a larger fraction of the market. Second, the method incorporates the best ideas of many of the best methodologists. Third, the process of merging the methodologies has resulted in the creation of a metamodel for OOAD that will probably become a de facto industry standard.

Wirfs-Brock is a widely used methodology that gained popularity by its early publication (1990) and ease of application. While the book is entitled Designing Object-Oriented Software, it is as much an analysis as a design method and can be considered a complete methodology. The emphasis is on the client/server relationship between classes of objects along with focusing on the responsibilities of these relationships.

A discussion of books about object orientation is not complete without including Bertrand Meyer's *Object-Oriented Software Construction* (1988). While it is not generally considered to be methodology, it is an excellent description of the foundations of object-oriented thought. The book established the idea of contracts between classes of objects and thus provided the foundation for Wirfs-Brock's responsibility-driven approach.

To reveal any bias I might have resulting from familiarity with particular methodologies, I will list for the reader my familiarity from most to least familiar: Wirfs-Brock, OMT, Booch, OOSE/Objectory, the Unified Method, Fusion, Coad-Yourdon, Shlaer-Mellor, then the remainder listed in Table 7.1. Of course, part of the reason I am more familiar with the above list, rather than others, is because they are among the most popular. Presumably there is some correlation between popularity and quality.

Although the methodologies with which I am least familiar will get shortchanged in the discussion of how well various methodologies satisfy the evaluation criteria developed in this chapter, the evaluation method described can be used for any methodology that the reader wishes to research. The discussion provided is just my contribution to alert the reader to aspects of the evaluation and methodologies that I consider significant. Additional sources of information need to be examined before completing an evaluation.

Sometimes methodologies are referred to by name and sometimes they are referred to indirectly by discussing the ideas of their authors. Remember that Table 7.1 contains a correlation between names and authors.

It would be more technically correct if I were to refer to selecting what Jacobson calls a "software-engineering process" (Jacobson, 1995a) rather than a methodology. A software-engineering process includes a methodology as well as all other procedures that are required for a software organization to do development. However, often one thinks in terms of selecting a methodology and not the process that needs to encompass it. Therefore, I simply use the words "complete methodology" to refer to the larger process.

7.2 Evaluation Method

The method involves evaluation criteria that are organized into categories. After a category is explained, the importance of the features in the category is discussed. Diamond-shaped bullets are used to indicate the individual criterion.

Using some form of a decision analysis evaluation procedure adds a degree of objectivity to selecting a methodology. The use of numerical weights and values in the evaluation of a specific criteria reduces the subjectivity that results from considering too many features collectively. The weights represent the relative importance of the various criterion relative to the other criteria. The value of each criterion represents the degree to which a methodology meets the criterion relative to other methodologies. By multiplying the weight times the value and summing these for all criteria, a numerical value is generated that represents the relative worth of the evaluated methodologies relative to the needs of the evaluating organization. Using values from 0 to 9 for the weights and for the values is one reasonable option. Different organizations and different applications will generate different relative worths for the same methodologies—no methodology can be expected to be the best for all situations.

Decision analysis entails separating needs into essential requirements and desirable characteristics. A methodology must meet the essential requirements or must be amenable to modification to meet those requirements; otherwise, the methodology can be immediately eliminated from consideration. To keep this book focused on object technology, however, I will not deal with the details of decision analysis. Those familiar with the topic can use a more sophisticated version of the process than the one outlined here.

The process is particularly valuable when the results show numerical totals whose order was unanticipated before the analysis. Individual assignments of values are subject to considerable uncertainty; however, the total value computed for all of the criteria may be useful provided the totals are not too close to each other. Methodologies with low scores may be eliminated, whereas a group with high scores should be considered further. If the values are quite close, then the exercise will simply indicate that any of several options will do fine. Unless one methodology scores markedly better than the others, the final decision will be largely subjective.

To select a methodology the reader should review the suggested criteria of the following section, choose those that are applicable to the development project, add any additional criteria that appear appropriate, consider the information about specific methodologies and applications provided in this chapter, consider your own information on the methodologies or that of your consultants, determine weights and values, and calculate and examine the results. The information sections that are provided here are intended to help with the evaluation by analyzing some of the more popular methodologies. Realize that because methodologies are constantly changing one will need to verify that any deficiencies discussed here about a methodology still exist at the time of the evaluation.

7.3 Evaluation Criteria

A methodology must satisfy many needs including the following major ones:

- Support for the development process
- Support for the development and maintenance of quality software

- Support for the methodology itself
- Support for the project and application domain

This section examines these major categories and their subcategories and suggests criteria that may be useful in evaluating candidate methodologies.

7.3.1 Support for the Development Process

The coverage of the full development process should be one of the first considerations of anyone selecting an object-oriented methodology. This includes coverage of the steps in the software life cycle, support for the activities of developers and managers, and support for object-oriented concepts. This section provides evaluation criteria for methodologies with respect to these topics.

7.3.1.1 Support for the Full Software Life Cycle

Most popular methodologies provide support for both analysis and design, so the following criterion is likely to eliminate only methodologies that are unlikely candidates anyway. It is essential for a methodology to cover both analysis and conceptual design, however.

◆ *The methodology supports both analysis and design.*

One of the major advantages of the object-oriented methodology over traditional methodologies is that it eliminates the chasm between analysis and design. Nevertheless, a perfectly smooth transition remains an ideal, and object-oriented methodologies still leave a gap between the life-cycle phases. The magnitude of this gap is very dependent on the methodology chosen. This is not of overriding importance for selecting a methodology, because all object-oriented methodologies do a much better job in smoothing the gap between analysis and design than structured methods, but it is still well worth evaluating.

◆ *The methodology supports a smooth transition from analysis to design.*

7.3.1.2 Support for Developer Activities

The object-oriented approach works best with an iterative and incremental development process, so it is important that a methodology's life-cycle model supports this. Those intending to use a strict waterfall model may want to give this a zero weight, however.

- *The methodology supports an iterative and incremental process.*

Most methodologies do not provide much support for programming and testing. The failure of a methodology to deal with programming is not a significant negative as far as selecting a methodology, because object-oriented programming techniques, unlike analysis and design techniques, are readily transferable from one methodology to another. Therefore, the following criterion is included to allow some credit for particularly complete methodologies, but it should be given little weight.

- *The methodology describes how programming languages can implement object-oriented constructs.*

On the other hand, testing is closely associated with how the requirements are specified, so the degree to which a methodology supports testing is significant.

- *The methodology supports requirements verification.*

7.3.1.4 Support for the Management Process

One purpose of defining a software life cycle is to allow management to monitor activities, measure progress, and control the process. A methodology should provide assistance in these areas. The following criterion assures that credit is given to methodologies that describe such a process.

- *The methodology provides a process to support management control of the project.*

The development process needs to be consistent with the style of management of the project if conflict between management and developers is to be avoided. This does not simply imply that a methodology should be picked that matches an existing style of management. Changing the management style to match the technology and methodology needs to be considered.

◆ *The methodology is consistent with the management style planned for the project.*

7.3.1.4 Support for Needed Views

A methodology must provide support for the modeling views needed by the application. A modeling view looks at one particular aspect of the system. For example, the control of processes is one such aspect commonly represented by a modeling view. If control is an important part of the application, then the methodology needs to be able to model it.

◆ *The methodology supports the modeling views needed for the application.*

7.3.1.5 Support for OO Concepts

As an alternative to the fairly general criteria, we could substitute criteria related to more specific content features of the methodology. The following features are among those that need to be considered: objects, types or classes, associations, aggregation, specialization or inheritance, constraints on types, states, events, event types, transitions, preconditions and postconditions, control flow, data flow, layering, designation of a system boundary, system interface, and agents or actors. Using these criteria will involve more evaluation time, but is more likely to uncover any deficiencies that exist.

◆ *The methodology fully supports the representation of object-oriented concepts.*

Most of the above features exist in all methodologies and therefore most are not really issues. Not all methodologies have incorporated the use case or have a construct with an equivalent function, however. As the list of benefits of the use case given in Section 6.4.2 indicates, the following criterion is quite important for many applications.

◆ *The methodology supports at least a limited implementation of the use-case concept.*

7.3.2 Support for the Development and Maintenance of Quality Software

By supporting the full software life cycle, the criteria of the previous section also help support the development and maintenance of quality software. This section adds some specific criteria related to such support. Three areas in which support is needed are terminology and notation, reuse, and adaptability to change.

7.3.2.1 Adequacy of Terminology and Notation

Nonstandard terminology is a common problem, but most notations are fairly clear and expressive. This criterion gives credit for methodologies that are good in these areas.

- *The methodology's terminology is standard and its notation is expressive.*

7.3.2.2 Reuse

The following criterion is important because reuse is such an important advantage of the use of the object-oriented approach.

- *The methodology provides support for reuse of analysis, design, code, and testing.*

7.3.2.3 Adaptability

The degree to which a methodology can provide support for the development and maintenance of quality software depends on the ease with which the methodology can be modified to handle unexpected situations. For example, the customer may impose special documentation requirements or the methodology may be required to interface with another methodology.

- *The methodology is adaptable to change.*

7.3.3 Support for the Methodology Itself

The selected methodology needs to provide a dependable foundation for future development; therefore, it needs to have longevity and support for future improvements by its originators. Trainers need to be available who are experienced in the methodology. The methodology should have tool support, and, ideally, have preexisting internal support.

7.3.3.1 Longevity and Stability

A methodology should be chosen that can be expected to last at least as long as a company expects to be using it. Otherwise, the pool of experts in the methodology from which a company might draw will quickly dry up.

◆ *The methodology is expected to have long-term support.*

7.3.3.2 Training Support

Training and mentoring support is essential to organizations newly involved with object technology, therefore the following criterion is needed.

◆ *Adequate training and mentoring are available for the methodology.*

7.3.3.3 Tool Support

A computer-aided software-engineering (CASE) tool is essential for large projects, but any methodologies likely to be considered will probably have at least one vendor supporting the methodology—otherwise no one would pay serious attention to it. The real question is how good the CASE tool is and what other environmental support tools are available.

◆ *High quality environmental support tools are available for the methodology.*

The above criterion assures that one can graphically represent the analysis and design and that one has debugging tools, etc. However, it does not ensure that the tools really support the process defined by the methodology or local extensions of the process model that may be needed to fill in the gaps left by the methodology. The following criterion places a higher requirement on tool support.

◆ *A fully integrated development environment is available for complete methodology support.*

7.3.3.3 Internal Support

If a company already has personnel trained in a particular methodology, this is a strong reason to favor that methodology. The following criterion takes this into account as well as more indirect forms of internal support.

◆ *The methodology provides a match with the existing expertise of personnel.*

7.3.4 Support for the Project and Application Domain

All of the previous criteria are, of course, related in some manner to supporting the needs of the application. This section adds some considerations that are more specific to the particular nature of the project and application.

7.3.4.1 Size, Schedule, and Budget of the Project

The schedule and budget of a project may limit the selection to less complex methodologies because of limits on training time and costs. On the other hand, a large project may require the use of a more complex methodology to be able to handle the modeling. Therefore, the following criterion is relevant.

◆ *The methodology is appropriate to the size, schedule, and budget of the project.*

7.3.4.2 Domain of the Application

The application domain can have a major influence on the selection of a methodology. Support for the application domain of a project provides evaluation criteria that are more likely to differentiate among competing methodologies than some of the other technical criteria. This is because conceptually the methodologies tend to converge, but detailed features of a methodology may be needed for particular applications. The following criterion is a bit general, but covers both high level and detailed features that relate to the application domain. The evaluator will need to describe the most important characteristics of the application domain and make the evaluation specific to those characteristics.

◆ *The methodology is well suited for the domain of the application.*

7.4 Evaluating Support for the Development Process

This is the first of four sections that examine the specific evaluation criteria and provide supplemental information about the criteria for selected methodologies. The criteria that are relevant to each section are relisted for the reader's convenience.

Many methodologies are not particularly noteworthy in either the favorable or unfavorable direction with respect to particular evaluation criteria. Therefore, my comments are limited to cases in which particular methodologies are especially good or bad in an area. The comments here cover the major topics as a whole; thus, subsections may not correspond to the individual evaluation criteria.

This section discusses the degree of support methodologies provide for the development process. It is important that a methodology cover all aspects of software development. If it does not, then before embarking on an OO project, one needs to determine the feasibility of borrowing some combination of methods that span all phases.

7.4.1 Support for the Full Software Life Cycle

The following criteria are related to this section.

- *The methodology supports both analysis and design.*
- *The methodology supports a smooth transition from analysis to design.*

Coverage of the life cycle is independent of the way in which analysis and design are defined; however, the different definitions do obscure what is being covered. To help deal with this problem, Chapter 4 introduced a prototype analysis-and-design model consisting of the steps relisted below.

Step 1: Creation of the problem statement

Step 2: Initial entity and relationship identification

Step 3: Creation of a customer-oriented behavioral specification

Step 4: Creation of a software-oriented requirements specification

Step 5: Creation of the conceptual system level software architecture

Step 6: Creation of the conceptual detailed level software architecture

Step 7: Creation of the implementation architecture

Step 8: Implementation

Step 9: Testing

Step 10: Evolution

Methodologies have interesting variations in how they implement the above steps. The following discusses these variations for some of the more popular methodologies.

Booch: Booch's methodology uses a macro model that roughly corresponds to all the steps represented in list and a micro process that involves the constant creation and refinement of types, objects, and object relationships at different levels of detail during the macro process.

Fusion: Fusion is unusual in the implementation architecture step in that it is not all done during design. Some additional translation of the design is done during the implementation step itself; for example, the life-cycle expression is translated into a state machine.

OMT-2: Rumbaugh's equivalent of step 3 was added after his 1991 book and is described in an article (Rumbaugh, 1994).

Shlaer-Mellor: The Shlaer-Mellor methodology is unique in that all of the steps are performed during analysis. The design step is a transformation of the analysis into design, so that the design is an implementation-oriented representation of the work done during analysis.

Wirfs-Brock: Wirfs-Brock's book was not particularly concerned with the life-cycle model; Lorenz adds a life-cycle model to Wirfs-Brock's methodology. Despite the name of Wirf-Brock's book, *Designing Object-Oriented Software,* the methodology can be used to describe both the design and the software-oriented portion of the requirements.

7.4.2 Support for Developer Activities

The following criteria are related to this section.

- *The methodology supports an iterative and incremental process.*
- *The methodology describes how programming languages can implement object-oriented constructs.*
- *The methodology supports requirements verification.*

7.4.2.1 Support for an Iterative and Incremental Life Cycle

Booch's (1994) methodology is probably the prime example of the iterative and incremental approach. Fusion and Shlaer-Mellor are closer to the waterfall model end of the spectrum. Fusion recognizes the necessity of an interactive and incremental approach, but places considerable emphasis on using a systematic process with well-defined steps intended to reduce the iterations. Regardless of the general philosophy of a methodology in this area, however, it is fairly independent of the rest of the methodology and can be easily changed to suit management. Therefore, I recommend that this criterion be given little weight. It is included largely to draw attention to the need to decide the extent to which the iterative and incremental approach will be used.

7.4.3 Support for the Management Process

The following criteria are related to this section.

- *The methodology provides a process to support management control of the project.*
- *The methodology is consistent with the management style planned for the project.*

Analysis, design, and implementation do not exist independently of the control and management of the project; the issue of how they interact must be considered. Does the methodology assist the user in areas outside of analysis, design, and programming? In particular, does it integrate well with the configuration control procedures that are needed for enterprisewide reuse of coding?

A methodology that provides a rigid set of procedures and defines a strict order to the process effectively supports management's tracking of the development effort. Unfortunately, this is very much at odds with how object-oriented software is best developed, so some other means of supporting the management process needs to be described by the methodology.

Management will want to choose a methodology that is consistent with the organization's management style and corporate culture. Although such consistency is desirable, management will probably need to adjust its style to the new technology more than the technology should be adjusted to the existing management style. Failure of management to adjust its style to the new technology is one of the primary reasons for the failures of object-oriented projects. Therefore, managing software development projects requires understanding the management implications of the object-oriented approach and adjusting procedures to the technology. The selection process should then consider the degree to which the revised management style and the methodology are compatible.

As discussed in Chapter 4, it is possible to use a modified waterfall model with the object-oriented approach. Management needs to decide in advance of choosing the methodology whether they are willing to adopt the iterative and incremental approach to software development recommended by most object-oriented experts or whether they prefer to use something closer to the traditional waterfall model of the life cycle. The issue is the relative importance of providing a high degree of management control versus the encouragement of innovation and efficiency. The level of expertise of the analysts, designers, and management is relevant to the issue.

Methodologies can support management control of the process by describing the nature of the monitoring and review activities needed. Booch provides a section on milestones and measures for each step of the development process. The Fusion book is an excellent source of information on items that need to be checked to assure the consistency of the modeling.

For the expert, Booch's conceptual approach of knowing what needs to be done at the appropriate time works fine. Booch's approach recognizes that a good software architect is constantly looking at the big picture. For example, the architect sees two equally good alternative ways representing the analysis and picks the one that will provide a smoother transition to the probable design. She or he recognizes the danger of having the design drive the analysis but does not put on blinders that would result in shortsighted decisions. The architect has an awareness of the implications that the specification of requirements will have in the testing phase. In short, her or his mind is constantly iterating though all phases of the life cycle and the implications decisions in one phase have on another. Such mental iterations can save a lot of physical iterations later on and a lot of work trying to maintain traceability though the life cycle.

Booch's interactive and incremental approach, which he describes as a micro process and a macro process, reflects the normal cognitive process by which people solve problems. However, it does not reflect the way managers normally wish to have a well-defined, orderly sequence of steps that can be measured and tracked to allow management control. Booch's approach is appropriate for designers of his quality and other experienced software developers who can be depended on to remember that adhering to a budget and schedule are essential parts of the process. Novices may need a more rigid process to follow than the free-flowing approach that Booch recommends.

For beginners, Fusion's technique of proceeding deliberately though a sequential process may be more appropriate. Certainly management will appreciate Fusion's approach better. However, it may not be the most efficient method once people have the experience needed to make intuitive leaps and land on their feet. On the other hand, the beginner who tries to make intuitive leaps may end up on his head.

If the waterfall model is used, it needs to be modified to assure that it is accomplished in a series of cascades so that individual tasks are being completed throughout the project. One can not be sure that "completed" analysis and design steps are really finished until coding has been created and tested. Only by periodically completing all steps of the life cycle for successive subsystems can one have confidence that a project is on schedule.

7.4.5 Support for Needed Views

The following criterion is related to this section.

- *The methodology supports the model views needed for the application.*

This topic requires an extended explanation to lay the foundation for understanding its role in selecting a methodology. It involves an understanding of two different evolutionary paths that have been taken in the development of object-oriented methodologies. These paths are related to the number of modeling views used to represent a system. This was discussed in Chapter 5.

7.4.5.1 Deciding Between the Unary and Ternary Approaches

The existence of the unary and multiple-view approaches has generated considerable argument as to which approach is best. Those in favor of the unary approach argue that it is simpler, easier to learn, and avoids the problem of requiring a separate step to integrate multiple views. Those in favor of the ternary approach argue that one needs to examine multiple views to arrive at an understanding of the system that promotes good analysis and design.

The unary methodologies have the advantage of being simpler and allowing for a refinement of the model during design rather than requiring a later reconciliation of multiple views. This advantage may have the disadvantage of encouraging developers to prematurely consider design during analysis, but this is no problem as long as developers are aware of it and guard against it. Starting with a unary approach makes it possible to start using an object-oriented approach earlier because less training is needed.

Good results in the application of unary methodologies are a strong point in favor of them, if Cockburn's (1994) study is typical. He found that the most successful projects were the ones with the simplest methodology (i.e., a unary one.) One should consider, however, that these results might be a result of the tendency of inadequately training personnel for the conversion to object technology and that if training is adequate, a multiple-view approach might be even more successful. Consider also that simpler projects are more likely to succeed than complex ones, and there may be a correlation between choosing a simple unary methodology for simple projects and a more complex ternary methodology for complex projects.

The main argument against unary methodologies is that they lack a state model. The unary model does describe both the control aspects of the system and the functionality of the system, however. Most accomplish this by implicitly containing information of the other views in the object model. For example, the object model can describe control in terms of functionally. However, this becomes awkward if the control aspects are complex. Complex changes of state can be handled very easily by adding a state model as needed on a class by class basis to a unary model. This can be done without making the unary method binary and without fundamentally changing the approach, as long as the addition does not drive the process at all. Thus, the state model in itself has little effect on the overall development philosophy for either approach. An exception to this is Shlaer-Mellor in which the state model is an important part of the foundation for the methodology.

The single view is not the natural evolutionary path for some developers, who are used to multiple views that are reconciled during design. Ternary methodologies provide the traditional three views of structured analysis and thereby provide a security blanket for transition from traditional methods. The use of three views is popular when making a transition from structured analysis and design, particularly when data-flow diagrams already exist for the software. My own feeling, however, is that in order to break the procedural mind-set, I would throw the data-flow diagrams away rather than let novices use them.

More important, multiple views provide a very thorough description of the problem. Although the traditional transformation problem from analysis to design is greatly reduced by the survival of the data model from analysis to design, the result of the more independent development of the data, control, and functional views in the ternary approach requires resolution of any conflicts between the views. The unary approach reduces this conflict by forcing functionality to fit the mold provided by the class structure as it is developed.

One could argue that using a single view of a system model, as the unary methodologies do, is like creating a single diagram to represent the electrical circuits, hydraulic system, and mechanical motion of an airplane, instead of the much clearer standard practice of using separate diagrams for the separate domains. The analog is not really a good one, however, because by representing the system in terms of objects, groups of objects generally describe separate systems independently anyway. A few high-level objects may indeed contain multiple functional components, but these objects are probably controller-type objects that unavoidably must deal with the interactions among the different subsystems of the airplane.

Despite that fact that a unary view is an extension of the traditional data model, it is not the case that the unary approach lacks the other two views. Let's look at this by way of an analogy. A typical way of creating engineering drawings for a three-dimensional object is to draw three two-dimensional orthogonal projections of the object. This partitions the complexity of the object into more easily comprehensible parts. Alternatively, a three-dimensional object can be represented in two dimensions with a single view by shading and other visual techniques that give the object a three-dimensional appearance. Just as this single view attempts to show all three dimensions in one picture, so does a unary methodology attempt to show all three aspects in a single view. Control and process are very much a part of unary views, they simply are not separated out. If they were not part of the view, they could not model any generally useful system.

Thus the essential difference between the unary and multiple-view approaches does not lie in what is represented. Both must represent data, control, and process. The essential difference in the approaches is that in the unary approach, the class is central and control and processing are directly derived and described in terms of class behaviors. In the ternary approach, the class is still the most important entity, but it is not so much the focal point for deriving the functionality of the system. Rather, control and functionality are viewed more independently and examination of them is intended to provide feedback later for the object model. In short, the unary approach attempts to consider all aspects simultaneously as one goes along, whereas the multiple-view approach looks at the different aspects one at a time and then reconciles them periodically.

Whether a methodology has a unary or multiple-view approach does not depend on the number of views alone. To be a ternary methodology, the three views need to correspond to the traditional three views. For example, the three major models in Fusion do not model data, control, and process in the traditional manner but represent an object model plus the equivalent of a use-case model; therefore I consider Fusion a unary methodology. If multiple views are well integrated into the object model and subsumed by it, then the methodology also might better be considered a unary methodology. Table 7.2 shows the number of views corresponding to the traditional model for the methodologies selected. Some of these are debatable because the views may not correspond well to the traditional three views, and some traditional views may be represented by multiple views.

Perhaps I have studied methodologies so much that they are all blurring together for me, but I can only conclude now that the current crop of unary, binary, and ternary methodologies are, at a fundamental level, equivalent at least if one makes some simple extensions to the unary ones when needed. This basic similarity does not imply that all methodologies are equally well developed or useful, however. It simply argues that either the unary, binary, or ternary approaches can be made to work for virtually any application. Of course, for some applications this issue is moot, because they do not require more than one view anyway, and the multiple-view approaches generally allow omitting the dynamic and functional models when they are not useful.

7.4.5.2 The Integration of Views

When one considers the three views of the ternary model, it is apparent that some mechanism is needed to unify all of the views. Data and behavior are the obvious candidates for providing the link among the views. Data links the processes and data stores in the structured approach, but this is not appropriate for the object-oriented approach in which data and operations are encapsulated into the object model. Looking at the three models it is apparent that each has "loose ends" in the form of behaviors that, when the models are developed separately, may not correspond from one model to the other. Whether a ternary or unary method is used, the behaviors represented in the classes by operations must be made consistent between the client and server classes. Assuring consistency is a painstaking task for which no methodology has offered a magic solution. The problem makes one grateful for the assistance a CASE tool provides.

7.4.4 Support for OO Concepts

The following criteria are related to this section.

- ***The methodology fully supports the representation of object-oriented concepts.***

- ***The methodology supports at least a limited implementation of a use-case-like concept.***

Knowing what an object-oriented methodology should contain is important to the selection process. This has been discussed in other chapters but is summarized here. Similarities and differences of

Table 7.2 *Methodologies and Views*

Object-oriented methodology	Number of views	Comments
Booch	2	Consists of the static model and the dynamic model.
Coad/Yourdon	1	Has a secondary state model, but basically a one-view method.
Fusion	1	Has an object model, operation model, and life-cycle model, but these correspond to an object model plus the use case and therefore constitutes a unary methodology.
OMT	3	Has an object model, dynamic model, and functional model.
OOSE/Objectory	1	Resembles the unary approach because of the unifying influence of the application of the use case.
Shlaer-Mellor	3	Uses data-flow diagrams in the process model that are local to a class.
Wirfs-Brock	1	Represented by collaboration diagrams.

methodologies in terms of their content are discussed for the following major areas:

- External behavior
- Classes and relationships
- Control
- Internal behavior

7.4.4.1 External Behavior

As discussed in Chapter 4, in creating a requirements specification a methodology needs to first focus on a customer-oriented view of the system. The terminology, objects, and relationships involved in the system need to be described, the system boundary needs to be determined, and the required behavior needs to be specified. An interface model is needed to describe the specification of the system inputs and outputs. This part of the process treats the system as a "black box"—the internal behavior is of no concern at this stage. The focus must be on the functional requirements of the system, not on how the developers might wish to design the system. Because of the nature of the object-oriented paradigm, the terminology, objects, and relationships used to describe the external behavior of the system will not only define the customer's requirements but will provide the foundation for the software representation of the system.

Use cases, or an equivalent such as that provided by Fusion, are needed to represent the externally visible requirements of the system. Although Jacobson built his entire method around the idea of the use case, most methods will probably not adopt this comprehensive approach. However, many methodologies use a more limited version of the use case to describe the interaction of the environment with the system, to allow specification of requirements in a manner easily verifiable by the domain experts, and to provide a mechanism for testing the code.

The methodologies that are adequate with respect to the specification of external behavior include (1) OOSE/Objectory; (2) the first batch of the second generation of object-oriented methodologies, which include Booch, Fusion, and OMT-2; and (3) the more recent converts to the use case that are occurring all the time.

7.4.4.2 Classes and Relationships

All the methodologies describe classes and their relationships. The main differences are in how much detail is provided in the class descriptions during different steps in the process. The description of relationships always includes specialization and almost always aggregation. Other relationships are described either in terms of constraints (like multiplicity) or contracts. Wirfs-Brock models aggregation, but only in terms of the responsibility of the aggregate to manage its parts.

Generally a model showing classes and relationships is referred to as the object model, even though the term *class model* would make more sense because these class diagrams may not show any objects. Usually separate prototypical diagrams showing the static relationships of specific objects is provided as part of the object model; however, these are illustrative rather than comprehensive. All methodologies provide the basic information needed in this content area.

7.4.4.3 Control

Separate descriptions of the dynamic behavior of the system are needed only when the control aspects of the system are significant. The traditional method of describing state behavior, state-transition diagrams, is still used with the object-oriented approach. State-transition diagrams are based on a single class and are used only as needed in most methodologies. Many methodologies use successors to the state-transition diagram. Several unary methodologies are not adequate in this content area.

7.4.4.4 Internal Behavior

Dealing with the internal behavior of the system is one of the most difficult aspects of development, because the need to represent particular behaviors becomes apparent only when dealing with the intricate details of the system. Behaviors may be made evident by considering the responsibilities a class should exhibit, by considering actions associated with events that occur, and by considering how data needs to be transformed by some process. Furthermore, behaviors involve communications among objects so that consistency must be maintained between the requesters of behaviors and implementors of the behaviors. How well a methodology deals with this complexity is one of the main characteristics that determines its quality.

Methods of dealing with this problem have been evolving and have resulted in several techniques directed at the problem. The most notable of these is the use of the object-interaction diagram or similar constructs with other names. Jacobson created interaction diagrams in mixed text and graphics form to show the activities of a use case in terms of classes (or design blocks), operations between the classes, and the duration of the active (control) status of the objects. Booch's object diagrams converted this from a table format to graphical format and added additional details. OMT-2's object-interaction diagrams are a continuation of the evolution and add a

Dewey decimal type of sequence number to order the operations. The result of this evolution is a diagram that shows objects, classes, operations, the sequence and iteration of operations, and roles in relationships that describe the details of either externally or internally driven behaviors. An object-interaction diagram is shown in Figure 7.1. The Unified Method extends these diagrams somewhat and calls them object-message diagrams.

7.5 Evaluating Support for the Development and Maintenance of Quality Software

The following criteria are related to this section.

- *The methodology's terminology is standard and its notation is expressive.*
- *The methodology provides support for reuse of analysis, design, code, and testing.*
- *The methodology is adaptable to change.*

Each of the criteria in this section are somewhat problematic to evaluate. Notation is significantly dependent on individual tastes. Support for the integration of reusable components by methodologies is uniformly weak. (This is in opposition to the technology itself, which provides strong support for reuse—methodologies are just poor at describing how to do the integration). Even if a methodology is adaptable, the CASE tools supporting it may not be. Nevertheless, these criteria need to be considered.

7.5.1 Adequacy of Terminology and Notation

The adequacy of terminology and notation is not usually a big concern — most are quite adequate. Although some methodologies use terminology that conflicts with general usage, this is usually is not of any concern to anyone except consultants who learn multiple methodologies. The criterion on terminology and notation does not lend itself to quantitative evaluation; basically, the question is whether the evaluator likes the terminology and notation. If so, it is worth giving the methodology some credit for it.

Depending on the methodology, inheritance or aggregation may be represented graphically either as tree structure or as nested contours; tree structures are more common for both. In Wirfs-Brock's graphical notation, layering of inheritance hierarchies is shown both ways, as tree structures in separate diagrams and as nested contours in conjunction with the collaboration graphs. This complicates maintenance, but both forms contribute to understanding the construct in different contexts.

One problem that graphical representations typically have is that they get very busy very quickly. If one had a line connecting each operation in a class to the class using the operation, any complex model would have a nightmarish tangle of lines. The most common approach in dealing with this is to simply not show the detailed behavioral communication between classes, but to show only that a relationship exists.

Most methodologies lack a mechanism for grouping related sets of operations so as to define the specific set of classes that use each such group; that is, they lump all publicly available operations in a class together. Wirfs-Brock remedies this by providing a tree structure of contracts consisting of responsibilities that are groups of methods. Because each contract is associated with a graphically defined set of other classes, this organizes the methods according to their relationships, as well as providing a hierarchy of role descriptions for the responsibilities provided. Wirfs-Brock's use of contracts shows more of the structure of the behavioral communication than other object model type views, still without having the diagrams swamped with lines for each method. Because each contract may represent many method calls, this visually simplifies the graphics and makes them more understandable. However, Wirfs-Brock doesn't handle other aspects of the relationship like multiplicity.

Fusion purposely keeps its notation simple and has the unusual feature of an appendix that actually formally defines the notation it uses. (The Unified Method also does this.) The use of a simple notation is based on the argument that notational overkill obscures what is really important in the diagrams.

Booch provides a comprehensive graphical notation to handle almost any situation. Some have complained that his notation is too complicated; however, this criticism is not justified because Booch delineates a frequently used subset of his notation and warns repeatedly against using advanced features unless they are really needed.

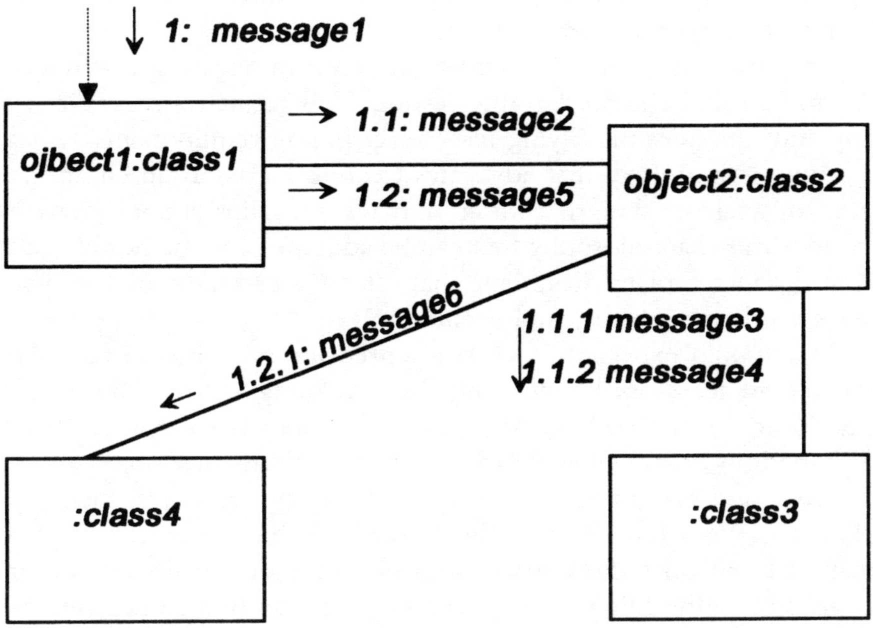

Figure 7.1 *Object interaction diagram.*

OMT-2, Firesmith, Ptech, Shlaer-Mellor, and the Unified Method also have comprehensive notations.

7.5.2 Reuse

The effect of reuse on the selection of a methodology is related to several issues. Does the methodology document the specifications so that it is easy to separate reusable analysis and design from the rest of the application? This is important because analysis and design, not just coding, should be reused for maximum benefit. Does the methodology include a means of testing the reusable code to assure its correctness? Code and design are not likely to get reused unless documentation and a method of testing are provided to give the user confidence that the design and coding meet the new user's requirements. Does the methodology provide for integrating existing reusable analysis-and-design components with the development of new software specifications? Otherwise, creating consistent interfaces and documentation can be a problem.

The use case provides support for reuse by creating a connection from the requirements through testing. This facilitates regression testing and simplifies modifying tests for changing requirements.

Any methodology that advocates treating a class as an encapsulated unit of analysis, design, coding, and testing helps support reuse. Of course, this is a philosophy that can be added to any methodology, and any support tool environment that allows association of files with a class can help with the implementation.

One would expect the object-oriented life-cycle model to improve on its predecessors by defining how to integrate reusable software specifications and code into a project. It is somewhat ironic, considering the importance of reuse to object technology, that object-oriented process models have little to say about factoring reuse into the process. This may be a reflection of the infancy of object-oriented reuse as a national industry. Presumably, as more reusable software becomes available, methodologists will devote more attention to describing the introduction of reusable software into the process. Fusion is one methodology that does address the question of reuse as part of the methodology.

7.5.3 Adaptability

Well-integrated methodologies, many of which are proprietary, are not as amenable to change as methodologies that are assembled more independently from multiple sources. The later case is typified by Booch, who provides a comprehensive collection of methods with no overriding central theme (other than the object-oriented paradigm). This makes it easier to change than a methodology like Shlaer-Mellor that is integrated around the concept of state. Thus, tightly integrated methodologies such as Shlaer-Mellor may have an advantage in more easily reconciling the different modeling views, but may also be more difficult to extend with methods from other methodologies and arguably may be less generally applicable to all applications.

Some methodologies like Booch and Fusion have "lite" versions that are a subset of the full version. This adaptability makes it easier for beginners to use. It is easy to reduce comprehensive methodologies to what is actually needed, but it is hard to extend skimpy methodologies because the extensions have to be made to fit and there is always the problem of having tool support for any extensions. This greatly favors the more comprehensive methodologies over ones that require extensions.

7.6 Support for the Methodology Itself

The following criteria are related to this section.

- *The methodology is expected to have long-term support.*
- *Adequate training and mentoring are available for the methodology .*
- *High quality environmental support tools are available for the methodology.*
- *A fully integrated development environment is available for complete methodology support.*
- *The methodology provides a match with the existing expertise of personnel.*

7.6.1 Longevity and Stability

A methodology should be chosen that can be expected to have continuing long-term support from its originators. Many dozens of object-oriented methodologies exist, but most of these few people have even heard of. Methodologies that are not either already popular or have major corporate backing can be expected to fall by the wayside. A company does not want to choose one of these when there are many well-supported methodologies to choose from.

Fusion came from Hewlett-Packard and therefore has corporate backing, which will help promote it. OMT, Booch, and the Unified Method are supported by Rational Software Corporation. OOSE/ Objectory was first backed by Ericsson and then by Lockheed Martin Corp. (formerly Martin Marietta), and most recently by Rational. Each of these methodologies is virtually assured to survive in some form for the foreseeable future. The merger of OMT and Booch into a single methodology is being performed in a manner that will allow a smooth transition from either of the original methodologies.

Other methodologies besides those with major corporate sponsors can be expected to do well if they already have a large following and a staff of significant size. For example, Project Technology, Inc. is certainly a well-established company that virtually guarantees that the Shlaer-Mellor methodology will be among the long-term survivors. Some other methodologies will survive on their merits, but consolidation can be expected as the industry matures and it is difficult to tell in advance which of the minor methodologies will survive.

OO methodologies do not have a record for stability because the technology is new and the need for improvements in methodologies has been obvious. The lack of stability in the past is no guide to the degree of stability in the future; in fact, those methodologies that have rapidly adopted new techniques may be more stable in the future because they have fewer improvements that need to be made.

7.6.2 Training Support

Even for those methodologies that can be expected to have long-term support, availability of training and mentoring may be a problem. The methodologies that have been popular for some time will probably have many consultants available for training and mentoring. Newer popular methodologies may be growing faster than one can grow experts with several year's experience in them.

Proprietary methodologies tend to be more complex to learn, more comprehensive in dealing with a particular category of applications, and possibly less general in the variety of applications for which they are suited. Consulting organizations with proprietary methodologies have considerable incentives to meet all of a company's training and mentoring needs. Because the training is part of the selling of the particular methodology, one can expect excellent quality in the training. However, proprietary organizations have little incentive to tell you that another methodology is better suited to your project. So one should be certain of the suitability before undergoing the training. I recommend starting with general object-oriented training before looking at proprietary methodologies. A good general understanding of the technology is needed before attempting to select a methodology. When beginning a conversion to object technology, methodologies are of secondary importance compared to understanding the concepts.

7.6.3 Tool Support

Are configuration management, traceability, browsing, statistical, and consistency cross-checking tools available and how good are they? Details on tool support is not a good topic for a book because the rapid changes that are occurring in products of this type would quickly render specific comments obsolete. *Object Magazine* is a good up-to-date source of product information. The availability of individual tools that may represent a piecemeal collection of products is only a minimum requirement. Ideally, a complete integrated development environment that supports the process of a methodology is needed. The tools should be integrated so that each development phase smoothly connects with the next. Full traceability from analysis though testing and back should be automatic. Developers should not have to invent necessary details of the process to make it work; the tools and their documentation should provide a complete guide to development.

The criterion on the fully integrated development environment may need to be relaxed simply to allow any methodology to qualify. Jacobson and Jacobson (1995a) reports that over $10 million was spent on Objectory's integrated support environment. Because this development was directed at integrating the process for a particular methodology as opposed to developing a general-purpose CASE tool, one can expect comprehensive CASE tools to require even more effort to perfect. Many object-oriented CASE tools exist, but it is questionable how many of them deserve the label of being an integrated development environment; calling a set of tools integrated does not make them so. Well-defined semantics that are consistent throughout the life cycle are needed to allow full integration; therefore, one should view quite skeptically any vendor claims of having a fully integrated development environment for a methodology that does not have such semantics. Other methodologies that have significant CASE tool support that arguably could be called integrated development environments include Shlaer-Mellor, OMT, and Booch. I have not studied the spectrum of CASE tool products, so I may be omitting mention of some others that are supported in an integrated manner.

Because there are a multitude of object-oriented tools that may be devoted to a particular methodology or may span many methodologies, one needs to determine what methodology is to be used before spending too much time evaluating tools. The need to understand the methodology first makes the criterion related to tools problematic to use as an evaluation criteria for selecting a methodology; however, one can at least perform a cursory examination of the tools to get an idea of what is available. Once the candidates are narrowed down further, effort to determine the quality of the tools can be applied and the evaluation figures can be recalculated for the reduced number of candidates.

7.6.4 Internal Support

The existing expertise of personnel in traditional software engineering usually does not have much influence on the selection of an object-oriented methodology. One exception to this is that a few methodologies, usually proprietary ones, are object-oriented extensions of a traditional methodology. In this case, the advantage of continuing with the object-oriented extension of the familiar traditional approach should be considered in the evaluation. Of course, in the rare case in which a substantial amount of expertise already exists in one object-oriented methodology, this will become a very strong factor in the selection.

7.7 Evaluating Support for the Project and Application Domain

The following criteria are related to this section.

- *The methodology is appropriate to the size, schedule, and budget of the project.*

- *The methodology is well suited for the domain of the application.*

7.7.1 Size, Schedule, and Budget of the Project

The principal consideration with respect to the size, schedule, and budget of the project is that some methodologies require significantly more training than others. This may increase the budget initially and may or may not pay off because of greater productivity later. This favors using the simpler methodologies for small projects. However, the methodology selected should be able to handle the largest project anticipated for the entire organization.

The cost of a CASE tool is occasionally significant. If the budget and project size are small, the cost of the available CASE tools may be an overriding factor. If the project is large, then one needs a methodology that scales well to large systems and that has a CASE tool capable of efficiently handling hundreds or thousands of classes.

7.7.2 The Domain of the Application

The object-oriented paradigm can be applied to most kinds of software applications. This section points out a couple of areas in which the nature of the application is particularly important to the choice of methodology.

7.7.2.1 Adequacy for Event-driven Programs

Sequential systems are characterized by predetermined sequences of events. Computer programs that used batch-input processing and predetermined sequences of procedures built into the software handled sequential systems reasonably well. In procedural programming, one procedure calls another and waits until the called procedures completes before control returns to the calling procedure and it continues executing. This approach is very limited when one thinks about how unpredictable most events are in the real world, however. The procedural programs designed to handle predetermined sequences can work well running a payroll program, but how would one simulate the activities on a battlefield? For example, one can not simply call a tank routine and have it merrily firing away, because it may fire when it should no longer even exist—at any instance an event may have occurred in which the tank was destroyed. Some mechanism is required to constantly poll for events and respond to them.

Graphical user interfaces (GUI) are another area in which sequence-driven programming is not feasible. The use of graphical user interfaces requires quick response to a highly variable set of keyboard and mouse input events generated by the user of the program. The actual sequence of actions in the program is not determined until execution time. Systems that must respond to external events in this manner are known as event-driven systems.

Event-driven systems require a different program design than systems in which the entire sequence of events can be established in advance.

Because many events can occur more rapidly than the system can respond, a central controller of events called a dispatcher is needed to record and direct the responses to the events. Operating systems have long used this architecture because they must respond to the events of many users. The Windows, X-Windows, and some vendor-specific windowing systems use this architecture and make operating-system-level support for event-driven programming for GUI applications available to developers.

Event-driven programs need a methodology that can define the requirements in terms of the external events. By now you already know that the use case or equivalent approach is ideal for this type of situation. The need to model complex event combinations also indicates the need for a good control model. Thus, OOSE/Objectory, OMT-2, and Booch (and, therefore, the Unified Method) are better candidates for this kind of application than are Wirfs-Brock and Lorenz. The client–server focus of the later two does not lend itself to problems such as event-driven systems that do not decompose well by considering only functionality. All methodologies without a dynamic model are also handicapped here. Because of its emphasis on state modeling, Shlaer-Mellor should also be considered for event-driven applications.

7.7.2.2 Adequacy for Dynamic Simulation

A dynamic simulation is a system that models real-world objects in which the inputs are predetermined. For example, modeling the trajectory of a rocket from the earth to the moon is a dynamic simulation, provided that no input occurs during the flight. Even if some inputs occur it can still be considered a dynamic simulation provided that the nature and sequence of the inputs are predicted in advance. If we are dealing with a spacecraft in which the pilot is actively dodging asteroids, however, we have definitely passed into the realm of a real-time system. The client–server approach of Wirfs-Brock's responsibility-driven approach works well for many kinds of dynamic simulation applications.

The use case, as valuable a method as it is, is limited in its utility in some applications. The use case, as originally described, adds little to modeling dynamic simulations in which there are few inputs and outputs or when all inputs are predetermined at the start of the problem. Thus, the focus on external behavior of Fusion and OOSE/Objectory has no special value in some dynamic simulation problems.

For example, suppose software is needed to determine whether the reactor core will start to melt down or not when a pipe breaks in a nuclear reactor. The sole input event is the breaking of the pipe and the sole input parameter is the location and size of the pipe. The sole output is the peak temperature of the cladding that contains the nuclear fuel. (This is a gross oversimplification to illustrate a point.) The use case treats the model with a single use case because there is only one input and output. However, the physics of what happens between the input and output events is incredibly complex and requires a very large number of objects to represent the reactor system. The original use case offers no help in modeling the system.

Although I used Wirf-Brock's methodology for a nuclear-reactor model, this was because it was about the only alternative available when we began the project. When Jacobson's book came out, I of course asked myself how the methodology could be applied to nuclear-reactor modeling. It appeared to me that to make use cases useful when the external requirements and user interface are very simple but the internal requirements are quite complex, one needed to decompose the system into many domains.

Subsequent to the publication of his book, Jacobson (1995) has described how to apply use cases to large-scale systems by decomposing the systems into other systems and the use cases into uses cases within the subordinate systems. In the reactor example, this could be accomplished by creating subordinate systems for heat transfer, hydraulics, control system, and reactor kinetics with subordinate use cases for each. Then each subordinate system has its own inputs and outputs to the superordinate system.

At this high a level, however, this helps only a little to alleviate the problem of making use cases advantageous in dynamic-simulation modeling. One would need a much lower level decomposition that would create numerous subordinate use cases for the method to be useful for this type of problem. Jacobson has hinted at some thoughts along this line of reasoning (jacobson & Christerson, 1993). This implies a somewhat artificial separation of the system into a series of black boxes, and treating each as a separate domain that may receive multiple inputs from the other subsystems, as if they are separate systems. Then the internal interaction among the parts can act just as though they were receiving external stimuli, although they come from the other domains rather than outside the system boundary. Thus internal scenarios are used that are dependent on internal events within the system. Care needs to be take to make this decomposition on an object-oriented not a functional basis, despite the functional nature of the use cases. Although this approach may be useful, I believe that it only reduces, and does not eliminate, the need to describe internal behavior in terms of traditional software requirement's descriptive techniques for dynamic simulation applications.

7.7.2.3 Implications of the Language Selection

Because the programming language selected is somewhat dependent on the nature of the application, the implications of the language selection on the choice of the methodology needs to be considered. Some object-oriented methodologies have a bias in favor of a particular language. This shows up in the terminology and concepts modeled during design.

For example, Booch and OMT, among others, have a C++ implementation bias built into their design methods, as evidenced by their categorizing attributes as public, protected, and private, which are C++ keywords for access control. Language bias should not be a significant consideration in the selection of a methodology. When the language does not support the enforcement of some design specification, it is relative easy to implement the design either by enforcing it with special coding or through standard procedures. For example, implementing protected visibility in a language other than C++ might consist of comments in the design and source code advising that an operation should not be invoked except by a specified set of classes.

7.7.2.4 Assembling One's Own Methodology

Several years ago I wrote an article that discussed how to assemble one's own methodology by selecting the best features of several methodologies (Singer, 1993). I suggested this largely because of deficiencies in the methodologies that existed at that time. Methodologies have now progressed to the point that there is little reason to take this outdated advice. In addition, the article was written when object-oriented CASE tool technology was in its infancy; now, assembling one's own methodology would require foregoing the use of the extensive CASE tool support that is available for the major methodologies.

There is another meaning to the idea of assembling one's own methodology, however. This can be done by specializing a methodology framework, as explained by Jacobson and Jacobson (1995b). Here it is feasible and desirable to assemble a methodology applicable to a specific application domain.

7.7.2.5 CASE Tool Support

When determining the process model for a particular project or enterprise, it is generally a good idea to adopt the life-cycle model of the object-oriented methodology selected, if one is provided. If one is using a complete methodology and the vendor provides fully documented quality-assurance procedures and supporting CASE tools in an integrated development environment, then it is essential to adopt and closely adhere to the process defined by the methodology.

If one is using a methodology without an integrated development environment provided by the vendor, however, then one may have considerable freedom in adapting an existing life-cycle model to the methodology. The organization can choose some combination of what the selected methodology recommends and what the organization is most comfortable with by drawing on existing tools and procedures. Although there may be short-term benefits to continuing to use a legacy life-cycle model, it will be best to eventually use the life-cycle method of the selected methodology or at least an interactive and incremental life-cycle model.

7.8 Application Example

This section describes a sample application in detail to illustrate how the application affects methodology selection. I chose a prediction of the stock market using a neural network because of the wide range of applications of neural networks. The following discussion of neural networks is a bit heavy in details about the application domain that are not related to object technology, but I feel the topic is of sufficient general interest to warrant the space. Those who disagree may wish to skip to the last two paragraphs of the section that discuss the reasoning process in considering various methodologies for this type of application.

7.8.1 Neural Networks

Computers have been very useful in solving problems with mathematical algorithms. They have solved problems in minutes that would have taken an army of technicians with pencil and paper years to solve. Until recently they have been no match at all for people in jobs requiring intuitive skills, however. Because the human brain is a marvel of flexibility, computer software is now being written to model the manner in which the brain works in an attempt to solve categories of problems that have resisted solution by traditional software methods. One of these computer models based on the operation of the brain is called a neural network. Neural networks are a part of the field of artificial intelligence (AI) that includes other methods like expert systems, fuzzy logic, and genetic algorithms.

The application of neural networks is as useful as it is fascinating. Neural networks can solve problems that are not very successfully addressed using either functional algorithms or statistics. The applications include predicting the stock market, solving problems involving optimization, and recognizing patterns that allow discriminating between benign and malignant tumors when examining mammograms. The main reason neural networks are better for these types of applications is that they require minimal preconception about the nature of the problem. For example, in predicting the stock market, functional and statistical methods require considerable effort in determining the importance of the various input parameters. With a neural network, one can simply list all input parameters that may be important, and the software will determine what really is important.

Ultimately we wish to determine how the salient features of a neural network model affect the choice of a methodology. Therefore, let us first review how the brain works, how the neural network models this, and then how the nature of the calculation affects methodology selection.

Imagine that you are throwing darts at a dart board. You throw and the dart is below the center. Your brain compares the position of the dart to the desired position and makes some adjustments. The adjustments can be considered values of various parameters. For simplicity, let us ignore horizontal adjustments and just consider the vertical adjustments. The parameters of interest to your brain are the distance to the target, the strength of your throw, and the angle of your throw. Suppose you decide that you need to increase the strength of your throw; this corresponds in a neural network to increasing the weight (a measure of importance) associated with the strength.

You throw your dart again and this time you are high. You decide to decrease the angle of your throw. This process continues and you become better at darts. If we wish to make a dart-throwing machine, we would not have to model this process because there are well-known laws of physics that let us calculate the force and angle needed to hit the center. Problems like predicting the stock market can not be solved using the laws of physics, however. Formulas have been developed for predicting the stock market, but these assume that some precisely defined relationships exist. What we really need here is software that can learn from experience like people (occasionally) do.

But how can we make a computer learn like we learn? Well, a computer has a central processor and a memory like the brain. It can use its memory to store information it receives, and it can use its central processor to process the information and store its conclusions back into memory. In the dart-throwing model, the computer can take the information for processing the information: "For throw number 1, the strength of the throw and the angle was such and such and the dart fell below the center of the target." The computer does not even need to know that if the angle of the dart is upward, then a stronger throw will make the dart land higher. Just like a child learns by trial and error, all the software needs to do is look at the data from other throws. If the angle is the same and the throw is weaker and the dart is even lower on the target, then the computer has learned something about the relationship between strength of throw and where the dart will land.

In a neural network, the computer would not learn relationships as such, rather it adjusts weights associated with connections between neurons. In the brain, neurons receive and transmit electric impulses. In the computer model, neurons are functions with multiple inputs and a single output. In the dart example, the neural network adjusts the weights associated with the strength of the throw. After much practice, a person gets better at throwing darts. Similarly, after processing many inputs of angle and strength of throw, the computer will have calculated better weights for combinations of the input parameters. If the computer were to control a dart-throwing machine, the machine would behave much like a human. Give it more practice (i.e., input and output data) and it will get better at hitting the target.

Let us now consider how we might model a prediction of the stock market using the same type of process that the human brain uses to throw darts. Incidentally, throwing darts has been a fairly successful method of picking stocks—a monkey reportedly used this technique and outperformed a group of stock brokers, but that is not the point. The point is that we can create a computer model that will actually learn from history.

Suppose we own a stock index fund and wish to predict what the Dow Jones Industrial Average (DJIA) will be at the end of the week. A typical neural network will consist of the following: a vector (i.e., array) of input neurons, a vector of hidden (interior) neurons, a vector of output neurons, and between each of these a matrix of synapses. The synapses store the "knowledge" of the network in the form of weights that describe the importance of the connection between the sending and receiving neuron in calculating the desired result. Once the neural network has been trained using historical data it can be tested for accuracy using additional historical data. When training and testing is complete, the network is ready to recall its stored knowledge and to predict future events.

For example, we could create a simplistic neural network to predict the DJIA for the end of the week that consists of three input neurons to represent the current DJIA, the DJIA for one week earlier, and the DJIA for two weeks earlier. A single output neuron will represent the end of week's DJIA. We could also add a fourth neuron in case the weather on Wall Street might affect the results. Suppose we input historical data and we find that the average rise of the DJIA was 0.3% if the weather was good and 0.1% if the weather was bad. If we keep doing this for many weeks and the general pattern holds and we find no correlation with the relative values of the DJIA on previous weeks, then the model will calculate a synapse matrix with a relatively high weight for the weather parameter and lower weights for the historical data. Of course, this is an unlikely result, but if it really were the case, the neural network could detect it or even detect the effect of multiple interdependent variables on the outcome, whereas other methods would detect these only if someone were to specifically trying to test for a particular type of anomaly. The more variables involved, the less likely other methods are to predict unanticipated correlations.

This example is so simplistic that we really do not need a neural network to model it; however, if we had a realistic model that contained multiple parameters (e.g., price, volume, and volatility) associated with each of the 30 stocks in the DJIA plus the federal discount rate, current average yield, inflation rate, and the values of major world-stock indexes, the neural network model is ideal.

The calculations within a neural network typically consist of summations of products of weights and other factors in the neurons to determine how to adjust the weights held in the synapses. Because the neuron layers are represented by vectors and the synapses by matrices, vector and matrix multiplications and additions are common operations. If many input and output parameters exist, then the matrices in the network can become very large and exceed memory capacity. Because this data is of a temporary nature and entirely predictable in its usage, no database management system is needed to keep track of it.

Therefore, despite the versatility of the neural network, from a modeling point of view it is rather simple; it is characterized by being high in functionality, low in data structure, and low in control. For such an application, we want a methodology that handles functionality well. This would point us toward Wirfs-Brock, OMT, and Booch, and away from Shlaer-Mellor and OOSE/Objectory, because the latter two would require learning a complex methodology to do a relative simple modeling job. Because both Jacobson and Shlaer-Mellor have methodologies that are process and control oriented and that integrate these tightly with other features throughout the methodologies, it might be more difficult to extract from these the particular methods needed to model the neural network. On the other hand, Wirfs-Brock's methodology is easy to learn and its contracts can well represent the client–server relationships between the main program and the neuron and synapse layers. If we use Rumbaugh, then we could simply ignore his dynamic and functional models and use his object model. It may appear strange to ignore the functional model in a problem that consists mainly of calculating functions, but the object model itself should provide sufficient information and structure for modeling neural networks. Adding the data-flow diagrams of the functional model would increase the amount of documentation maintenance and would require the merging of two different views of the analysis during the design phase. Booch's object model will also handle the problem well, as will Coad/Yourdon's methodology.

For neural network applications, C++ may be preferred over Smalltalk, mainly because of execution-time considerations. Training a neural network usually requires processing a huge amount of data and performing very time consuming vector and matrix operations. Although Smalltalk usually has the advantage of having a comprehensive built-in library, many C++ libraries are available for using vectors and matrices.

7.9 Summary and Recommendations

Evaluating a methodology is important even if its selection is a foregone conclusion. Going through the evaluation procedure familiarizes the evaluator with the characteristics that a methodology ideally should possess and flags any deficiencies that must be remedied using other resources.

Four different categories of evaluation criteria were discussed. The evaluator needs to determine the relative importance of each criterion within the four categories and the degree to which candidate methodologies satisfy the project needs. The question of which methodology is best can be answered only relative to the needs of a particular organization and the nature of its applications—no methodology is the best for all applications.

Object-oriented methodologies generally favor modern life-cycle models that use an interactive and incremental approach, although the use of the traditional waterfall model in conjunction with concurrent development is a feasible alternative if continuity with existing procedures is an overriding concern.

Anyone selecting an object-oriented methodology should ignore arguments that one methodology is better than another because the other does not define analysis and design "properly." The critical question is whether the required steps in the combined analysis-and-design process contains the steps needed to efficiently produce a high-quality specification. One of the essential steps that is lacking in some methodologies is a customer-oriented scenario-based requirements specification. Methodologies that excel in this are those that follow Jacobson's use-case method in some form. These include OOSE/Objectory, Booch, OMT-2, and the Unified Method. Fusion has an interesting variation of this that is not as general but is simple to use. Methodologies that are deficient in this aspect of the life cycle should not be rejected, despite the importance of using Jacobson's approach. First, not all applications profit equally from this approach. Second, the use-case approach can be prefixed to the existing steps of almost any methodology without adversely affecting the other steps, but without full benefits. Also, lack of tool support may be a problem.

The object-oriented methodology selected can affect the entire nature of the development process because different methodologies take different approaches. The decision also affects the degree of difficulty of the transition, the availability and quality of training and consulting, management style, the appropriateness of the methodology to the application, and the costs and benefits of the entire technology. Although successful projects may be conducted with many different methodologies, the degree of success may well depend on the methodology selected.

7.10 References

Booch, G. (1994). *Object oriented design with applications.* Redwood City, CA: Benjamin/Cummings.

Booch, G. & Rumbaugh, J. (1995). *Unified method for object-oriented development documentation set, version 0.8.* Santa Clara, CA: Rational Software Corporation.

Coad, P. & Yourdon, E. (1990). *Object-oriented analysis.* Englewood Cliffs, NJ: Prentice Hall.

Coad, P. & Yourdon, E. (1991). *Object-oriented design.* Englewood Cliffs, NJ: Prentice Hall.

Coad, P. & Nicola, J. (1993). *Object-oriented programming.* Englewood Cliffs, NJ: Prentice Hall.

Cockburn, A. A. R. (1994). In search of a methodology. *Object Magazine, 4*(4), 52–56.

Coleman, D., Arnold, P., Bodoff, S., Dollin, C., Gilchrist, H., Hayes, F., Jeremaes, P. (1994). *Object-oriented development, the fusion method.* Englewood Cliffs, NJ: Prentice Hall.

Ellis, J. R. (1994). *Objectifying real-time systems.* New York: SIGS Books.

Embley, D. W., Kurtz, B. D., Woodfield, S. N. (1992). *Object-oriented systems analysis, a model-driven approach.* Englewood Cliffs, NJ: Prentice Hall.

Firesmith, D. G. (1993). *Object-oriented requirements analysis and logical design.* New York: Wiley.

Jacobson, I., Christerson, M., Jonsson, P., Overgaard, G. (1992). *Object-oriented software engineering.* Workingham, England: Addison-Wesley.

Jacobson, I. (1995). Use cases in large-scale systems. *Report on Object-Oriented Design, 1*(6), 9–12.

Jacobson, I. & Christerson, M. (1995). A growing consensus on use cases. *Object Magazine, 8*(1),18.

Jacobson, I. & Jacobson, S. (1995a) Beyond methods and CASE—The software engineering process with its integral support environment. *Object Magazine, 4*(8), 24–30.

Jacobson, I. and Jacobson, S. (1995b). Building your own methodology by specializing a methodology framework. *Object Magazine, 5*(7), 96–95.

Lorenz, M. (1993). *Object-oriented software development, a practical guide.* Englewood Cliffs, NJ: Prentice Hall.

Rumbaugh, J., Blaha, M., Premerlani, W., Eddy, E., Lorenson, W. (1991). *Object-oriented modeling and design.* Englewood Cliffs, NJ: Prentice Hall.

Rumbaugh, J. (1994). *Getting started using use cases to capture requirements. Journal of Object-Oriented Programming, 7*(5), 8–12,23.

Shlaer, S. & Mellor, S. J. (1992). *Object lifecycles, modeling the world in states.* Englewood Cliffs, NJ: Prentice Hall.

Singer, G. (1993). An eclectic approach to developing an O-O methodology. *Object Magazine, 3*(4), 36–41.

Wirfs-Brock, R., Wilkerson, B., & Mener, L. (1990). *Designing object-oriented software.* Englewood Cliffs, NJ: Prentice Hall.

Chapter 8

Object Database Management Systems

For projects requiring a database management system, the decision to use only relational database management systems or to adopt newer technology is a critical one. This chapter describes the capabilities of Object Database Management Systems (ODBMSs) to help in making this decision. The following chapter provides a guide to aid in the selection process for managers who decide to invest in an ODBMS.

Although the primary focus of this book is on object technology, this chapter includes some discussion of database technology in general to lay the foundation for understanding the ODBMS. Other sections help the reader determine whether an ODBMS might be of use for a particular application. The advantages inherent in the marriage of the object and database technologies, as implemented by the ODBMS, are discussed throughout this chapter.

8.1 Database Management Systems

A database is an organized collection of data that may be shared among multiple users. Software tools to manage and maintain databases are known as database management systems (DBMSs). A DBMS provides an efficient way of managing databases, ensures the internal consistency of the data, improves flexibility in the use of the data, allows for data backup and access security, and includes numerous other features that may vary from vendor to vendor.

Software technology supporting the development of databases has moved through five evolutionary steps: file, hierarchical, network, relational, and object. Each step was initiated by the necessity to control the escalation of costs of development, maintenance, and upgrades to application programs (Kim, 1971). One of the more recent driving forces in the evolutionary process has been the need to meet the complex modeling requirements of some applications.

Although the object-oriented approach is the most recent evolutionary step, this does not imply that it replaces the earlier developments. Each approach is still useful for appropriate applications. The focus of this chapter is on object databases, but relational databases will be described to contrast the two most recent database technologies. As both technologies continue to improve, the overlap of application areas in which they compete expands, making it more difficult to determine which technology to use. The following sections help provide an understanding of the differences between the two technologies and when it is appropriate to use one or the other.

8.1.1 ODBMS Application Areas

Object Database Management Systems offer many advantages over earlier ways of managing data, particularly for certain types of applications. However, if one examines a list of areas in which the ODBMS excels, such as the following one, it is not readily apparent what these application have in common.

- computer-aided design (CAD)
- computer-aided engineering (CAE)
- computer-aided manufacturing (CAM)
- computer-integrated manufacturing (CIM)
- computer-aided software engineering (CASE)
- simulation
- office automation
- natural language processing

- geographic information systems
- knowledge databases used in artificial intelligence systems
- applications requiring the use of variable length data structures
- multimedia databases for digital text, image, graphic, or audio data

The answer to what these applications have in common is simple: complexity. This chapter will explain why the ODBMS is better than its predecessors at modeling complex objects and relationships.

8.1.2 Two Points of View

Earlier chapters approached object technology primarily from the traditional point of view of the programmer. This view focuses on the solution to a problem without much consideration of the input/output aspects of the problem. From the application programmer's point of view these are secondary considerations. Database programmers approach the problem from an entirely different viewpoint, however. This view focuses on the need for data to exhibit persistence and for this persistent data to be well managed. Many applications require a tool that provides both points of view. An ODBMS is based on a merger of two technologies, object technology and database technology, and thus satisfies both points of view.

8.2 Object Data Management Systems

Object database management systems are a subset of a more inclusive group of systems that manage data using objects, object data management systems (ODMSs). According to Cattell (1994a), the set of ODMSs includes DBMSs based on object-oriented, semantic, functional, extended relational, and some other data models. This chapter is directed at the ODBMS, but explains extended relational models for the purpose of contrast and as a possible alternative, particularly to users with legacy relational systems. The other systems are outside of the scope of this chapter. Because there is disagreement on precisely how an ODBMS should be defined, this chapter describes the characteristics exhibited by most ODBMSs rather than attempting a definition.

Object database implementations did not begin until the 1980s with the first commercial ODBMS becoming available in 1987. End-user applications of commercial ODBMS were created in the early 1990s, mostly as tools for computer-aided design and computer-aided software engineering. Object-based commercial multiuser applications are becoming increasingly popular with dozens of ODBMS products available or near commercial release.

Companies from a wide variety of industries have discovered that the performance offered by relational database management systems (RDBMSs) is unacceptable for their particular applications. These applications are characterized by requiring the management of complex data types. Classical relational and prerelational systems cannot address these applications well because of the limited capabilities inherent in representing everything in terms of tables. The appeal of an ODBMS is in its ability to model complexity in a straightforward manner while improving performance over the relational model for such applications. The growing popularity of object-oriented programming languages has been synergistic with the increased recognition of the utility of the ODBMS.

8.3 Relational Database Model

Any reader interested in ODBMSs is probably familiar with either relational databases or object-oriented programming languages. This section is provided for the benefit of those in the later group only—the section contains nothing new to database programmers and may be skipped by those familiar with database theory.

In 1970, E. F. Codd proposed the relational model as a simple, yet powerful, alternative to the existing methods of managing data (Codd, 1970). He then provided a rigorous theoretical foundation for the model that resulted in the creation of a multibillion dollar industry. Some are predicting that this incredible growth will be duplicated by the fledgling industry based on the object model. Others believe that the relational model will be extended to include the object model and thus extend the phenomenal growth of the relational vendors at the expense of the newcomers.

Features that distinguish the relational model from its predecessors are simplicity and data independence. The simplicity is in the uniform method of treating all data in a tabular format using a consistent set of rules for managing it. Data independence is the separation of the logical view of data from its physical implementation, allowing the user of data to avoid dealing directly with storage structures and devices. This contrasts with the file and hierarchical models that require the user to know how the data is stored. If a user must know how the data is stored, then any changes to the storage structure impact the user, requiring changes in the accessing program. In the relational model the user is shielded because she or he thinks of the data as consisting of tables, but the system managing the data is free to manage the data as it chooses.

Codd's model also offered the potential for standardizing the communication between users and developers. The potential was partially realized by the creation of a language that is referred to as a structured query language (SQL). SQL (pronounced sequel) is now the standard interface for relational databases. SQL is a nonprocedural query language for accessing the rows and columns of a table; it allows retrievals, insertions, deletions, and updates to be executed in a universal way.

SQL supports two modes: interactive and embedded. Interactive SQL statements allow the user to access the database without use of a separate programming language. Interactive SQL is limited by not being computationally complete. Computationally complete means that a language "allows any arbitrary arithmetic computation to be performed on data values" (Brown, 1991, p. 35). Embedded SQL provides this capability by use of a separate programming language in conjunction with SQL statements, and with it the ability to perform complex data manipulation.

8.3.1 Use of Tables

For many kinds of data, it is easy and natural to organize and view the data in tables. Because the table is the basic data structure in the relational model, an RDBMS interfaces with an application to give the user the impression that the data is organized into table form. The physical storage may be accomplished in any way the RDBMS vendor sees fit, however.

Several terms used in the relational model need explanation; these include "relation," "row," "column," and "key." A named table is called a relation. The rows of a table are referred to as records (also known as tuples); each row represents a real or abstract entity. The same row can appear only once in a table. The columns in a table are called fields or attributes; each column represents a property of a record.

The idea of a key is essential in the relational model to allow identification of rows and thus allow management of data among multiple tables. Rows in a table are identified by a primary key. The value of a primary key is unique within a table by definition. Primary keys do not have to be numbers or even be confined to a single field. A foreign key is a primary key of a table that is used in another table.

8.3.2 The Three-Schema Model

The three-schema model is a generally accepted strategy for relational database design. The purpose of the three-schema model is to allow users to work with a separate representation of data than that needed for the physical implementation of the data in a computing system. If the user were forced to work directly with the actual physical representation of the data, it would require great attention to numerous mechanical details. For example, the user would have to be concerned about the addresses of data, the internal organization of the data, and numerous possibilities as to how various forms of storage should be accessed and updated. It is much more convenient for the user to concentrate on the real-world entities that the data represents, such as an account, an inventory, or a spreadsheet, rather than minutiae of machine mechanics.

The three-schema model accomplishes this separation of representational views by creating an external schema to represent the user's view, an internal schema to represent the database implementation view, and a conceptual schema to provide an essential model of the system, which prevents the adverse effects of directly linking the internal and external views. The problem with directly linking the internal and external schema is that there may be multiple internal schema for each external schema and vice versa; that is, a many-to-many relationship exists between the internal and external schema. The conceptual schema converts this many-to-many relationship into two one-to-many relationships. This, in turn, allows independence between the internal and external schema so that one may be changed without affecting the other.

8.4 Object Database Model

The object-oriented approach offers a better framework for working with complex relationships by providing a more accurate representation of the problem. An ODBMS accomplishes this by applying the object-oriented concepts introduced in earlier chapters: the use of abstract data types to encapsulate data and methods as objects, the use of classes to generate objects, and the application of the concepts of generalization and specialization to make use of polymorphism. To these, the ODBMS adds the concept of persistence with database features. Most of the database features provided are similar to those of the relational model.

8.4.1 Principles of the Object-Oriented Database Model

The object database model shares all the concepts of the object-oriented paradigm. In addition, the database model extends the paradigm with some features of its own. This section will emphasize concepts that are not included in the paradigm but that must be included to implement the database model.

8.4.1.1 Object Identity

An essential characteristic of an object is that it have a unique identity. This is in contrast to the nature of the relational counterpart of an object, namely, a row in a relation (i.e., table). Rows in a relation have an identity that depends on the values of certain attributes of the row. These are the values of the fields representing the primary key, which may change and thus create an entirely new meaning to what the row represents. On the other hand, the identity of an object is tracked by a system-generated identifier that is associated with an object for as long as the object exists. The identity is totally independent of the value of any or all of its attributes and will not change even if the values of all attributes change.

In a programming language the system-generated identifier may be a pointer to an address in memory. In an object-oriented database, using a memory address is not practical because an object stored on disk will probably be reloaded into a different memory location than it originally held. Therefore, each object in the database is uniquely identified by an object identifier (OID) that is not related to a memory location. Because objects have an identity that is external to the data values of the object, an ODBMS can track an object through time despite changes to attributes and behaviors.

Identifying an object by an OID instead of by data values provides a considerable advantage over the relational counterpart because it means one no longer needs to manage keys and be concerned about normalization; the object identification is inherent in the database. The object data may be shared among applications independent of value-based considerations.

The nature of class attributes is very limited in relational compared to object databases. A relational environment requires attributes to be atomic values in first-normal form. In an ODBMS, a class attribute can be any type — anything from a simple data type to a complex abstract data type that has been defined by the user.

8.4.1.2 ODBMS Storage Philosophy

The philosophy behind the object-oriented database is not only that the object-oriented paradigm be applied, but also that the entities in the program's memory and the database's storage be of the same form. The object embodies this common form, allowing both data and methods applied to the data to be stored together. (This applies at least conceptually, if not physically.) To access an object from the database, all the application has to do is request the execution of one of the object's methods in the database. If the needed object is not available in memory, an ODBMS can automatically fetch it. Thus the database is coupled with the programming language that can fully model object behavior.

Thus the object model couples the database to the programming language without altering the form in which the data is stored; there is a one-to-one correspondence between the object in the program and the object in the database. The object model requires no special code to retrieve or store information in a database; only a declaration that the data is persistent may be needed to inform the compiler that the data is to be automatically stored and retrieved as needed. In the ODMG-93 standard for a C++ language binding, an object of a persistence-capable class can be created using an overloaded new() operator (Strickland, 1993).

8.4.1.3 Persistence

For objects to be shared by other applications, a mechanism is needed to make selected programming data persistent. *Persistent data* is data that will continue to exist after the program that created it is no longer in online use, unlike transient programming variables that are lost when the program is terminated. An object-oriented programming language like C++ creates objects but has no means of storing and managing them after termination of the program. The Smalltalk language can store an image of an entire application program, but cannot store individual objects so that they may be used in other programs. Therefore, this way of providing persistence is not suitable for sharing data.

The use of a file system is the traditional approach to persistence. Read and write commands are used to transfer the data from the storage space to the application. This approach may be conceptually simple, but it can quickly become unmanageable as a project's complexity increases. Data stored in this manner is very difficult for other programs to use. A change to the content of the data or the order that the data is written in requires modification of the coding of all programs reading the data. Object database management systems provide not only the persistence capability needed for applications using shared data, but also provide additional data-management features such as those provided by relational database management systems (Loomis, 1993a).

8.4.1.4 Navigational versus Associative Access

Both navigational and associative access are natural processing modes of the human mind. The emphasis in navigational access is in the relationship among things without regard to actual content. Associative access works by considering the values of things rather than the fundamental relationships between them. Navigational access is typified by typing on a keyboard. The mind knows the "address" of each key and quickly accesses it as needed. Associative access is a very common mental process that considers the values assigned to objects and includes brainstorming, daydreaming, and association of words (such as the free-association tests that psychologists and psychiatrists administer), as well as more deliberate thought processes such as sorting silverware. In the later example, we sort by examining the "value" of each piece of silverware as being a knife, fork, or spoon.

As another example, consider a family's home-filing system that is contained in a four-drawer filing cabinet. Navigational access requires planning. One should organize the filing system in some manner that reflects the natural order of members of the family. If each member operates fairly independently then one drawer per person is reasonable.

If one member keeps track of everyone's bank accounts and another keeps track of insurance, then a division along these lines is reasonable. Suppose we have the former case; if we wish to locate Jim's Western Bank records, we would go immediately to Jim's file drawer, the banking section of drawer, and the Western Bank folder. Notice that we only had to thumb through one section of one drawer to locate the folder, and if we alphabetized each section, this process was efficient also.

Using associative access for a filing system, instead of following natural relationships among the objects in question, we would simply look for the value "Western Bank folder." If every folder is organized alphabetically by name, this process can be done reasonably efficiently without examining the name of each folder. We can immediately go to the drawer labeled "T through Z." Notice that if we also wanted to look at the First Interstate Bank account, we would go to the drawer labeled "A–H," whereas with navigational access we find this account in a nearby folder.

Navigational access is the natural type of access between objects. In terms of software, navigational access is retrieval by use of memory addresses. Each object has a well-defined relationship with a set of other objects with which it can communicate efficiently because the object knows the address of other specific objects. If an object does not know the address of another object, it may be able to locate it though a series of navigational accesses using intermediate interconnected objects. Queries can quickly locate information that involves a relationship between two objects or a series of related objects as long as the chain is not too long. If there is not a natural association between objects, then an object-oriented application may need to resort to a method less natural to the paradigm, associative access, in which unrelated objects are queried.

Because associative access is not natural to the object-oriented paradigm, additional effort is required for an ODBMS to provide this type of "ad hoc" access. Nevertheless, this capability is needed to provide the equivalent capability that is a fundamental part of every RDBMS; therefore, associative access is currently provided by most ODBMS products.

8.4.2 ODMG Standardization

An understanding of the common features of ODBMSs, as reflected in database-management standards, is a prerequisite to understanding the differences among the various products. A general understanding of the relationship between database management standards and related standards is also needed. These related standards include the Object Management Group (OMG) standard (which can be considered a standard for standards) and standards for distributed computing on which handling heterogeneous database management systems depends. For a summary of the relationship between the OMG, the Object Database Management Group (ODMG), and the American National Standards Institute (ANSI) standards committees, see Barry (1995). The article also discusses current efforts toward reconciling relational and object-query language standards.

The purpose of the OMG is to create standards for the interoperability and portability of distributed object-oriented applications. It does this by creating a common architectural foundation for various technology domains, such as the ODBMS domain. These technology domains are represented in the OMG Object Model as profiles that are composed of components that may be common to more than one profile. Figure 8.1 shows the profiles of interest to this chapter and to the following chapter on distributed computing.

OMG members can submit proposals of detailed specifications that are consistent with the required architecture to the OMG. The profile of interest in this chapter is the ODBMS profile. The Object Database Management Group was formed in the summer of 1991 and released the Object Database Standard, ODMG-93, in the fall of 1993. ODMG-93 is a standard that extends the OMG standard for database management purposes. The standard is described in detail by Cattell (1994b); most of the information in this section is from this source. The primary goal of the ODMG was to create a standard that allows customers to write portable database applications. A secondary goal was to promote interoperability among ODBMS products. The foundation for this interoperability of heterogeneous distributed databases is the CORBA standard (Ben-Natan, 1995) that allows communication among objects created by different languages and on different operating systems.

Anyone familiar with the usual pace of standards committees should be impressed by the speed with which the ODMG created the ODMG-93 standard. For example, FORTRAN language standards are spaced over a decade apart and the first C++ standard will have taken about ten times as long as the ODMG-93 standard.

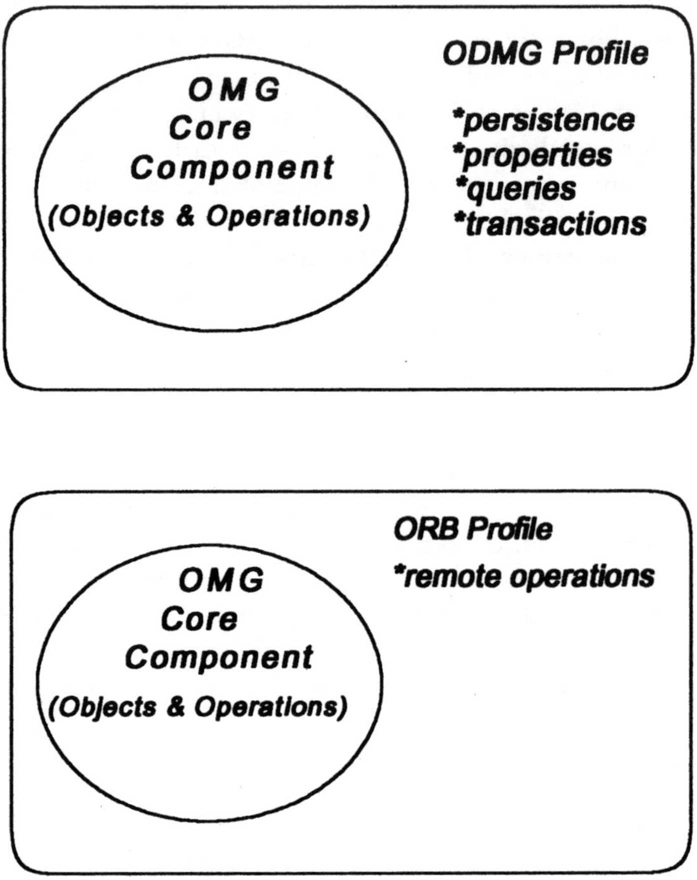

Figure 8.1 *OMG object model components and profiles.*

The ODMG is a separate organization from the OMG, and thus the ODMG-93 standard required independent acceptance by the OMG to become part of the OMG standards. However, the ODMG-93 standard became an immediate de facto standard because the ODMG is a group of ODBMS vendors representing over 80% of the commercially available ODBMS products.

The motivation behind the rapid development of ODMG-93 was economic. Widely accepted standards imply an endorsement of the object-oriented approach to database management by the industry. Thus, they give customers confidence in the stability of the technology on which their applications will depend. Furthermore, customers recognize the importance of the portability and interoperability of the product that can only occur through the use of widely accepted standards. Customers are more likely to risk a new technology if they do not have to be dependent on a single vendor's implementation of that technology.

The ODMG-93 standard was not intended to be a final standard; rather, it is intended to be a foundation for further development of the technology in a predictable fashion. The standards adopted were chosen to allow the vendors to achieve an early implementation of the standard. They were also chosen to describe the future evolution of the standard to prevent the various vendors from diverging in areas involving code portability. Divergence in other areas, however, such as specialized functionality for specific market niches, is not discouraged. To further guard against divergence in the future in critical areas, the ODMG-93 includes a description of the elements of the next update to the standard. The SQL3 standard can be considered competition to ODMG's standard, but the real competition here is between the products themselves: the extended RDBMSs that will use the SQL3 standard and the pure ODBMSs that will use the ODMG standard.

The foundation of the ODMG standard is the Object Model (ODMG/ OM), which is a superset of the OMG Object Model (OMG/OM). The ODMG/OM describes types, objects, operations, and an inheritance hierarchy as does the OMG/OM, but extends the model for database management purposes. In addition to the object model, which provides the conceptual framework for the standard, the standard includes an object definition language, an object query language, an object manipulation language, and C++ and Smalltalk language bindings and provisions for additional language bindings. The object definition language is a specification language used to define the interfaces to object types that conform to the ODMG object model. The object query language is used for querying and updating database objects. The bindings provide the full power of a programming language to the database management system.

8.4.2.1 ODMG-93 Languages and Bindings

There are two opposing philosophies about how database and programming language capabilities should interact. The primary purpose of database language is to query the database, whereas the primary purpose of the programming language is to perform calculations. One approach is to have a database query language that is entirely independent of the programming language. This approach was adopted by RDBMSs using SQL and has the advantage that only one query language syntax needs to be learned. There is a disadvantage to this approach, however, in that constant transformations are required between the database variables and the programming language variables because the type systems are incompatible. The ODMG-93 standard defines an embedded query language that adopts the second approach, namely, that database and programming should be integrated with a common type system. This eliminates the need for transformations between the two representations and greatly simplifies their interaction. The standard also provides a stand-alone query language, but it is the embedded versions that can be expected to receive the heaviest use as the stand-alone version is of limited use without the language support.

The language definitions used in the ODMG-93 standard are separated into three categories: the object definition language (ODL), the object query language (OQL), and the object manipulation language (OML). The object definition and query languages can be defined independently of any particular implementing language, such as C++ or Smalltalk. However, the object manipulation language is tied to the syntax of the implementing language and is, therefore, defined separately for each language as part of the definition of the language binding.

The language binding is the definition of how the ODMG-93 standard is implemented using an existing language. The binding is implemented by using a class library and by extending the syntax of the language and applying a preprocessor to translate the extended syntax. From the point of view of a programmer, the language binding combines the ODL, OML, and OQL into a single coherent language that uses the natural syntax of the language. OQL is actually the subset of OML that supports associative access. In the following discussions of the components of ODMG-93, the object manipulation language is discussed as a part of the discussion of language bindings because there is no OML defined independently of an implementing language.

8.4.2.2 Object Definition Language

The object definition language is a declarative language for the specification of interface signatures that conform to the ODMG Object Model. The purpose of ODL is to define object types, not to be a full programming language; it needs an OML to be complete. ODL is language independent; however, the actual language implementations of it require a translation from the ODL. Although the ODL does not provide interoperability for heterogeneous ODBMSs, it is does contribute toward that goal.

ODL allows for the capability of integrating schemas from many applications and sources. The ODL was designed to provide a level of insulation protecting applications from variations in programming languages and ODBMS products by providing a common language for integration. Thus ODL functions similarly to the traditional database data definition language (DDL). It is compatible with the OMG's Interface Definition Language (IDL) that is part of the Common Object Request Broker Architecture (CORBA) standard for the ORB profile.

8.4.2.3 ODMG Object Query Language

The ODMG object query language provides declarative access to an object database consistent with the Object Model. Declarative access does not require the program to know how to navigate database structures but only to specify the conditions on the data to be retrieved. This is in contrast to the procedural access that was commonly used before relational databases were available in which the programmer had to understand the details of the database structure in order to access data.

OQL was kept somewhat similar to its relational counterpart, SQL, to minimize the amount of relearning by programmers. However, the Object Model has considerably greater capability and corresponding complexity than does the relation model. Therefore, the ODMG's main goal was to implement capabilities needed by ODBMSs, not to maintain full SQL compatibility.

Features of OQL include the following as listed by Strickland (1993):

Booleans: *and*, *or*, and *not*

Collection operations, like intersect, union, test membership, use subrange, flatten

Nested queries

Selection from classes or sets

Sorting and ordering

Universal and existence quantification

Calling methods on objects

OQL, like SQL, is not computationally complete. The object manipulation language described in the following section is required to provide the needed logical manipulation capabilities.

8.4.2.4 ODMG C++ and Smalltalk Language Bindings

The ODMG-93 standard is designed to allow a language binding to be developed for any object-oriented programming language. The goal of the binding is to create a database capability within the language that does not violate the spirit of the language. A binding for Smalltalk is described by ODMG-93. It is included in the ODMG-93 standard to give a sense of the multilingual capability of the ODMG/OM. The standard provides a complete definition of the binding for C++, the most commonly used programming language among ODBMSs.

8.5 Limitations of the Relational and Object Models

The creation of relational databases was driven by applications requiring flexible processing of simple fixed-format data that fits naturally into tables. As expected, relational databases excel in handling this type of data. The creation of object databases fills the need for handling complex data that does not adapt to tabular form. Again, as one would expect, object databases excel in applications that model complex entities.

Each approach is currently limited in its ability to handle the type of application for which the other was originally devised. Vendors in both camps are working hard to overcome product limitations, however. RDBMS makers are adapting their products to become more object oriented. By making these changes, they hope to discourage customers from defecting to ODBMSs. In many areas, ODBMS vendors must play catch-up with the relational vendors who have had more time to improve their products. Therefore, ODBMS companies are working to provide customers with products that offer data management features comparable with RDBMS products. The sections below discuss some of the challenges that face the particular models.

In many cases in the explanation of the limitations of the relational model below, a comparison will be made with the object model to highlight the deficiency and demonstrate that it can be overcome. In many, but not all of these cases, the limitation could also be removed by extending the relational model.

8.5.1 Limitations of the Relational Model

Although the simplicity of the relational model is appealing, particularly to developers who have had to deal with the complexities inherent in the hierarchical and network models, the relational model is limited in two major areas: the ability to handle complexity and the ability to achieve acceptable performance levels for many types of applications (Kim, 1994). This section examines these major areas and discusses more detailed features that contribute to the major problems. Finally, the section examines the ongoing effort to extend the relation model to deal with its limitations.

8.5.1.1 Modeling Complexity

The reason that the relational model does not handle complexity well is due to the restrictions necessitated by its rigorous mathematical foundation and the resulting restrictions on its tabular representation. One of these restrictions is the requirement for normalization of data. The normalization of data is used to ensure predictability about how a database functions, to help ensure data integrity, and to avoid duplication of data, but this places severe limits on what can be effectively represented. For example, because first-normal form disallows structure within cells of the table, one cannot place another table within a cell of a table. Thus even the modestly complex modeling concept of nesting is inhibited. This is just one of many instances in which the format is too rigid to represent complex data types.

In order to achieve data independence, the relational approach forces all data into a tabular form and uses a common language (SQL) to manage it. One problem with this approach is that many types of data are not best represented as tables. For example, parts explosions and organizational structures are naturally hierarchical in nature, and data within these structures can be most efficiently accessed navigationally rather than by association, as done by the relational model. In the past, this lack of efficiency has been accepted as the price to pay for data independence.

The number and variety of data types allowed in a relational model are quite restrictive when compared to an ODBMS. The relational model allows for predefined data types, such as integer, character, and string. Some RDBMSs allow date, money, and time types, but there is no way for users to create their own data types. In contrast to the relational model, the object model allows an unlimited number of different data types that may be defined by the developer. Thus the object model is more powerful than the relational model in its ability to express application semantics because it can model abstract data types that represent real entities in the problem domain.

The relational model does not allow modeling of natural hierarchical specialization relationships. Although one could consider a table as representing a class, there is no way in the classical relational model to represent a subclass. This is not possible in classical relation theory because there is no way to model the concept of one table being made up of other tables. The relational model also does not represent the aggregation or composition relationship in which a whole consists of parts. This limitation is being circumvented in the nested relational database model that extends the classical model to allow nested tables (Rao, 1994). In contrast, the object model can represent hierarchies that occur in the real world by using generalization, specialization, and aggregation, without stretching the paradigm at all.

Specialization relationships exist in the real world, and if one is using an RDBMS the relationships must be represented using the relational model. There are many ways to implement inheritance using the relational model, but none are pretty. One can model each class of objects by a separate relational table. (This is called a "relation" in database terminology; do not confuse this with the word relation sometimes used in describing associations or relationships between objects.) However, there is no way in the relational model for the relations to be related in a hierarchical manner to implement inheritance. Alternatively, one can use a single table that contains all the attributes of both the parent and child objects, but this means that many attributes will be null. Another alternative, having each child object contain the common attributes, causes redundant data. When modeling a specialization relationship, only the object model provides an elegant and efficient solution.

As mentioned previously, deficiencies in the relational model frequently may be eliminated by extending the relational model. In the case of modeling complexity, however, extending the relational model is quite limited, as will be discussed later.

8.5.1.2 Modeling Mismatches

Relational tables are used to represent real-world objects. For some objects, like a spreadsheet, this representation occurs naturally. Most real-world objects do not have a tabular structure and must be adapted to relational form, however. The more complex the object is, the less smoothly this adaptation is achieved.

The mismatch between the relational interface (e.g., SQL) and programming languages causes much of the difficulty in making this adaptation. This difference in data structures results in what is often called "impedance mismatch." Although the relational model requires data representing objects to be saved in tabular form, the programming language requires the data to be placed in variables in a data structure. This is needed to allow procedural manipulations on the data and to exercise full computational logic. Dealing with the mismatch requires obliterating the object's structure every time an object needs to be stored in the flattened form required by the relational model and reconstructing the object on retrieval.

Considerable additional work is involved in flattening objects and partitioning them into homogeneous structures to allow storage in records consistent with the relational model. References to these relations must be added to the object. Considerable extra programming is involved in maintaining the two separate representations of the objects.

Colley (1992) points out that the additions needed to maintain the transition between the relational and object model corrupt the objects, because the relations that have been added are not characteristics of the real-world object. The point of using objects is to free the programmer from the burden of having to deal with the details contained in the object; adding the relations necessary to retain the object in a nonobject environment exposes the programmer to detail beyond the methods needed to manipulate objects.

Using an RDBMS to store objects is analogous to the well-known example of disassembling your car every time you park in the garage. (This analogy was originated by Tom Atwood or Mary Loomis; each is willing to give the other credit for it.) To store a car object in a relational environment, the car must be disassembled into its component parts. The tires go into one table; the spark plugs into another, and so on until the whole car is disassembled and stored in tables. The next time the car object needs to be used it must be reassembled. As the analogy emphasizes, this is not a particularly efficient solution.

In contrast, the ODBMS does not need to transform the in-memory representations of the object programs to a different form to fit into the ODBMS data model because the in-memory and in-storage representations of an object use a common model. In terms of the above example, the car would not be subject to disassembly in order to be parked in the garage. Both the car and garage would be treated as objects and could simply be designated as have the property of being persistent.

Colley points out that many organizations attempt to make the transition to object technology by using an object-oriented programming language to reduce development and maintenance costs, but lose many of the benefits by attempting to retain the use of an RDBMS for data storage. This mismatch does not occur between ODBMSs and object-oriented programming languages. A separate database language, like SQL, is no longer required (although it may still be a convenience), because an ODBMS can integrate database capabilities with an object-oriented programming language. Use of an ODBMS with the object-oriented programming language (OOPL) eliminates the extensive programming effort needed for the translation of every storage and retrieval of objects (Colley, 1992).

8.5.1.3 Lack of Semantic Content

The data in relational databases lacks any semantics beyond being in a relational format; therefore, operations on the data are limited to simple operations like SELECT, JOIN, and UNION that have meaning to all tabular data. More complex operations that are based on the physical or conceptual meaning of specific data types are not allowed.

Because the relational model does not handle semantics, the application, not the database, must interpret the meaning of the values in the database. This independence of the data from function makes the use of the data very flexible; however, this flexibility comes at a high cost—the lack of semantics in the database means that sharing is limited to data and the potential for also sharing the meaning of data is lost. This results in duplication of effort because each application must maintain its own meaning of the data; this requires extra programming to add semantics to the data. Furthermore, it increases the likelihood of errors occurring in multiple applications' interpretation of the semantics.

As discussed in Section 8.5.1.1, "Modeling Complexity," the relational model lacks the semantics of relationships such as the ability to represent generalization, specialization, and aggregation relationships. On the other hand, the object model allows all of these kinds of relationships. As a simple example, it is natural for an ODBMS to represent the fact that a car object has four wheel objects and to enforce this constraint — if records were entered that recorded the assembly of only three wheels then the ODBMS would know that the multiplicity of the relationship had been violated. At a more sophisticated level, the leather seat upholstery type could inherit attributes and relationships from a seat upholstery type. All of these capabilities are simply those that one should by now expect an object-oriented model to exhibit. However, the ODBMS adds persistence, checking of the consistency of the relationships, and numerous other typical database features as well.

8.5.1.2 Performance

The increasing size of databases and the advent of new types of data that need to be stored, such as multimedia and topographical information, require greater efficiency than can be obtained by the relational approach. Relational database performance is compromised by several characteristics of the model. The need to flatten data, discussed previously, requires extra processing both to create and modify the tables from program data structures and to access data and redistribute it into the program variables. Normalization of the data into multiple tables simplifies avoiding the duplication of data, but the increased number of tables increases the amount of processing required to utilize the data. In particular, a greater number of tables requires more validation logic, record locking, and error handling (Colley, 1992). An ODBMS does not require either the flattening or the translation process, because objects are stored in the same form in memory by the programming language and on permanent storage by the database. Therefore, the object model does not suffer from the performance hit from these sources.

The total dependence of the classical relational model on associative access is a major limitation of the model with respect to performance. In the words of Loomis (1993b, p. 78), "Joining and sorting compete for being the slowest operations possible in relational systems." A *join* is an associative retrieval of data from more than one table. Because joining tables requires every row to be compared with every other row to determine if values meet some condition, the time required increases with the product of the number of rows in each table. For example, even joining two tables of length N may require N^2 comparisons. In effect, the relational model rebuilds relationships as needed rather than permanently maintaining the relationships.

In contrast, the navigational access inherent in the object model does not require such reconstruction because it maintains the addresses of related objects and can access the data in these objects directly. When the object model uses navigational access it avoids the poor performance of associative access for large tables. The use of navigational access is restricted to use within a planned framework of object relationships, however. Of course, when the object model finds it necessary to use associative access it is no more efficient that the relational model and for some ODBMSs may be less efficient, so far, because of more immature optimization techniques.

The high cost of associative access can be alleviated by the use of parallel processing, particularly the use of associative processors that can perform query processing without sending all of the data to the central processing unit (Krikelis & Weem, 1994). However, improving associative performance by use of associative processors is independent of whether a relational or object-oriented approach is used.

8.5.1.3 Application Programming Interfaces

Relational database application programming interfaces (APIs) are needed to shield developers from some of the intricacies of RDBMSs, but are not entirely adequate for the job. Vasan (1992a) describes many problems with the existing APIs. It can take numerous lines of code just to connect a database to an API. Extensive coding is necessary to perform even simple queries and APIs force a programming style that is likely to cause errors. Each time that a user requires a query, there is significant repetition of code. Vasan further describes how using C++ and an object-oriented approach solve many of the existing problems.

8.5.1.4 Standards Problems

To overcome some of the limitations of SQL, vendors added extensions to SQL to make it more complete. As a result, only 30%–40% of the calls in an application are actually in the "standard SQL," which means the remaining 60%–70% use vendor-specific extensions (Cattell, 1994b, p. 146). Therefore, the proprietary extensions of SQL by Oracle and Ingres, for example, are incompatible. Although such extensions increase the ability of the SQL to handle complexity somewhat, this comes at the price of decreased portability.

8.5.2 Extending the Relational Model

Some vendors have produced hybrid forms of a database management system that attempt to marry the capabilities of ODBMSs and RDBMSs. Not only may these extended RDBMSs be a better option than RDBMSs that conform to the classic relational model, they may provide a smoother transition toward object technology for companies with a substantial existing commitment to relational technology.

On the other hand, the extended RDBMS approach may impede the complete transition to object technology and may leave a company just short of meeting its real needs. The most important elements in the decision to choose an extended relational model or an ODBMS are the size and nature of the legacy system, the nature of the application, and long-term plans. Loomis (1993a) assists with making this decision with a list of user needs correlated with the capabilities of RDBMSs, extended RDBMSs, and ODBMSs.

Vasan (1992b, p. 42) includes the following advanced features as possible additions in extended RDBMs: "indexes, views, defaults, domains, rules, stored procedures, referential integrity, and triggers." Some of these have been in existing RDBMSs long enough to no longer be consider advanced features. More flexible data types and binary large objects (BLOBs) should also be included in the list. Another possible extension is to violate first-normal form to allow nesting of tables. The items of particular interest in comparison to ODBMS capabilities are stored procedures and BLOBs.

Extended RDBMSs add stored procedures because normally an RDBMS can store only data, not operations to manipulate the data. Loomis (1994, p. 77) defines a *stored procedure* as "a set of SQL statements, to be stored and executed by the DBMS server rather than the application space." By storing procedures, not all of the operations on the data are the responsibility of the application code to maintain, but some can be maintained by the database itself. This has the advantage, in many instances, of reducing the amount of communication between server and client that would otherwise be required to move the data to the client for processing by the application program.

The BLOBs provided by extended RDBMSs to represent arbitrary data structures attempt to deal with the problem that the relational model provides an extremely limited number of types. BLOBs are needed because tables require data to be homogeneous. For example, each value in a row must be of identical type, such as all integers, and each row must have an identical set of types for its fields. Furthermore, the number of fields (attributes) must be a fixed number. This makes managing variable length data problematic. BLOBs allow storing variable length data of varying types.

8.5.2.1 Limitations on Extended RDBMSs

Although extended RDBMSs go a long way in solving some of the limitations of RDBMSs, the extended versions have some fundamental limitations themselves that are imposed by the paradigm. Many of the areas in which RDBMSs are limited remain to a greater or lesser extent a limitation of the extended RDBMSs. The ability to handle complexity is improved somewhat by the addition of BLOBs and stored procedures. However, both are limited compared to the use of objects in an ODBMS to model complexity.

BLOBs are aptly acronymed—they have no structure and they add little to typing capabilities because no semantics are associated with the type. In contrast, objects have strong typing and associated semantics. BLOBs also lack the ability that objects have of possessing associated behaviors. Lacking most of the capabilities of objects, BLOBs also cannot be organized hierarchically so as to model inheritance or aggregation. The effort of interpreting BLOBs and most of the management of BLOBs falls on the application program rather than being supported by the extended RDBMS (see Figure 8.2). BLOBs must be sorted into a meaningful structure in the application program every time they are retrieved to memory from permanent storage.

Stored procedures are not the same as object methods. A stored procedure is not associated with a particular row or table, whereas a method is associated with a particular object and its class. Stored procedures provide behavior, but they are not encapsulated in BLOBs or even with any other type. Again, the burden of applying stored procedures to the appropriate data and assuring the appropriateness of their use is the responsibility of the application.

The limitations related to the mismatch between the use of a relational model for the database and the object model for the programming language still exists in the extended relational model. The flattening and translation of in-memory representation to in-storage representation is still required for extended RDBMSs.

RDBMS models are limited in performance compared to ODBMS

Figure 8.2 *BLOBs are the responsibility of the application.*

for applications requiring navigational access, although extended versions are now adding this capability. The performance problem that cannot be solved with the relational model is the extra time that is required for the translation processes.

All RDBMSs are limited with respect to distributed computing by not being able to distribute objects that contain both data and the operations associated with that specific data. The advantages of APIs using the object model rather than the relational are simply the same advantages of using an object-oriented language for development in general. These advantages, discussed in more detail in other chapters, include ease of extensibility and maintenance. The advantage retained by the object model over extensions of the relational model with respect to standards includes the fact that the ODMG-93 standard was created from scratch with future growth in mind. The new SQL-3 standard that extended relational databases will be adhering to requires compatibility with the original SQL standard that was not well thought out with respect to how it might evolve. The multiple varieties of extensions to it that relational vendors have made is witness of this.

Stein (1992) expresses some additional concerns about extended RDBMSs. First, extending the relational model invalidates the formal model that gave the relational model a rigorous foundation. (Incidentally, he also challenges how elegant and simple the formal model is.) Second, he is concerned that delays in the release of extended capabilities will cause people to forgo the transition to object technology while waiting for these capabilities. Third, he feels that extending the relational model sacrifices its simplicity without achieving the full benefits offered by the object model.

Overall, the extended model falls short of what the object model provides, but one must also consider the state of current implementation of the two models. Extended RDBMSs, leveraging off well-established technology, currently provide more features than do the ODBMSs. As will be discussed, the object model also has limitations.

8.5.2.2 Extended RDBMS Products

Examples of extended RDBMSs that include enhancements to incorporate object-oriented concepts include UniSQL/X by UniSQL, and Persistence by Persistence Software. Many more examples exist but these represent two different approaches to extending the RDBMS.

An RDBMS may be extended in either of two ways. An extended RDBMS can either look very much like a traditional RDBMS to the user (by having an SQL type interface) or it can act internally very much like a traditional RDBMS (by using relational "machinery" rather than object-oriented "machinery") (Friedman, 1993). (If it looked like an ODBMS to the user and used object-oriented implementation then it would qualify as an ODBMS.) UniQSL/X is an example of the former approach and Persistence of the later. UniSQL/X provides a relational data type of model using object-oriented software underneath by using an SQL-like language that has object-oriented extensions to the SQL language. With this object-oriented foundation it is certainly reasonable to call UniSQL/X an ODBMS instead of an extended RDBMS. UniSQL/X allows both the associative access characteristic of RDBMSs and the navigational access characteristic of ODBMSs. Persistence is a gateway product to other RDBMSs like Oracle and Sybase rather than having its own underlying RDBMS.

Although an ODBMS may theoretically be the best general solution to modeling complex situations, the use of an extended RDMBS may be a better solution for some users for reasons discussed earlier. Those interested in pursuing the latter option can find a discussion of available products in Cattell (1994a). This also discusses simpler ODBMS products like object managers that simply provide persistent storage without full database capabilities.

8.5.3 Limitations of Current ODBMS Products

There are few limitations on the object model in comparison with the relational model from a theoretical point of view. Rather, the limitations are in the capabilities of existing products in achieving the full potential of the object model—object database technology is not fully mature. Many of the current problems in ODBMSs will be solved as vendors continue to respond to the needs of their customers. Some problems will be addressed as ODBMS and RDBMS assimilate each other's features.

One problem that can be considered a limitation, but also an advantage, of the object model compared to the relational model deals with how queries are handled. Relational models allow convenient access to information in any table; this is sometimes referred to as "ad hoc" queries. The object model, however, limits access to information by encapsulating it and allowing access to objects where a predefined relationship exists. Of course, ODBMSs can and do extend the model's capabilities to allow ad hoc queries, but some argue that this is at odds with the general object-oriented philosophy of information hiding. Kim (1995) takes the opposite view arguing that encapsulation is not violated; the user is still shielded from directly accessing the database because the database management system, not the user, examines the data.

The relational model is good at modeling simple entities and is simple itself. The object model is good at modeling complex entities and is correspondingly a lot more complex than the relational model. Therefore, the use of ODBMSs requires a higher level of development expertise. More attention must be paid to design, because there are more opportunities for novices to make mistakes that either hurt performance or inhibit growth. This problem can be reduced by the use of sophisticated development environments; however, this also is an immature field and products have limited capabilities.

From a theoretical point of view, performance in many application areas is one of the strong points of ODBMSs. Generally this is also true for ODBMS implementations, but full testing for all sets of conditions, like very large numbers of concurrent users, large amounts of data, or a very high volume of transactions has not been demonstrated for all ODBMSs.

There are also many long-standing problems in achieving good performance in database management for which the object model adds no new solutions. For example, the number of times data is accessed compared to the number of times it is updated affects the choice of technique used to manage the data. If, as is most common, data is accessed much more frequently than it is updated, the technique used should minimize access time. Sorting and indexing techniques are used to reduce the access time, but straightforward techniques cause index table size to increase linearly with the increased size of the data, regardless of whether the data is rows in a table or objects. Hash tables may be used to reduce the cost of searching for and maintaining indexes, but hash tables are not efficient for some queries. Therefore, other techniques such as the use of B-trees are also used. Balancing all of these conflicting needs requires considerable forethought; Stein (1994) discusses these trade-offs in more detail. Because there are many cases in which an ODBMS can not use navigational access, all of these traditional problems remain to be dealt with using traditional techniques, and application-dependent optimization must continue.

Although having a common model uniting database and programming-language capabilities is an advantage of the object database model, not all features integrate together smoothly. Loomis (1993b, p. 79) lists the following areas of tension: "access control, schema dynamics, query scope, and deletion."

8.5.3.1 Standards Problems

As someone once facetiously said, the nice thing about standards is that there are so many to choose from. Unfortunately, there are two major competing standards related to the use of databases with object technology. Fortunately, these standards are not in direct competition. The ANSI SQL3 standards committee is developing object-oriented extensions to the SQL2 standard that will be used by RDBMS vendors who are extending their products to take advantage of object technology. The ODMG-93 standard will be used by new ODBMS companies that have taken the pure object-oriented approach. Although having two standards is not ideal, they may eventually converge.

8.5.4 The Convergence of the Relational and Object Approaches

David Taylor (1992) predicted several years ago that the two database models will converge, thus making the decision of whether to go object or relational irrelevant. He attributes the intense polarization of the debate to competition among vendors rather than the difference in the technology. To support this assertion he gives examples of how the technologies are merging. One RDBMS vendor has implanted unique object identifiers into stored relations. This allows for efficient navigational access, instead of associative access mechanisms. Numerous ODBMS vendors have released versions with variants of SQL to access methods and data interchangeably through queries. This allows users the freedom of not having to know how a value is computed, retrieved, or stored from some other object.

8.6 Summary

Many applications require the use of persistent data that may require access by multiple users; therefore, various methods have evolved for retaining and managing data. The most recent such methods are the relational, extended relational, and the object-oriented databases.

Relational databases were produced to allow the users of data to avoid dealing directly with storage structures and devices. Relational databases are still the database of choice for data that is naturally represented as a table. However, limitations of relational databases became apparent as applications became more complex.

Although this chapter focused on the object-oriented approach to dealing with these limitations, readers should be aware that for many applications, the extended relational database adequately avoids many of the limitations. The extensions are particularly valuable in providing a gradual evolution of legacy relational systems whose growth has exceeded the capabilities of the underlying relational model.

Many applications can best be managed using an object-oriented database management system, however. ODBMSs are attractive for several reasons. First, they allow the creation of arbitrarily complex persistent data types. Second, unlike the situation with programming languages in which standards were developed late in their evolution, the ODMG attacked the problem early and a widely accepted standard exists. Third, performance improvements may be quite dramatic compared to the use of an RDBMS. This applies especially for applications in which navigational access rather than associative access is appropriate.

For those who feel that the use of an ODBMS may be of value for their applications, the following chapter will assist in selecting one.

8.7 References

Barry, D. (1995). The ODBMS industry is maturing. *Object Magazine, 4*(9).

Ben-Natan, R. (1995). *CORBA: A guide to the Common Object Request Broker Architecture.* New York: McGraw-Hill.

Brown, A. W. (1991). *Object-oriented databases: Applications in software engineering.* London: McGraw-Hill.

Cattell, R. G. G. (1994a). *Object data management: Object-oriented and extended relational database systems* (P. 2, Appendix A). Reading, MA: Addison-Wesley.

Cattell, R. G. G. (Ed.). (1994b). *The Object Database Standard: ODMG-93.* San Mateo, CA: Morgan Kaufmann.

Codd, E. F. (1970). A relational model of data for large, shared data banks. *Communications ACM, 13,* 377–387.

Colley, G. (1992). Retain the object model and retain the benefits. *Object Magazine 2*(1), 27, 28.

Friedman, J. (1993). New options for object databases. *Object Magazine, 2*(6), 67–71.

Kim, W. (1991). Object-oriented database systems: Strengths and weaknesses. *Journal of Object-Oriented Programming. 4,* 27–34.

Kim, W. (Ed.). (1994). *Modern database systems* (p. 5). New York: Addison-Wesley.

Kim, W. (1995). p. 267.

Krikelis, A. & Weems, C. C. (1994). Associative processing and processors. *Computer, 27*(11), 13.

Loomis, M. E. S. (1993a). Making objects persistent. *Journal of Object-Oriented Programming. 6*(6), 25–28.

Loomis, M. E. S. (1993b). Object programming and database management. *Journal of Object-Oriented Programming, 5*(9), 78, 79.

Loomis, M. E. S. (1994). ODBMS myths and realities. *Journal of Object-Oriented Programming, 7*(4), 77.

Rao, B. (1994). *Object-oriented databases.* (p. 39). New York: McGraw-Hill.

Stein, J. (1992). "Butter, margarine, or both?" muttered my mother. *Journal of Object-Oriented Programming, 5*(7), 21.

Stein, J. (1994). It's about time—it's about space. *Object Magazine, 4*(1),26.

Strickland, H. (1993). ODMG-93: The object database standard for C++. *C++ Report 5*(8), 46,48.

Taylor, D. A. (1992). The coming convergence of object and relational databases. *Object Magazine, 2*(3),16–18.

Vasan, R. (1992a). Integrating objects and relational databases. *Object Magazine, 2*(2), 59.

Vasan, R. (1992b). Relational databases and objects: A hybrid solution. *Object Magazine, 2*(5), 42.

Chapter 9

Understanding and Evaluating ODBMSs

Although determining whether to adopt an object database management system (ODBMS) is no simple matter, choosing a specific product poses an even greater challenge. The decision is important and difficult because the products vary considerably in the features they offer, the performance they provide, and the applications for which they are best adapted. The buyer is faced with the challenge of matching his company's needs with the scores of features that the products offer. Selecting an ODBMS for a particular application from among the many products can require a major investment.

This chapter provides a method for evaluating ODBMSs. The intention of the evaluation method is to assist in reducing the number of systems that should receive a more extensive (and more expensive) evaluation. Therefore, the method is designed to be the first step in the selection process. For those who have already selected or are already using an ODBMS, this chapter should still be of interest because it explains many of the important features of an ODBMS.

Currently, very little information is widely available on ODBMS products other than what is provided by the product vendors. One exception to this is that Barry (1995) provides a concise summary of the features of 16 ODBMSs. *Object Magazine* provides a compilation of available ODBMS products and contact information (1996a).

Examining all the features of the major ODBMSs is a very time-consuming task; benchmarking all the major ODBMSs would be a very expensive one. Based on Barry's (1994a) statement that it is easy to spend over $100,000 doing a reasonable benchmark on a small number of products, it could cost a company hundreds of thousands of dollars to perform benchmarks to determine the performance of all the major ODBMS products. Eliminating ODBMSs using simple inexpensive criteria reduces the number of ODBMSs requiring benchmarking.

Therefore, managers need a process that examines the most significant ODBMS features that are required to meet a company's database management system requirements and that will winnow out ODBMSs that are unlikely to satisfy the requirements. The method presented in this chapter involves evaluation criteria that will be referred to as *initial selection criteria*. The development of the initial selection criteria provides such a process and thus simplifies studying vendor materials and reduces the number of benchmarks that need to be performed. The abbreviation ISC will be used for both the singular (criterion) and plural (criteria) cases of the phrase.

This method provides only a first pass at eliminating ODBMS products from consideration. A second pass is recommended in which additional essential criteria are considered to cover cases in which vendor sales information is not adequate for evaluation. The second pass may use vendor manuals, demonstration versions, public benchmarks, and information from ODBMS users; these sources may provide sufficient information for narrowing the field further without resorting to expensive benchmarks. However, Barry (1994b) warns that public benchmarks do not often match actual application domains. Ultimately, application-specific benchmarks on a carefully selected set of candidates are advisable to ensure a match between the application's domain and usage and the ODBMS.

Another goal of this chapter is to flag important features that should be considered in selecting an ODBMS, but that do not lend themselves to easy determination as required by the method presented. These issues should be pursued after the initial elimination process has been accomplished.

9.1 Evaluation Method

Numerous issues must be considered when attempting to select an ODBMS. No one ODBMS is the best; one is best only relative to the needs of a particular organization and the nature of its applications. There are at least 650 different features that can be used to compare ODBMSs (Barry, 1994a). Barry (1993) provides a detailed list of such features. Barry's list is long and is not presented in a convenient format for making comparisons from vendor to vendor. It would be very difficult for an organization to select likely ODBMS candidates from such a detailed list. Barry (1994a) also describes a shorter list; however, it is still relatively long. The features were chosen based on their importance. However, some of the features in the short list cannot be said to either exist or not exist, but rather they exist in varying degrees. This considerably complicates using those features in an evaluation.

This section describes a method that provides a simple evaluation process and allows an evaluator to efficiently narrow the field of viable ODBMS candidates. This winnowing process uses initial selection criteria as a basis for eliminating products. All ISC must be answerable with a yes or a no response. The ISC are derived by examining information from each vendor that is a member of the ODMG and by determining what capabilities constitute "discriminating features." The term *discriminating feature* is used in the following sections to mean that some of the reviewed ODBMSs have the feature and some do not. Only discriminating features are included in the initial selection criteria. In addition, the features used in the initial selection criteria are based on importance to the customer and the ease of determining the presence of the feature.

The criteria must be unambiguous—one must be able to determine that a product possesses or does not possess a capability. Capabilities that are partially satisfied by some products are not used as initial selection criteria. Also, vendor material must be sufficiently explicit on the topic to determine the presence or absence of the capability.

Each of the following sections explains the important features of ODBMSs and determines which of the features are appropriate for use as initial selection criteria. Diamond-shaped bullets are used to indicate the initial selection criteria. The features are organized into categories. After a category is explained, the importance of the features in the category in providing a winnowing strategy is determined. If a feature is useful in accomplishing the goal of efficiently determining a small set of ODBMS candidates, then it may be used as an ISC. If the feature is not useful for this purpose, either because it is not sufficiently important or cannot easily be evaluated, then the feature is not used as an ISC.

9.2 Organizational Requirements

An organization's requirements for an ODBMS are dependent on what one wishes to do with the ODBMS and on the nature of the organization itself. The choice of an ODBMS depends to some extent on whether a legacy database system is involved. The nature of the software development culture is the primary characteristic of an organization that may affect the selection of an ODBMS.

In examining the first issue, one needs to determine how an ODBMS is going to interact with an organization's existing system. Is the ODBMS to be integrated with an existing RDBMS? Coexistence may be required by (1) the need to add new applications that require ODBMS capabilities while continuing the use of existing databases, (2) an intentional plan to use each type of DBMS where it is most appropriate, or (3) the need to provide portable applications for both types of systems (Loomis, 1993a). Is the ODBMS to be used only for new applications in a stand-alone mode or is the legacy system to be migrated into an ODBMS framework? Is the intent to eventually replace the legacy system with an object-oriented one, or are they to coexist indefinitely?

The answers to these questions will affect the choice of the initial selection criteria that the evaluator wishes to apply in the later sections. For example, if the ODBMS is to be used only for new applications, then the existence of a SQL-embedded language becomes a less important feature for an ODBMS to have. If existing relational databases are to be migrated into an object environment, and if existing personnel lack experience in the object-oriented language to be used with the ODBMS, the existence of a SQL-embedded language might be an important short-term consideration for efficiency of conversion.

Examining the second issue, Loomis (1993b) has pointed out that object database developers have roots in one or both of two normally separate cultures: the database culture and the programming culture.

Individuals with roots in one culture think differently about database development than people with roots in the other culture. Object-oriented programmers tend to think that a database should be transparent, like virtual memory. No separate language should be required to manage persistent data. Database people think that it is natural to have one language for programming logic and another for database functions. ODBMS vendors favor the single-language approach, but they realize that it is important to provide database programmers with capabilities they are familiar with using. Most organizations have a predominance of one type of developer; therefore, it may be important that an ODBMS cater to the background of the prevailing type. Both of these organizational issues relate to the issue of the training of existing personnel. The heart of the issue is the use of SQL or a SQL-like language in an ODBMS. Therefore, this topic is resolved later in the section on queries capabilities.

9.3 General Characteristics of the ODBMS

This section examines global aspects of ODBMSs including the overall system architecture of the product, what the system costs, whether it conforms to standards, on what platforms it is operational, and the stability of vendors.

9.3.1 Product Structure

An ODBMS is more than just a database engine that provides database functions such as data access, updating, and protection. At a minimum, an ODBMS is a system that includes capabilities that support the conceptual schema, provides a means for physical storage, and provides a language binding to the database engine. The system may also include a graphical user interface to simplify the use of the language bindings and additional tools for the administrators and developers.

Vendors create these capabilities as modular components to allow ease of modification and addition of new capabilities (such as a new language binding). The organization of these components is similar among the various vendors. Although the structure of the product may affect the productivity of the vendor in further development of the ODBMS, it only indirectly affects the customer and will therefore not be used as an ISC.

9.3.2 Cost of System

Companies must always be cost conscious and the cost of the system is a discriminating feature. However, the cost of the system is not usually a good criterion to use for selection because the quality of the ODBMS tends to increase with cost. Nevertheless, sometimes one has strict budget limits, so this criterion is included.

Because the initial selection criteria must be expressible as a yes or no decision, the evaluator should determine the maximum acceptable cost of the system and compare the product costs to this figure. Conservative cost limits may be shortsighted and are unlikely to maximize the return on investment. Therefore, the evaluator is encouraged to use the highest feasible cost figure to avoid arbitrarily eliminating the best products.

- *The cost of the system is less than a value selected by the customer.*

Two costs need to be considered: the purchase price of a development license and the price of a run-time license. The cost of learning to use the ODBMS should also be considered even though it is not included in the criterion because it is difficult to estimate.

9.3.3 Conformance to Standards: The Object Model

Although at the time of this writing differences still remain in the object models of the ODBMSs most of these fundamental modeling differences should not exist by the time of publication of this book. The members have committed to implement the ODMG-93 standard object model and have considerable incentive to do so; any vendor not satisfying the standard will be at a competitive disadvantage because users want adherence. Therefore, although elements of the object model might currently provide discriminating features, the rapid convergence of models will make a criterion based on this obsolete. Therefore, no object-model features are included in the initial selection criteria.

9.3.4 Operating Systems

Operating systems perform two basically unrelated functions. One function is to conceal the complexity of the hardware from the users. The operating system provides an easy-to-use file-oriented interface. The other function is to manage all the parts of the system, such as processors, memories, and input/output devices (Tannenbaum, 1992).

Individual ODBMSs do not support all operating systems or hardware so it is important to make sure that the ODBMS is compatible with the user's existing and future platforms. Therefore, the ability of the ODBMS to function on the customer's specific operating system and hardware is an initial selection criterion.

◆ *The ODBMS supports required platforms.*

9.3.5 Programming Language

Because all the reviewed ODBMSs have a computationally complete language interface, the computational power of the language is not a discriminating feature. Nevertheless, the programming language or languages available for the ODBMS is an architectural feature of great interest to some organizations. An organization that has C++ or C programmers may be interested only in an ODBMS that uses C++, whereas an organization with Smalltalk programmers may restrict their selection to ODBMSs that use Smalltalk. The ability of an ODBMS to interface with a particular language is certainly one of the clearest and easiest ways to evaluate an ODBMS and is therefore one of the initial selection criteria. The ODBMS of the members of the ODMG have C++ bindings, so its availability is not a discriminating feature for at least seven major vendors, however, the ability to use the ODBMS with Smalltalk is a discriminating feature.

◆ *The ODBMS supports the required programming languages.*

9.3.6 Vendor Support and Longevity

If the history of RDBMSs is any indication, then only a few of the initial group of vendors will thrive. It is too early to determine which ODBMSs will become the next Oracle or Sybase, but one should keep in mind that some ODBMS vendors may end up with a shrinking fraction of the market and may therefore lag behind others in developing new features and supporting customers.

ODBMS vendors may suffer either from competition among themselves or from competition with RDBMS vendors who are extending their products to make them more objectlike. Francois Bancilhon of O2 Technology argues that ODBMS vendors are not threatened by RDBMS vendors who are extending their products to make them more object oriented. To compete with ODBMSs built from the ground up on object-oriented principles, RDBMS would have to rewrite their core technology, and they are not about to do this for the 7% share of the market that is forecast for ODBMSs in 1995 (Johnston, 1992). Major RDMBS companies are quite involved in object technology, however, as indicated by the commitment of Oracle (Stewart, 1995a) and Sybase (Stewart, 1995b) to help develop and adhere to the object-oriented standards for distributed computing, so this may be wishful thinking.

Because vendor information cannot credibly include a statement as to whether the company will still be in existence in 10 years and since this would be difficult for anyone to predict, vendor longevity is not used as an ISC. Nevertheless, after the initial selection, part of the final selection should include a look at the company's financial statement and strategic alliances. Currently all the reviewed ODBMS companies appear to be growing rapidly, but eventually as the market approaches saturation and if some ODBMSs take a clear lead in market share, this may become an important consideration. Of course, even if a vendor captures only a small fraction of the market share, their product may be the one to choose if it provides the best features for the particular market niche of interest to the customer.

Although the position of a couple of the vendors may appear more tenuous than the rest, it is much to early to discount any one. The experience possessed by the personnel in ODBMS companies is of considerable value to large relational vendors and other software companies and makes them prime takeover candidates; the major financial backing and distribution network of a large database management system vendor or user could quickly reverse the prospects of a small ODBMS company in trouble.

9.4 General Database Management Features

This section defines and explains some of the general database management features that may be considered during an evaluation of ODBMSs.

9.4.1 Client/Server Architecture

A customer may feel the architecture an ODBMS uses is unimportant compared to capabilities it possesses. Although this is a reasonable attitude from a user's point of view, the architecture does have a pervasive influence on ODBMS capabilities. Therefore, although this section will not include any architectural feature as an ISC, later features that are a result of the architecture chosen will be selected as initial selection criteria. Particularly, one needs to understand the client/server architecture that is common to all the reviewed products to understand the importance of the distributed features of an ODBMS.

To understand the meaning of client/server architecture, it helps to understand the common and desirable features of the architecture. A client/server system usually uses a graphical user interface (GUI) as a presentation interface with the user. It frequently has a centralized database management system on one or more servers. Occasionally it has an object-oriented database management system in which most of the database processing is performed on the client side. Ideally, it has a distributed ODBMS in which database management processes may be conducted on either the client or server side depending on which location is the most efficient for a particular situation.

There are three common approaches to implementing a client/server architecture. The architecture can have a server emphasis, a client emphasis, or a balanced emphasis. The approach used may have a significant impact on how other features are handled and may have a significant affect on the performance of the ODBMS. The server emphasis is the architectural approach used by the RDBMS, and is rarely used for an ODBMS. The three basic approaches are sometimes referred to as the database server (server emphasis), page server (client emphasis), and object server (balanced emphasis). The different approaches affect computing costs, flexibility, and performance in various ways.

The database server approach gives most of the processing responsibility to the server, whereas the client passes messages requesting action on to the server, receives results from the server, and sends results back to the application. This approach may be more efficient or less efficient depending on the nature of the processing being done. A database server requires minimal network traffic as long as the client passes simple requests containing small amounts of data and receives back simple answers also containing small amounts of data. For example, a database server functions expediently and efficiently when asked to find the name of an owner of a car when given a license-plate number.

However, if the request requires moving large amounts of data between the server and the client, the database server may be able to perform the search efficiently, but may backlog the communications network receiving and sending data. For example, suppose an architect has an image of a building on the client screen. If he wishes to view the building from a different angle using a database server, the database server must send the entire new view over the network. In addition, the server approach does not exploit the power of modern client machines, which results in underutilization of client hardware.

The page-server approach does the majority of its processing in the client. It is implemented using paging, a virtual memory technique. This approach heavily exploits the client side's processing power. Referring to the architect example again, the page server could have the needed information as pages on a client machine. It could show the planner many different views of the terrain without ever having to move screen images over the network; thus less network traffic is required as compared to the database-server approach.

Problems do still develop under this method. The page-server approach reduces the server to simply providing bulk data to the client because query processing is performed on the client. This can result in increased network traffic as the page server is unable to perform data-manipulation functions. Although this is not a problem in stand-alone systems, it can be a problem on client/server systems because all the data must be transferred from the server to the client for query processing. However, it is only a problem when the client needs a lot of data and does little processing of that data. If the client does not need a lot of data compared to the amount of processing it does on the data, then there is no problem.

The object-server (balanced) approach divides the processing responsibility between the client and the server. Processing queries in the server ensures that only requested data needs to be transmitted, reducing network traffic. The object-server approach allows computationally intensive calculations to be performed on the client side, efficient processing of common resources on the server side, and minimized traffic between the client and server. Obviously, this is the more flexible and the generally preferred approach, although some applications may work quite well with one of the other two approaches.

One tends to think of a server as being a mainframe and a client as a smaller computer, but the terms refer to the role of the computer in the relationship, not the nature of the computer. Therefore, a mainframe could act as a client to a PC.

The X Window System is illustrative of the arbitrariness of the client and server roles concerning hardware. One might expect that a mainframe acting as the host would be the server for the terminals (workstations or X-terminals) using the system. For the X Window System, however, the purpose of the mainframe in the relationship is to execute a program that may or may not require considerable computation, whereas the purpose of the terminal is to graphically display the results. Therefore, the host is actually the client (application program) and the terminal is the server. The X server runs on the terminal to display the control of and results of the application program (Johnson & Reichard, 1990).

The meaning of client/server with respect to distributed computing differs somewhat from expert to expert. For example, Wade (1994) does not consider server-based or client-based client/server architectures to be "distributed," but uses the word "distributed" to indicate a balanced client/server approach.

Despite all the interest in client/server architecture, a peer/peer architecture is a superior model with respect to capabilities. In a peer/peer architecture all computers have equal ability to provide services to each other, by acting as both servers and clients. This allows more effective allocation of workloads and available disk space. The client/server approach is more popular because it is easier to implement.

9.4.2 Active Versus Passive ODBMSs

Another architectural issue of interest is whether an ODBMS is active or passive. An active database is one that stores the methods of an object in the database; a passive database is one that stores the methods separately. One would think that ODBMSs would be active; rather, most are passive. The advantage of an active database is that the objects in the database are complete and can be used by any program, whereas the objects in a passive database are usable only by programs that maintain the methods. Of course, the classes for objects that are widely used can be placed in a library so that many programs can use them; the difference is that maintaining and accessing the library is a separate task and not part of the ODBMS capability. The active/passive nature of the

ODBMS is a discriminating feature and is an initial selection criterion. David Taylor, a former Director of Applications for GemStone Corporation, which provides one of the few active ODBMSs, considers this to be "the most important selection criterion" (Taylor, 1996).

◆ *The ODBMS is an active database.*

9.4.3 Transaction Properties

Transaction properties include atomicity, consistency, isolation, and integrity. These properties are basic characteristics that all ODBMSs share, but each product's characteristics differ in specific ways. Although these properties are not a good discriminating feature, they are fundamental to transactions; therefore, the meaning of the four terms is explained below.

The term *transaction* refers to a unit of processing and information exchange. Any time a transaction is performed, atomicity ensures that either the whole transaction succeeds or that it completely fails. If the transaction succeeds then the database is permanently changed as prescribed by the transaction. If a transaction fails, it fails entirely and does not change the original state of the database. A system must ensure atomicity because if the system allows part of an operation to change data and part of the operation to be lost, the data in the database may become inconsistent.

A transaction maintains consistency when it changes from one consistent internal state to another consistent internal state. Consistency could be violated if a partially completed transaction were to be saved before the full transaction were completed. A potential cause of this happening is an abort of the transaction, which could be the result of a person changing his or her mind about the transaction or a power failure that terminated the program. Maintaining consistency is essential to the functioning of a database.

Internal inconsistency is allowed during a transaction but not before or after the transaction. Because a transaction in progress may not reflect a consistent state, the internal state of a transaction should not be visible to other transactions. This rule is referred to as isolation. Integrity is the guarantee that recovery from a failure results in a consistent state and that no changes successfully entered into the database by previous transactions are ever lost.

9.4.4 Types of Transactions

Many applications require "long transactions," which can be much longer than the online transaction processing (OLTP) that is common in RDBMSs. OLTP is typically measured in seconds or minutes, whereas long transactions may require months to complete. A very common example of the need for long transactions is in the development of software by two or more people. Developing a single new class or set of classes can require weeks or months of work. Provision must be made to ensure that either the version on which the work is based is not changed by one developer while another is modifying it, or there is some provision for merging changes. Long transactions of this nature can be protected by long (persistent) locks, that is, checkin and checkout capabilities that span the termination of many transactions and applications.

Nested transactions, in which one long transaction can consist of many short transactions, are needed to support the long-transaction capability. Versioning capabilities are also an important form of support for long transactions. The ability to handle long transactions and support for nested transactions are important for some applications and are discriminating features. Therefore, these are included in the initial evaluation criteria.

◆ *The ODBMS provides the ability to handle long transactions by support of nested transactions and versions.*

9.4.5 Query Capability

The English meaning of the word "query" indicates that a database query refers to retrieving data. This includes the extraction of data from a database depending on specified conditions on the data contents (predicates). Because the predominant query language, SQL, supports general database management functions, the meaning of "query" with respect to databases frequently refers to processing and updating data as well as retrieving data.

A query language is a DBMS capability that allows general declarative management of data, that is, provides management by allowing the programmer to declare what is to be accomplished without requiring any knowledge of how it is to be accomplished. In an RDBMS, a query returns a relation. In an ODBMS a query returns an object or set of objects. Interestingly, both use the message-passing philosophy that is considered one of the hallmarks of the object-oriented paradigm.

As discussed earlier, whether the ODBMS provides some form of SQL interface is an important issue for many organizations that need to interface an ODBMS with an existing RDBMS. This section provides additional background and deals with questions about using SQL within an ODBMS. Under what circumstances and to what extent is it important to make use of the existing knowledge of relational database programming personnel in an object-oriented environment? To what extent do ODBMSs cater to this need, and to what extent is it useful to do so?

All the vendors reviewed favor the object programmer in that they integrate a programming language seamlessly with the ODBMS. This is demonstrated in the way the vendors approach the three ways that an ODBMS can provide a query capability. These methods are to (1) provide a class library containing query functions in an object-oriented programming language, or (2) extend the programming language to contain query functions, or (3) embed a SQL-like language in the programming language (Loomis, 1994a). Currently some use methods 1 or 2, but once all comply with the ODMG-93 standard they will be using methods 2 and 3.

Because some vendors recognized early the importance of appealing to the large existing clientele of RDBMSs, they already allow embedded SQL statements, allowing SQL programmers to leverage off their existing knowledge. Extended RDBMSs provide another alternative for those who feel strongly about leveraging existing SQL expertise.

As convenient as extended RDBMSs are for people with a relational database background, they lack the feature possessed by the pure ODBMSs of having a single language for both programming and database operations (Friedman, 1993). Utilizing existing SQL knowledge makes sense from a practical point of view, but it does not make sense conceptually because having different on-disk and in-memory representations of data forgoes the advantage of a seamless transition between object-oriented programming and database usage. On the other hand, if one is using a conventional language like COBOL, then one would have great difficulty in implementing an object-oriented design and a seamless transition would be unlikely anyway. Therefore, an extended RDBMS is particularly attractive for this situation.

One might think that having an ANSI standard SQL interface in an

ODBMS would be essential in interacting with a relational legacy system, but according to Loomis (1993c, p. 40), "it is not necessary for the ODBMS to support full standard SQL. It is only necessary to be SQL-like." Close compatibility with ANSI standard SQL may be of significant concern if there is much legacy code that needs to be migrated to an ODBMS. In the short run, such compatibility can be quite convenient. However, insisting on this simply to avoid the need to learn the programming language can limit the ability of programmers to make effective use of both the object-oriented paradigm and the ODBMS. In the long run, the value of seamless integration of database management with an object programming language by use of a common type system is of much greater value than maintaining compatibility with existing SQL commands. Rather than applying similarity to the ANSI standard SQL as a criterion of elimination, it would be preferable to count it as a desirable feature when comparing the ODBMSs surviving the elimination process.

To some extent one can leverage off the existing knowledge of SQL, but converting to an object environment involves a lot more than a translational process to a new DBMS. In addition, ANSI standards SQL and SQL2 are inadequate to deal with the capabilities provided by ODBMSs, and limiting usage of the ODBMS in this way would defeat the purpose of the product. Although providing an embedded SQL in an ODBMS may provide database people with a greater sense of security, it only disguises the fact that fundamental changes are required in how one thinks about and implements database management in migrating to an ODBMS. The ability to use the ANSI standard SQL or SQL2 statements inside an extended object-oriented language provides only a subset of ODBMS capabilities. ODBMSs now extend query capabilities over those of traditional RDBMSs by adding the following to access based on the value of attributes: access based on relationship paths and access based on predicates involving the execution of methods contained in objects. The SQL3 standard narrows the differences in capabilities considerably.

The existence of a SQL-like language is not included as an ISC because once vendors adhere to the ODMG-93 standard, all will implement Object Query Language (OQL) and this feature will not be a discriminator.

9.4.6 Associative and Navigational Access

The ideas of associative and navigational access were described in Section 8.4.1. This section considers whether the ability of an ODBMS to provide declarative associative access should be an ISC.

Data in an RDBMS may be accessed only by use of the query language (e.g., associative access). All the reviewed ODBMSs use navigational access, which is the natural method for the object-oriented approach. Unique object IDs are used to retrieve objects that have relationships with a given object. This type of access is particularly valuable in retrieving objects that are component objects of an aggregate object.

A key reason for an ODBMS to add associative access is to provide the explicit joins that RDBMS users are familiar with. Bertino and Martino (1991) describe the reason that some ODBMS vendors do not provide this capability. They say that joins are used mostly to support relationships and recompose entities that were decomposed for normalization. Because the object model supports relationships directly in a more natural way and because normalization is not needed in an ODBMS, there is no real need for a query language to provide explicit joins.

Despite this argument one can expect to see most ODBMSs provide associative access if for no other reason than for marketing purposes. Many people feel strongly that this convenience is important. This group includes the ODMG, as evidenced by the OQL being included as part of the object model of the ODMG-93 standard. OQL is a query language in the original sense of the word—it provides only read access to the database. Modifications to the database are made using the database programming language.

Some ODBMSs already allow associative assess. Once the vendors have implemented the ODMG-93 standard, they will all support OQL, which provides declarative access, so that this will no longer be a discriminating feature. (Whereas declarative access simply implies a nonprocedural access with implementation not specified, the implementation of OQL can use associative access). Therefore, associative access is not used as an ISC.

9.4.7 Schema Modification

Schema modification or evolution refers to changing the structure of data in a database, preferably without long delays for unloading and loading complete databases. For example, to add a ZIP code to mailing addresses, the schema of databases has to evolve to add a field (attribute) to tables containing addresses. A good RDBMS can accomplish this task incrementally with little impact on daily operations. Schema modification is an inevitable result of the need to change and improve systems, so ODBMSs must deal with this problem just as RDBMSs have been doing for many years.

The schema evolution of adding attributes to an object in an ODBMS is similar to changing the schema in an RDBMS by adding new columns to tables. Adding new objects in an ODBMS is similar to adding new rows in an RDBMS table, and adding classes in an ODBMS is similar to adding a new table. The process is more involved for an ODBMS, however, as objects can be arbitrarily complex—they may contain or be contained in other objects and may be created using a parent class or have a child class in an inheritance hierarchy. With an ODBMS, attributes may be changed, methods may be changed, and superclass/subclass relationships may be changed. Various operations, such as add, drop, and delete, may or may not be allowed. This added complexity makes it difficult to maintain referential integrity among hierarchies of related objects.

For example, if one modifies a class that has a subclass, the subclass schema is also affected. Therefore, considerable effort is required to allow an ODBMS to handle all the complex possibilities in the dynamic schema evolution of an object model. The degree to which various ODBMSs handle schema evolution varies widely; therefore, this can be used as a discriminating feature once precise conditions are described defining what level of schema evolution is required.

Probably the main interest to users is whether the database must be taken offline to accomplish schema modification. Whether it can remain online or not may depend on what type of schema modification is being undertaken. Companies with 24 x 7 applications (applications that must be available 24 hours per day 7 days per week) will require that at least certain types of schema modifications be allowed without going offline. At a minimum they may require the same level of dynamic schema modification that is available with an RDBMS, that is, dynamic schema modification of tablelike structures without inheritance being involved. Therefore, this is used as an ISC. This requirement does not include capabilities specific to the object model, such as dynamic modification of subclasses in a class inheritance hierarchy.

◆ *The ODBMS provides online schema modification for the type of capabilities also present in RDBMSs. (Thus, this criterion does not require online modification of inheritance structures.)*

Although this criterion may be useful to eliminate potential candidates because they definitely do not have any online schema modification capability, the ones that do claim this ability will need to be tested. For example, there is a big difference between an online schema modification that must lock users out of 50% of the system's files to perform the changes and one that can modify 5% of the files at a time while maintaining consistency and operability.

9.5 Data Protection

Data must be protected from everything from system crashes to two people trying to update the same data at the same time. This section examines various means of protecting data and how ODBMSs deal with data protection.

9.5.1 Locking and Concurrency Control

Concurrency control is the process of coordinating requests for access to objects so that applications can share objects without interfering with each other or compromising the database. Locking is the most common method used for concurrency control. Locking is a method of controlling access to objects; its primary objective is to ensure that only one application at a time can change an object. This ensures that changes are completed in an orderly way.

There are two types of concurrency control: pessimistic and optimistic. Pessimistic concurrency control assumes conflicts are common and checks for access conflicts at the time the lock is requested. Thus, a pessimistic system guarantees that no conflicts will be present at commit time. The pessimistic approach is the most common approach.

Optimistic concurrency control assumes that an object is rarely accessed by multiple users simultaneously; therefore, conflicts are only checked at commit time. If conflicts occur it may be possible, under some circumstances, to automatically apply the changes sequentially, effectively merging the multiple changes. In other cases, conflicts may be able to be resolved by manual methods, such as presenting the user with results for acceptance or rejection. In many cases in an optimistic system, conflicts present at commit time will require a transaction abort. Nevertheless, as long as conflicts seldom occur, there is considerable advantage in not locking out other applications.

The type of concurrency control is a discriminating feature because although all ODBMSs have pessimistic control, some also provide optimistic control. However, optimistic control has not been a common feature of RDBMSs; therefore most managers will not feel that it is a critical feature. Also, the use of optimistic concurrency control is mainly of value in improving performance, but because there are much more important issues affecting efficiency, the type of concurrency control is not a good initial selection criterion.

Lock granularity describes how much data is protected from access when a lock is performed. Typically the unit of granularity is either an object or a page (which may contain many objects). If an ODBMSs has page-level locking, a user will lock out all other users from all the objects on that page even if the user is only changing a single small object on the page. If object-level locking is available the user can lock just the object that is of interest, leaving all other objects available to other users.

Although it may appear that the smaller the lock granularity the better, this may not always be true. If an ODBMS has page-level locking, it means only one lock is needed per page. On the other hand, object-level locking could require the ODBMS to have many more locks depending on object sizes, requiring more processing time for lock management. The page-level lock tends to have less locking overhead and thus fewer processing resources are used (Barry, 1994c).

Both extremes of locking granularity can cause performance problems. To determine what level of granularity is optimal, the developer must determine how the data is used. Page-level locking is best when one can cluster many related objects together on a page for use by one user at a time. Object-level locking is best when there is high demand for objects within a group of objects by multiple users. In the later case, the use of page-level locking would tie up frequently used objects on a page, preventing the other users access.

It is not likely that a company will be able to use the following ISC because a company normally has a wide variety of applications that do not all work best with one particular type of locking. However, for the rare instances in which a particular type of locking is clearly superior for a set of applications, the criterion is included. Another reason to be cautious about using this criterion is that some ODBMSs use techniques for mitigating the problems with either type of locking (Barry, 1994c).

◆ *The ODBMS has the type of locking (e.g., object or page locking) that is most appropriate for the customer's applications.*

9.5.2 Security Authorization

In general, most ODBMSs have been weak in the area of security. The design of a multilevel secure database management system (MLS/DBMS) is needed if ODBMSs are going to be used in organizations requiring a high level of security, such as the military. MLS/DBMS identifies users by security level, so that sensitive data can be kept on a DBMS that is accessed by many users who may have different levels of security authorization. Thuraisingham (1990) describes issues related to security in an ODBMS and proposes solutions to the problems. Several of the issues are of interest in our search for ISC.

The basic level of security is login security, which prevents unauthorized users from obtaining access to the database. However, this level of security is adequate for the relatively few applications in which every user is equally trusted with all parts of the database. A finer granularity of security is needed if for no other reason than to allow some users to read the data and to allow selected users to modify the data. Beyond this, selective access control is frequently required for various parts of the database. For example, a person's salary and health records would warrant greater security than the person's office location. Control at this level requires protection at the object level or a similar level of detail.

Some ODBMSs claim that they have security features because they protect data from unauthorized access at the file or database level. This is a minimal level of security that is equivalent to the type of access control provided by the UNIX operating system. For many applications this is totally unacceptable. Rather, control is required at the object level. Therefore, the ISC selected allows the user to differentiate among ODBMSs that have minimal access control and ones that have detailed (object level) control. If it is feasible to maintain sensitive information in a separate database from nonsensitive information, then this might not be an essential feature even when the application requires distinguishing levels of control among various users.

Many organizations have security requirements that are important but not as critical as they are for the military. The ability to handle security at a more detailed level than database or file security is therefore both a discriminating feature and is a critical item for some applications. Therefore it is used as an initial selection criterion.

◆ *The ODBMS has access control at the object level.*

Access control at the object level is just the start of what is needed for comprehensive security. Ideally, one would like to control access to individual methods and attributes as well as to files and objects. One would also like to be able to base access permission on the contents of the data in the database. For example, the government might want to allow general access to the names of Agriculture Department county agents, but not to the names of undercover agents of the Drug Enforcement Agency, so that the name of the department might be used to control access.

One would also like to be able to base access control on the nature of a relationship between two objects. For example, consider a database for a hospital. Many employees may need to know the names of patients. All employees might have an interest in all the current diagnoses of patients, so that anyone might recognize an epidemic of staph infection, for instance. Most employees should not have access to the combination of a person's name and diagnosis, however, particularly if the diagnosis is politically or legally sensitive. Thus, the individual objects would have one level of access and the relationship between them would have a more restricted level of access. Currently no ODBMS comes close to having these advance access control capabilities so they are not included as ISC.

9.5.3 Backup and Recovery

A backup and recovery capability is essential for a DBMS. Some ODBMSs are quite competitive with RDBMSs in this area (Loomis, 1994b). Other ODBMSs have not yet created backup and recovery capabilities adequate for systems requiring continuous availability.

The most primitive means of data protection is accomplished by maintaining offline backups, which normally use a tape device. This may be adequate for some applications, but is inadequate for most database uses, because it is not feasible to make offline backups very frequently and because it takes considerable time to restore the system. A considerable amount of updated data can be lost between an offline backup and the time of a later failure.

Therefore, online backup is a priority for many applications. The objective is to lose as little information as possible if a problem occurs and to continue transactions as quickly as possible. This can be accomplished using a logging technique that maintains a history of transactions, or by using a shadow system that maintains a replica of information on disk.

Even online backup is insufficient for many applications such as online transaction processing (OLTP). For OLTP the backup must not only be online, it must be done in a manner to ensure that, at worst, the only transactions that may be lost during failure are ones currently in progress. The logging technique is well suited to maintain the continuous recording of the data needed to ensure this. For the shadowing technique to ensure preservation of all but the in-progress transactions, frequent incremental backups are necessary. Although recovery time is very quick from the backups, the overhead of storing the backups will normally exceed the time needed to create a log of transactions. On the other hand, if the transactions require extensive computations characteristic of some scientific applications, the reverse is true.

Almost all ODBMSs provide an online recovery capability. The critical consideration of some users will be whether this capability is adequate for OLTP. This level of backup and recovery is a discriminating feature and is essential for many types of applications. Therefore, the following is an ISC.

◆ *The ODBMS provides transaction recovery based on an online backup capability that is adequate for online transaction processing. This requires that no transactions be lost during failure other than those in progress at the time of failure.*

It is assumed that all the ODBMSs with an online backup capability that use the logging technique provide the currency of backup required for OLTP. The ones using the shadowing technique may or may not be adequate for OLTP.

9.5.4 Versioning

Versioning is the management of ongoing changes in a product by keeping track of the product's state during its evolution. Each such state is called a version. Versioning is placed somewhat arbitrarily within the larger category of data protection because versioning protects older versions and is used to support backups. However, it is also used to support schema modification and concurrency control (Bertino & Martino, 1991) and could therefore have been listed in either of these categories. As mentioned in the discussion of transactions, versioning capabilities are also an important form of support for long transactions.

Versioning is also used more for the general purpose of configuration management. This use of versioning could be considered an application rather than a database management feature. Version management allows multiple release versions of the code to be distributed and multiple permanent and temporary development versions to be maintained. Versions are sometimes maintained in a simple sequential series of versions, usually by saving changes (deltas) to a base version or by maintaining the ability to recreate earlier versions from current versions. Version management planning should strive to maintain a single linear path of versions to reduce maintenance problems that can multiply rapidly if version branching is used. Frequently, branching of versions cannot be avoided, however. The branching of versions implies that multiple current versions of the product exist concurrently. The duplication of maintenance functions, including tracking of error reports and corrective action, should provide strong motivation for terminating or merging branches whenever feasible.

Version management includes the ability for multiple users to work together on a single project. Here the versioning system may provide support for workgroup development by allowing the merging of modifications of a common base version by multiple developers. Although the version management system may simplify the mechanics of integrating the separate changes of many developers, this process can never be fully automated. Not only does one have to consider programming conflicts, but one must also consider conceptual conflicts. The best tools available here are no substitute for careful project management to divide a project into largely decoupled tasks before beginning modifications. The object-oriented approach does contribute here by making it easier to achieve effective decoupling.

Although database management systems are not versioning systems, they do provide a convenient means for building such systems. Object versioning has become important in marketing ODBMSs; however, versioning is independent of whether the relational or object-oriented paradigm is used. The reason for the importance of versioning to ODBMS vendors is that they want to please users in the largest current market for ODBMSs, engineering applications, where versioning is a particularly important feature (Colley, 1992).

The usual way for an ODBMS to provide a versioning capability includes providing a user with version manipulation commands that allow users to develop their own version hierarchies. This provides great flexibility, but imposes a burden on the developers. Hsieh (1994, p. 74) analyzed the versioning methods of three ODBMSs (Versant, Objectivity/DB, and ObjectStore) and concluded that the methods and capabilities were similar enough that the selection of an ODBMS "is likely to be dominated by considerations other than version management." Therefore, the particular method of versioning is not considered a discriminating feature among the ODBMSs providing versioning capabilities. However, the existence of a versioning capability is a discriminating feature and is included in the ISC.

◆ *The ODBMS supports a versioning capability.*

9.6 Distributed Computing Systems

Although the following chapter will discuss distributed computing in general; here we are interested in how distributed computing relates to evaluating ODBMSs.

9.6.1 Distributed ODBMS Features

The need for many users to share persistent data was the reason driving the creation of databases and database management systems. The need to allow object interaction on a distributed system was a driving force in the creation of distributed object management. The combined needs drove the creation of ODBMSs for heterogeneous environments. The need for efficiency in such an environment is driving the development of ODBMSs with a balanced client/server architecture.

One can define a distributed ODBMS as a system that contains two or more ODBMSs connected on a network. This definition could be tightened by adding the condition that the system be fully transparent. A distributed system is transparent if the system appears from a logical view to behave as if it were a single system. Just as data independence allows the user of data to deal with the logical form of the data instead of its physical representation, the broader concept of transparency allows the user to deal with data independent of where it is located. Achieving transparency is a primary goal of a distributed database management system.

Requiring full transparency would turn the definition into a currently unattainable ideal of what a distributed object database management system should be, however. The problem is that there are many types of transparency, some of which are extremely difficult to achieve. Ideally one would like to have location transparency, migration transparency, replication transparency, fragment transparency, schema-change transparency, performance transparency, transaction transparency, parallelism transparency, and heterogeneity transparency.

Although a vendor may claim that its ODBMS is "fully" transparent, their meaning of "fully" does not include all forms of transparency. For example, no RDBMS or ODBMS is close to achieving parallelism transparency (Tanenbaum, 1992). Parallelism transparency means that a system can automatically select an appropriate set of central processing units (CPUs) within a distributed system for execution of a multithread program. Of the forms of transparency, the ones that are the mostly likely candidates for inclusion as ISC will be examined: location transparency, migration transparency, replication transparency, transaction transparency, and heterogeneity transparency. For definitions of types of transparency not discussed here, see Loomis (1993a). All of the reviewed ODBMSs are distributed systems; therefore, this is, by itself, not a discriminating feature.

9.6.1.1 Location and Migration Transparency

Location transparency means that the user does not need to know where in the network an object is located. In particular, one does not need to specify a machine ID to identify an object. Location transparency is a prerequisite to migration transparency, which means that objects may be moved from one location to another without having to change their names. Location and migration transparency reduce maintenance costs because references to objects do not have to be changed when an object is relocated.

Location and migration transparency are the most important forms of transparency in a distributed system. Because they are essential for all distributed systems they are not discriminating features.

9.6.1.2 Replication Transparency

Users need a system that provides shared access to resources and allows the sharing of companywide business information. Users also want nodes to function independently, however. A system that allows shared access while still allowing nodes to function independently protects users from many of the problems that result from system failures. If nodes can function independently, failures will be localized and users will be able to operate on some basis even if the network or other nodes are down.

The only feasible way of accomplishing both access to common shared data and individual node autonomy is to use replication. Replication can be defined as creating a semipermanent copy of an object. Replication transparency means the user does not need to know how many copies exist or where they are—the application does not have the responsibility of dealing with replicas. Replication transparency is needed across network nodes because copies of objects are needed for back-up purposes and to allow multiple users to efficiently access the objects on various server machines. ODBMSs bear the burden of assuring that updates to objects synchronize the updating of the replicas in an efficient and predictable manner.

It is important to distinguish between an object that is identical to another object including the object identifier (OID) versus two objects that are identical except for the OIDs. In the former case, the objects are considered the same object and effort must be expended to ensure that the implementations of the object are kept the same. In the later case, it may be permissible for the objects to change independently.

To distinguish between these two cases, two terms may be used: replication that produces replicas and duplication that produces duplicates. In the English language, neither of these options naturally implies that two objects are really the same object. Therefore, the industry has picked the words *replication* and *replica* to refer to implementations of the same object that have the same OIDs. The words *duplication* or *duplicate* can be used to mean the objects were created identically except for the OID.

Replication can greatly improve efficiency by making objects available on a computer that is using the object intensively. Maintaining object integrity when there are multiple replicas in a distributed environment is difficult, however. Integrity is threatened whenever replicated objects are updated. This requires the ODBMS to synchronize updates to the database.

One method of synchronizing object updates is to have a server designated as the owner of the object. Whenever a replica of the object on a nonowner server is to be used, a message is sent to the owning server. If the message determines the local replica is not current (by comparing the time stamp or version of the updated object with the object on the owning server), the replica can be replaced by a current replica. Any changes in the local replica must be made in the owner copy, and in all other replicas, at least before they are used. The timing of the updating of replicas is a complex matter if efficiency is considered and it is very dependent on the nature of the application (Loomis, 1993e).

Only recently have vendors added the ability to manage replicated objects. Before, the application was given the responsibility of managing multiple copies. Some ODBMSs support the checkout and checkin of objects that implements replication (Loomis, 1993e). If an object is checked out and retains its identifier from the source object, then there has been replication. If the object loses its identifier, the duplicate object will be treated as a different object.

Replication can be a critical efficiency issue for some network configurations. For example, a network that consists of local area networks (LANs) connected by a wide area network (WAN) might need replicas of objects on the LANs to avoid excessive network traffic over the slower WAN lines.

Replication transparency is important for three reasons: site autonomy, availability, and performance. The performance advantage does not lend itself to becoming an ISC and is best left to benchmarking. Availability and site autonomy may prove to be important to customers, however. Therefore, replication transparency is an ISC.

◆ *The ODBMS has the capability to replicate either objects or a group of objects along with the capability to coordinate updates among the replicas.*

9.6.1.3 Transaction Transparency

Transaction transparency means that local and distributed transactions occur in the same way from the application's point of view. Making a distributed transaction behave the same way as a local transaction requires more sophisticated transaction management than is required for a nondistributed system.

As an example of the added complexity required for distributed transactions, consider the following example of updating a distributed database as the result of the sale of a computer. There are two servers involved, one at the local dealer that contains the local inventory and one at the regional distribution office that supplies the local dealer. The transaction needed is to update databases on the two servers to reflect the change in the local inventory and to automatically send a replacement computer. If the local transaction were to commit and then a failure occurred that prevented the regional server from committing its part of the transaction, the results would be inconsistent.

The most common method of avoiding this problem is by use of the two-phase commit. A two-phase commit protects the integrity of transactions that involve multiple nodes. The first phase determines if all the servers participating in the transaction can commit. All participating servers then must complete writing log records. Not until all servers have ensured that the update will survive in case of a failure, are any of the servers allowed to commit the update to persistent storage. If servers were allowed to commit before all the servers were ready, and any servers were unable to commit, consistency would be violated. Even after all servers have indicated readiness to commit, and the ODBMS coordinating the transaction has issued the general commit command, there is still the possibility of failure. Consistency is protected against this event by requiring all participating servers to signal back to the coordinating ODBMS that the commit was successful. If indication of success is not received in a specified time, then the entire transaction should be aborted. This may require a rollback of each ODBMS to a pretransaction state. Consistent with the requirement for transparency, the application should not even know whether a single or two-phase commit or alternative mechanism is being used. Because transaction transparency is fundamental to all distributed ODBMSs, this is not a discriminating feature.

9.6.1.4 Heterogeneity Transparency

Many organizations have accumulated a mixture of computing equipment and operating systems either because of lack of planning, or lack of predictability of a dynamic computer industry, or because of legitimate varying needs of different organizational units. For such organizations, adoption of an ODBMS restricted to homogenous computers would severely limit communications among the disparate types of platforms. Therefore, a requirement that an ODBMS serve a heterogeneous collection of platforms is a reasonable ISC. It is not vital that an ODBMS be fully heterogeneous for all platforms. It is only important that the ODBMS provide heterogeneity for the set of platforms that the customer needs. Therefore, the following ISC is phrased in terms of a customer-selected set of platforms.

- ***The ODBMS provides full heterogeneity for customer-selected platforms.***

9.6.1.5 Scalability

Scalability refers to the ability to grow without requiring significant alterations to the structure of an application or system and without disproportionately hindering performance. The areas of growth that need to be provided for include an increase in the number of users, the amount of data, and the number and type of platforms handled. An ODBMS that has good scalability manages such increased demand on the system transparently to the user.

Scalability is closely tied to transparency. The various forms of transparency make it easier to change an application or system with little effort and little change in performance. For example, the transparency with which objects can be distributed around a system allows for easy redistribution of workloads as new platforms are added. The transparency that is possible in distributed ODBMSs is key to the scalability of applications.

An automobile is a good example of a product that is not scalable. If one's family grows and a car's space is no longer adequate, one replaces the car rather than adding additional room. One definitely does not want to follow this procedure with ODBMSs. One needs to anticipate growth and ensure that the product selected will scale to handle growth. Starting over with a more scalable ODBMS would usually be unnecessary and very disruptive.

Because scalability is a result of many other ODBMS features, all of which contribute to it, scalability is not an easily quantifiable characteristic. Benchmarks are the only practical way to determine scalability. Therefore, scalability is not used as an ISC.

9.7 Performance

Performance is determined by the functioning of numerous features. One feature to look at that has a significant effect on performance is the nature of the client/server architecture. This feature, the degree of balance in the client/server architecture, was discussed earlier. The balanced client/server approach with the ability to do most processing on either the client or server sides provides a major performance advantage. Therefore, if an organization has an overburdened mainframe and overburdened communication channels with underutilized workstations, it may be very important to have a client/server architecture that is not server oriented. Although a balanced client/server emphasis is ideal, a client emphasis may be satisfactory in cases in which applications on workstations tend to use the same objects for long periods of time.

An evaluator might decide what type of client/server architecture is required and choose an ODBMS based on anticipated performance due to the architecture. Although performance-related features sometimes give a rough idea about what to expect in the way of performance benchmarks, surprises can easily occur. Performance on two different products can differ tremendously based just on the order in which a programmer specifies database operations (Loomis, 1994c). An ODBMS that optimizes the order of a particular set of operations has a great advantage over nonoptimized or poorly optimized code. Because each ODBMS may focus on different areas to optimize, even a detailed examination of the optimizations might not be sufficient for predicting overall performance for a particular application. For this reason and because optimization becomes much more difficult for the complex objects that ODBMSs deal with, benchmarks are the only reliable way to predict performance for an application domain. Therefore, features related to execution performance are not used here as initial selection criteria.

9.8 ODMG-93 Compliance

ODMG-93 compliance is a final extremely important criterion that I hope will be irrelevant by the time you read this. As of early 1996, most ODBMS vendors had not achieved full compliance with ODMG-93. See *Object Magazine* for a table that describes the degree of compliance as of the first quarter of 1996 (*Object Magazine,* 1996).

◆ *The ODBMS is ODMG-93 Compliant.*

9.9 Summary of Features

Table 9.1 provides a summary of the features that have been examined in this chapter. Each feature is listed, and a short explanation of why the feature was included or not included as an ISC is provided.

9.10 Evaluation Process

This section recommends an evaluation process that allows one to compare the suitability of the various ODBMS products for an organization or project. Table 9.2 provides a summary list of the initial selection criteria and additional columns to assist in the evaluation. One copy of the Table should be completed for each ODBMS considered. The scoring scheme is designed to eliminate candidates not meeting the requirements and to also provide a rough idea of the comparative value of the remaining candidates.

The first step in the process is to determine the importance of each criterion in meeting the organization's needs. Mark each criterion by using the numerical value shown in parentheses for the following cases: essential (100), very important (2), important (1), or not important (0). The second step is to enter a value for each criterion of 0 if the criterion is met and 1 if it is not met. The next step is to multiply each of the numbers in the importance column by zero or one in the value column to complete the score column. Of course, if a feature is not important and therefore has a value of 0, it will not matter what the value of the value column is; the product will be 0. The total score is calculated by assigning each ODBMS an initial score of 100 from which the sum of the values in the score column is subtracted.

Table 9.1 *Summary of ODBMS Features Considered*

Feature	Reasoning (NDF or ISC)[a]
Product structure	Lacks importance—only affects the customer indirectly.
Cost of system	ISC—only products that are under or equal to what the customer is willing to invest will be considered
Object model	NDF—ODMG-93 standard will standardize the object model
Operating systems	ISC—product needs to support customer's operating system and hardware
Programming language	ISC—important to customers with certain types of programmers
Vendor support and longevity	Ambiguous—cannot determine which vendors will survive
Active versus passive ODBMSs	ISC—valuable when a high degree of intelligence is needed in the database
Transaction Properties	NDF—basic characteristics to all ODBMSs
Support for long transaction	ISC—important to customers who are involved with software development in which more than one person is involved
Query capability	NDF—OQL will be adopted under the ODMG-93 standard
Navigational access	NDF—all ODBMSs possess navigational access.
Schema modification	ISC—important to customers who use applications that must remain online continuously.
Locking and concurrency control	ISC—the type of locking may be important depending on the customer's application

[a]NDF = not a discriminating feature; ISC = initial selection criterion.

Table 9.1 *Summary of Features Considered (continued)*

Feature	Reasoning (NDF or ISC)[a]
Access control at the object level	ISC—important to customers who require security greater than password access to the database
On-line Backup	ISC—important to customers requiring a back-up capability adequate for OLTP.
Versioning	ISC—important to customers who have multiple users working together on a single project
Location transparency	NDF—common to all ODBMSs
Migration transparency	NDF—common to all ODBMSs
Replication transparency	ISC—important to customers who require network nodes to function independently
Transaction transparency	NDF—common to all ODBMSs
Heterogeneity transparency	ISC—important to customers with mix of computing equipment and operating systems
Scalability	Ambiguous—many factors affect the feature
Performance	Ambiguous—many factors affect the feature
ODMG-93 Compliance	ISC—standard implies many critical features

[a]NDF = not a discriminating feature; ISC = initial selection criterion.

Evaluators should use considerable caution when deciding that a feature is essential. Don't adopt the attitude that the goal is to eliminate most of the candidates so as to simplify the selection process. The purpose of this evaluation method is to eliminate only those candidates who definitely can not meet the customer's requirements. After all, it would not be difficult to create unnecessarily stringent conditions that do not reflect real company requirements on the ODBMS and that would eliminate all candidates from consideration. For some criteria a choice of methods is required before a value can be assigned. For

Table 9.2 *Summary of ODBMS Evaluation Criteria*

Criterion	Importance (100=essential, 2=very important, 1=important, 0=not important)	Value (No=1, Yes=0)	Score (Importance times Value)
The cost of the system is less than a value selected by the customer (Section 9.3.2).			
The ODBMS supports required platforms (Section 9.3.4).			
The ODBMS supports the required programming languages (Section 9.3.5).			
The ODBMS is an active database (Section 9.4.2)			
The ODBMS provides the ability to handle long transactions by support of nested transactions and versions (Section 9.4.4).			
The ODBMS provides online schema modification for the type of capabilities also present in RDBMSs (Section 9.4.7). (Criterion does not require online modification of inheritance structures.)			

Table 9.2 *Summary of ODBMS Evaluation Criteria (continued)*

Criterion	Importance (100=essential, 2=very important, 1=important, 0=not important)	Value (No=1, Yes=0)	Score (Importance times Value)
The ODBMS has the type of locking (e.g., object or page locking) that is most appropriate for the customer's applications (Section 9.5.1).			
The ODBMS has access control at the object level (Section 9.5.2).			
The ODBMS provides transaction recovery based on an online backup capability that is adequate for online transaction processing. This requires that no transactions be lost during failure other than those in progress at the time of failure (Section 9.5.3).			

(Continued on next page)

example, the locking criterion requires that one decide whether page locking, object locking, or neither is required.

The effect of this scoring procedure is to subtract from the initial score—100 for each "essential" criterion not met, 2 for each "very important" criterion not met, 1 for each "important" criterion not met, and subtract nothing for any "not important" criterion. A 0 or negative

Table 9.2 *Summary of ODBMS Evaluation Criteria (continued)*

Criterion	Importance (100=essential, 2=very important, 1=important, 0=not important)	Value (No=1, Yes=0)	Score (Importance times Value)
The ODBMS supports a versioning capability (Section 9.5.4).			
The ODBMS has the capability to replicate either objects or a group of objects along with the capability to coordinate updates among the replicas (Section 9.6.1).			
The ODBMS provides full heterogeneity for customer-selected platforms (Section 9.6.1).			
The ODBMS is ODMG-93 compliant (Section 9.8)			
Total score (calculate as: 100 – sum of scores) =			

total score will eliminate the ODBMS from consideration. For the remaining ODBMSs, scores in the high 90s will certainly be worth pursuing. An evaluator may wish to eliminate an ODBMS that fails to provide many features important to an organization. The exact magnitude of the final number should not be taken too seriously, however, since the primary purpose of the initial selection criteria is to provide a means of eliminating unsatisfactory products, not to compare ones with similar capabilities.

Because vendors may claim to provide an important capability but the actual capability does not function to the standards expected, this process may not weed out all the products that should be eliminated. On the other hand, it is unlikely that a vendor would provide one of the ISC and not mention it, so the process will probably not eliminate ones that should not be eliminated. The exception to this is that vendor information may become dated quickly because of the rapid development pace of current ODBMSs. The reader is cautioned not to eliminate a vendor on a single criterion without checking with the vendor—there may be a newer version that provides the capability.

9.10 References

Barry, D. (1993). ODBMS feature listing. *Object Magazine, 2*(5), 48–53.

Barry, D. (1994a). Should you take the plunge? *Object Magazine, 3*(6), 24–27.

Barry, D. (1994b). ODBMS benchmarks. *Object Magazine, 4*(6), 24–26.

Barry, D. (1994c). The importance of understanding ODBMS features. *Object Magazine, 4*(2), 76–77.

Barry, D. (1995). Feature coverage in the current market. *Object Magazine, 5*(4), 24–31.

Bertino, E., & Martino, L. (1991). Object-oriented database management systems: Concepts and issues. *Computer, 24*(5),41.

Colley, G. (1992). Versioning. *Object Magazine, 2*(4), 32–34.

Friedman, J. (1993). New options for object databases. *Object Magazine, 2*(6), 69.

Hsieh, D. (1994). Comparing the version management features of commercial ODBMSs. *Object Magazine, 4*(6), 65–74.

Johnson E. F., & Reichard, K. (1990). Advanced X Window applications *programming*. Portland, OR: MIS Press.

Johnston, M. W. (1992). French OODBMS newcomer strong at starting gate. *Software Magazine, 12* (March), 000–000.

Loomis, M. E. S. (1993a). Object and relational technologies: Can they cooperate? *Object Magazine, 2*(5), 35–40.

Loomis, M. E. S. (1993b). Object programming & database management. *Journal of Object-Oriented Programming, 6*(2), 31–34.

Loomis, M. E. S. (1993c). Object and relational technologies: Can they cooperate? Object Magazine. 2 (5): 40.

Loomis, M. E. S. (1993d). Distributed object databases. *Journal of Object-Oriented Programming, 6*(1), 23.

Loomis, M. E. S. (1993e). Managing replicated objects. *Journal of Object-Oriented Programming, 6*(5), 65–71.

Loomis, M. E. S. (1994a). Querying object databases. *Journal of Object-Oriented Programming, 7*(3), 58–59.

Loomis, M. E. S. (1994b). ODBMS myths and realities. *Journal of Object-Oriented Programming, 7*(4), 78.

Loomis, M. E. S. (1994c). Querying object databases. *Journal of Object-Oriented Programming, 7*(3), 56–60,78.

Object Magazine. (1996a). Contact information for vendors of ODBMS and related products. *5*(9):23.

Object Magazine. (1996b). ODMG-93 Compliance. *5*(9):22.

Stewart, M. K. (1995a). Executive brief. *Object Magazine, 5*(6),8.

Stewart, M. K. (1995b). Executive brief. *Object Magazine. 5*(7),10.

Tanenbaum, A. S. (1992). *Modern operating systems.* (pp. 3–4, 387). Englewood Cliffs, NJ: Prentice Hall.

Taylor, D. A. (1996). Private communication.

Thuraisingham, M. B. (1990). Security in object-oriented database systems. *Journal of Object-Oriented Programming, 2*(6), 18–25.

Wade, A. E. (1994). Distributed client-server databases. *Object Magazine, 4*(1), 47, 50–52.

Chapter 10

Object Technology in Distributed Computing

Everyone is familiar with distributed computing in an abstract sense because this is how businesses work, irrespective of the use of computers. The distributed objects in the business world are people. They have their own tasks to perform and their own specialized abilities to apply to the tasks. They move about communicating with other people who have capabilities that assist with the completion of their tasks. This human model of a distributed system works very much like a distributed computing system needs to work for cooperating computers.

At a primitive level, distributed computing simply means that two or more computers or devices can communicate with each other (see Figure 10.1). With this definition, two computers on my desk could be considered a distributed system when I transfer data between them on a floppy diskette. Of course, this is not what is generally meant by a distributed computing system; normally we would expect, at least, some type of physical electronic connection joining the computers. More than this is required for what Tanenbaum (1992) describes as a "true" distributed system, namely, a system of computers with no shared memory that appears to the user as if they were a single computer.

Creating the illusion that a distributed system appears as if it were a single computer is a matter of making many aspects of the system transparent to the user and the software developer. It is a daunting

Figure 10.1 *A primitive distributed system*

task when one considers all of the aspects of the system that must be transparent to the user. The transparency must provide for machine, operating system, language, and location independence, to name a few. This means that a heterogeneous mixture of PCs, workstations, and mainframes must all behave similarly, despite such fundamental differences as storing integers in different byte orders within memory. Operating systems as vastly different as UNIX and DOS must be accommodated. Languages with strong philosophical differences, such as Smalltalk and C++, must be able to interface transparently. And the location of program entities must be made irrelevant to the user of the system. It is little wonder that prior to the advent of object technology, very limited progress was made in achieving all of these goals.

All these capabilities for transparent use of a distributed system can best be achieved with the development and acceptance of standards and with the use of a paradigm that facilitates the communication of both data and its associated semantics among the nodes of a network. Standards for open object interfaces have been developed; as a result, rapid progress in distributed computing is accelerating in all of these areas by using objects as the vehicle of distribution.

"Creating an illusion" has the ring of a magician's trick, but the benefits of creating this illusion are enormous. It means that the distributed system performs an immense amount of work with no effort on the user's part. It can allow sharing and processing of previously incompatible data. It can allow local autonomy of work groups and simultaneously can allow use of the work group's data for more global business purposes. It can save converting programs from one language to another to merge application capabilities. It also can save unused computation power on underutilized machines and relieve other overburdened machines and saturated network channels.

The use of object technology is ideal for distributed systems because encapsulation and the message passing philosophy are key principles of the object-oriented paradigm. Encapsulation ensures that only the interface of objects need to be considered and not the details of the implementation. This allows other objects to send messages to an object without caring how the object accomplished the requested service. These same principles that decouple the sending object from the implementation of the receiving object's behavior also allow the sending object not to have to know the physical location of the receiver. This is similar to dialing a phone number—one doesn't need to know if the callee is down the street or in a distant city. Looked at this way it would seem that this is the natural way for messages to work; however, traditionally, computing systems have worked as if one had to hand deliver a message to the person next door or in the next city.

This chapter first provides a brief introduction to distributed computing and client/server architecture to provide a foundation for the discussion of the role of object technology in this domain. Later, distributed computing standards and the implementation of distributed computing on the Internet are discussed.

10.1 The Evolution of Distributed Computing Systems

Distributed computing systems are closely associated with the idea of the client/server architecture, so first we will discuss the meaning of this term.

10.1.1 Client/Server Architecture

One of the first ways of sharing information was for the programmer to simply embed data into an application program. Then all users of the program were in effect sharing the benefits of the data. Of course, the embedded data was of no use in any other program, so next, data was also stored in "flat" files. Then the data could be shared with many users as long as they were using programs that knew the format of the data, could interpret the significance of the data, and could process it. Having to know all of these details about the data is the antithesis of the transparency that we are seeking in modern distributed computing systems, however.

The meaning of the words "client/server" has changed as technology has advanced. From the viewpoint of a single computer program, a client is a calling routine and a server is the called routine. From the viewpoint of early computer systems, the mainframe was the server for many individuals creating programs using punched cards or "dumb" terminals as client hardware. Thus, the original meaning of the words "client" and "server" was related to both the use of software and of hardware; however, now client/server architecture generally refers to a software architecture.

The evolution of technology displaced the earliest uses of the words, so when one refers to a client/server architecture today, one is unlikely to be referring to something as primitive as a mainframe with terminals that only provide input. The advent of workstations that possess significant computing power set the stage for a new relationship between the mainframe and the client hardware. Now, typically, client/server architecture assumes that the client-side terminals are capable of doing substantial computation. The advent of communication systems that allow the interconnection of many computers of many types to be interconnected on a network has further expanded the view of what a client/server system encompasses. Thus, client/server architecture is now considered in the context of a network of possibly heterogeneous computers and is closely identified with the idea of distributed computing.

The evolution of the term "client/server" has not stabilized enough to have established a commonly accepted definition of the term. However, Loomis (1992a) describes criteria, summarized below, that define the meaning of "client/server architecture" in a manner that is consistent with earlier uses of the term, describes the current common usage of the term, and distinguishes it from the associated concept of distributed computing.

- There exists a functional separation between the client and the server.
- Client and server portions are able to operate on separate machines but don't have to.

- Multiple clients are able to access the server concurrently.
- Servers may be replaced or distributed to multiple servers without adversely affecting clients.
- Clients may be added or deleted without adversely affecting the other clients.

10.1.2 Distributed File Systems

The creation of distributed file systems was an important first step toward the goal of fully transparent distributed computing. As an example, let's look at one of the best known network operating systems to provide a shared global file system, the Network File System (NFS) of Sun Microsystems. A goal of this system was to create a transparent file system using multiple computers. The users of NFS can simply request files by name without specifying where the files are located; they may be local or on a remote computer. (One does need to specify initially what file systems of the remote server are to be mounted for use by a local machine, but this can be done just once during setup.)

NFS achieved a couple of forms of transparency: location transparency and limited heterogeneity transparency. The latter is limited to a selected set of computers but adaptable to the addition of other computers. A limitation on NFS is that it is centered around input/output, which is involved with low-level machine-dependent implementation details. A higher level of abstraction not so close to the hardware is needed as a basis for a distributed system. A further limitation on this advance is that it achieved transparency only for data, not for processes; separating the data and methods reduces the semantic value of each. An object-oriented approach eliminates this limitation. For the same reasons that one needs data and methods encapsulated as objects, as provided by the object-oriented paradigm, one needs them encapsulated as objects for distribution in a distributed system.

A distributed file system provides only a small portion of the desired single-image illusion, because there are many other aspects of a distributed system that need to be transparent besides those related to file access. A distributed object database management system (ODBMS) is needed to create a realistic illusion, because it can provide many additional types of transparency. This was discussed in the previous chapter, so a single example of an additional type of transparency is provided here, namely, distributed transactions—there are no distributed transactions in a system like NFS.

The next step in the evolution of distributed systems was to make processes transparent across computers on the system. This was accomplished by the method of remote procedure calls (RPCs), which makes calls to remote machines look just like calls on the local machine (with some exceptions, such as when a failure occurs). HP Apollo's Network Computing System is an example of an architecture that implements RPCs.

Distributed systems are evolving simultaneously in three independent dimensions from centralized, relational, homogeneous systems toward decentralized, object-oriented, heterogeneous systems. As shown in Figure 10.2, these dimensions represent the following:

- the evenness of the distribution of the responsibilities among the computers on the network
- the degree of compatibility of the computers in the system
- the degree of intelligence of the distributed entities

The origin of what I call the distributed computing cube in the figure represents the centralized, relational, homogeneous system that is only nominally distributed; this will be referred to as *basic distribution* or a *basic distributed system*. It is distributed because a central computer provides common data for multiple computers. The diagonal corner of the cube represents a fully distributed system that can be termed a balanced distributed, object-oriented, heterogeneous system; this will be referred to here as *ideal distribution* or an *ideally distributed system*.

The x-axis in the figure represents the distribution of the responsibilities of the computer; these may be centralized or relatively evenly distributed. The distribution of responsibilities among networked computers is a function of the implementing architecture. Within the client/server architecture there are three approaches, as described in Section 10.3, that determine whether responsibilities are centralized or decentralized (balanced). The section describes the "distribution of responsibilities dimension" of the distributed computing cube of Figure 10.2.

The y-axis in the figure represents the degree of compatibility of the computers on the network; they may all be of the same type (homo-

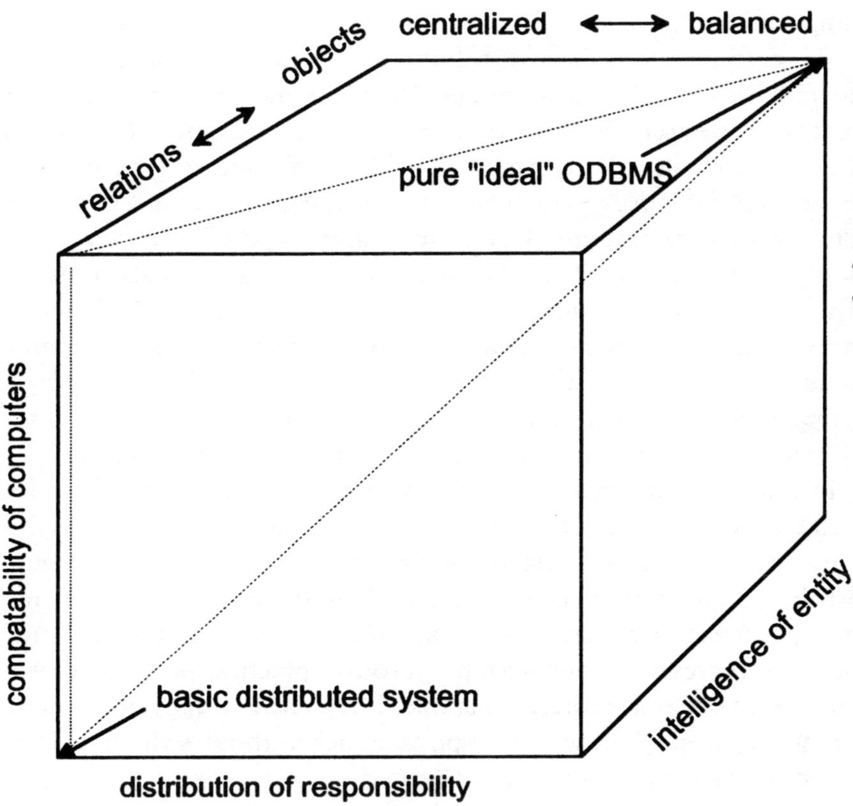

Figure 10.2 *Distributed Computing Cube*

geneous) or may be incompatible with respect to hardware, operating systems, and computer languages used (heterogeneous). Section 10.4 describes the "compatibility of computers dimension" of the distributed computing cube.

The z-axis in the figure represents the degree of intelligence of entities being distributed. The entities may lack intelligence; that is, the entities may be data without associated behavior. Alternatively, the entities may have intelligence; that is, they may be objects that have both data and behavior related to the data. The intelligence of the distributed entities is a function of the paradigm used. The data-structure paradigm distributes unintelligent entities (data) and the object-oriented paradigm distributes intelligent entities (objects). Section 10.5

describes the "intelligence of entities dimension" of the distributed computing cube.

Not everyone needs ideal distribution. For example, if all of one's computers have identical hardware and use the same operating system, the ability of the ideally distributed system to handle all types of computer is of no current value. Furthermore, the ideally distributed system may not be ideal for a company with a large installed legacy system. On the other hand, many organizations already are in great need of everything that an ideally distributed system has to offer. Section 10.2 provides an example of why a company would need an ideally distributed system. It provides an example of the evolution of a distributed computing system without attempting to precisely define the terms used. The sections following the example describe distributed computing in more technical terms by focusing on the three independent characteristics of a system.

In practice there may be a mixture of paradigms and database management systems used. For the purposes of explaining distributed systems, descriptions of systems represented by the vertices of the distributed computing cube are used. These represent the pure forms of the parameters under consideration. Intermediate points within and on the cube represent mixed systems. From a practical point of view the dimensions are not entirely separable, however. For example, it is difficult to achieve a balance of responsibilities without switching from a relational database to an object-oriented one.

The dashed lines in the figure show typical transition paths to a fully distributed object-oriented system. The diagonal path of the cube may be taken by a company with no previous investment in any form of distributed computing. Other companies may have a heterogeneous system of communicating computers using a server-based RDBMS. Thus they would start at the upper left vertex of the front face of the cube and might traverse the diagonal of the top face of the cube by obtaining an ODBMS with a balanced client/server architecture, as shown by the other dashed lines in the figure. The example in Section 10.2 describes how a company might take the former route.

10.2 A Distributed Computing Example

The following discussion of distributed computing uses a real estate company as an example. The company, which we will call RECo, started with a central office in a large metropolitan area with a staff of realtors specializing in residential property. RECo started when paper and ink were the media for conducting business; but we will skip past the dark ages to the time when their housing data and accounting information were placed on a mainframe computer. We will follow this hypothetical company through its evolution from simple information processing to a file sharing system to a distributed system with a balanced client/server architecture using an ODBMS. At each stage we will examine the computer needs of the company and the characteristics of the various systems used. Subsequent sections will describe distributed computing in more technical terms.

Originally RECo maintained computer files containing property information in record format, but found it necessary to constantly modify their processing software to locate property meeting combinations of conditions that customers were interested in. By switching to a relational database, RECo was able to quickly identify property meeting the unpredictable requests of their customers, without constant reprogramming.

During the 1980s RECo began expanding throughout the country. Local offices purchased PCs and workstations to do accounting, maintain local listing information, and to provide data for the central database. Initially, updates to the central files were made by carrying or mailing floppy diskettes to the main office for inclusion in the database. Although the central office could provide comprehensive nationwide listings and sophisticated processing of requests, because of the geographical dispersion of the company, considerable time delay occurred in transmitting information between the central and local offices.

RECo wanted to quickly provide a customer at a local RECo office with information about what houses were for sale in any location of the country. So RECo invested in network software to connect their computers, allowing each local office to transmit information about houses between the central office and local offices. Some offices near the central office were connected with a local area network (LAN) and the remaining offices were connected with a wide area network (WAN).

RECo's needs are similar to that of many national and international companies—they are physically distributed and need a distributed computing system to allow easy sharing of information. Typically these communication systems use a client/server architecture, frequently with a central database server that stores data, processes the data, and sends results back to the client computers in local offices.

Although RECo's networked system of computers can be considered a distributed computing system because of the physical separation of the computers, the actual architecture of the system differs little from that of the traditional mainframe with punched card input. The remote terminals are used mainly as input/output devices to a centralized storage and processing system. RECo found that despite the communication speed advantage of the new system, it still had some of the same problems as before.

Occasionally the central computer would be down, taking most of the capability of the entire computing system down with it. Even though the local offices had powerful workstations with a lot of free time, the mainframe was overloaded and had to be replaced with a larger model. The downtime during the transition to the larger computer wreaked havoc on local offices that were dependent on the central database for not only national listings but local listings as well. In addition to the reliability problem, they discovered an economic one—replacing a computer with one with twice the capacity was more than twice as expensive.

Despite some sporadic customer dissatisfaction, the company was keeping up with the latest technology, giving it a competitive advantage that kept it growing. Although RECo management was delighted with their increased business, the increase in the number of offices using the central database was overloading their network communications, causing delays. After an expensive upgrade of the network hardware, the new system eventually worked smoothly and RECo happily continued in this mode indefinitely raking in profits.

No, you know better. The only thing constant in business is change. Soon RECo observed that they were losing customers to another company that was making use of a virtual-reality program that was simply dazzling customers and selling houses that the customers had never even visited.

Here's what RECo found that the rival company could do for a customer in Kalamazoo who was moving to Kankakee. The customer goes to the Kalamazoo office and sits down in front of a computer. He clicks a mouse button to choose Illinois then another click to choose

Kankakee on a map of the state. He selects a region of town, a price range, and other preferences. He sees pictures of the outside of the houses that meet his criteria. He selects a house he likes and the monitor displays exactly what he would see as he enters the door and walks throughout the house, spending as much time in any part as he wishes and looking in any direction he chooses. He see what looks like a flaw on the wall and zooms in on it to find that it is just a fly.

RECo realized that to compete it must have the virtual-house program available to every office, but quickly discovered that the existing network architecture could not handle the job. The problem was that the amount of data needed to visually represent a house dwarfs all other data about the house. Buying an even bigger mainframe and network hardware would not solve the problem this time. Just transferring all of the visual data on houses from the server to the client computers in the local offices would put a great burden on the network. Even more serious, transmitting updated images of the interior of the house every time the view is changed requires all of the information needed to repaint the entire display screen to be transmitted over the network many times per second. If users at local offices attempted this, all communications would come to a standstill.

RECo hired a consultant to deal with the problem and got some good news. They already had all of the computing power and disk storage they needed to handle the virtual-house software. No hardware purchases were needed; all they had to do was make better use of the largely idle capacity of the computers in the local offices. Furthermore, with the plan the consultant outlined for them, when they add new local offices they would be able to buy a workstation for the local offices without having to replace the mainframe for the foreseeable future.

They followed the consultant's advice and purchased an ODBMS with a client/server architecture. The solution to their potential problem of bogging down in network traffic was solved because their client machines handled the computationally intensive calculations and the graphical interface, using the remote server only to locate housing information meeting specific customer criteria and to download the objects describing a particular house.

RECo started with a centralized relational homogeneous computing system and went directly to a balanced distributed object-oriented heterogeneous system. In terms of the distributed computing cube, they took the diagonal path. Because of the gradual evolution of this technology, many companies first take a route along one axis. For example, to interconnect a variety of existing computers, they first move from a homogeneous to heterogeneous distributed system using remote procedure calls (RPCs).

We now switch to technical issues raised by the example. To understand the role of ODBMSs in a distributed computing system, one needs to understand something about client/server architecture (discussed in Section 10.1), distributed computing in a network, and the relationship between distributed computing and client/server architecture. The latter topics are discussed below.

10.3 Centralized versus Balanced Distributed Systems

This section explores the first of the three dimensions of the distributed computing cube that represents the distribution of the responsibilities of the computer. The earlier section on client/server architecture discussed many of the issues related to the use of a balanced distribution of responsibilities versus centralized responsibilities. The following sections clarify the distinction between a distributed system and a client/server architecture and reiterate key differences in the two approaches.

10.3.1 Distributed Computing versus Client/Server Architecture

Section 10.1 described what is meant by a client/server architecture, but it may not yet be clear what the difference is between the closely related concepts of client/server architecture and distributed computing. Some authors [e.g., Berson (1992)], describe client/server architecture as a type of distributed computing. Many others use the term "distributed client/server." Apparently they do not consider client/server to be a specialization of distributed computing or the use of the word "distributed" would be redundant. Thus, there are two views of the meaning of client/server architecture.

By adopting Loomis' earlier definition of client/server, one can keep the definitions of the client/server and distributed computing independent. The second item of Loomis's (1992a) criteria ("Client and server portions can operate on separate machines *but don't have to.*"), allows a client/server architecture on a nondistributed system. From this it is apparent that the two concepts are independent using her definition. The client/server model deals with the logical relationship between units of software. Distributed computing involves a relationship among pieces of hardware that must be implemented by some software architecture. The client/server model describes how the hardware units work together via the use of software—the client/server model is a software concept not a hardware concept. Thus, client/server architecture is one way of utilizing a distributed computing system.

As an example of an alternative method to the client/server approach, a master–slave model could be used. The master–slave model is useful for one device selecting and controlling another device, such as a mainframe controlling the selection of a tape drive. The master–slave model would certainly not be a generally appropriate model for connecting workstations to a host, because making slaves of the workstations would waste their intelligence.

10.3.2 Centralized Distributed Computing Systems

The distributed computing system in the example began with a centralized architecture. The main advantage of this type of a system is that it is easier to create. The disadvantages of having a lopsided workload are in the economics and reliability. The economic problem is that mainframes have a higher price-to-performance ratio than PCs and workstations. The reliability problem is that if the mainframe goes down the peripheral computers are badly crippled too.

10.3.3 Balanced Distributed Computing Systems

A centralized distributed computing system, in which all of the data is maintained on and processing is done on a central computer, does not model the effective manner in which people perform cooperative work. A decentralized, fully distributed model does parallel human cooperative work and provides a solution to many problems of the centralized model. ODBMSs perform a critical role in achieving the distributed computing capabilities needed for many applications.

10.4 Distributing Data versus Objects

This section discusses the second of the three dimensions of the distributed computing cube that represents the nature of the entities being distributed. A distributed RDBMS distributes data and an ODBMS distributes objects. The relational model is deficient in its generalized modeling capability compared to both the human model and the object model, because it provides only data and very limited intelligence with which to manipulate the data. However, a distributed object model can adequately represent the human model of cooperative interaction. Although the distributed object model has this potential and the relational model has more limited potential, this does not imply that existing ODBMSs fulfill this potential.

The objects in the system need to have their own knowledge and intelligence (data and the ability to execute methods on the data). The objects also need to be mobile and to communicate with other objects anywhere in the system. Ideally in a distributed system, servers provide services of general utility to a wide array of applications, and applications request these services with minimal knowledge of how the services function and without knowing what location in the network provides the services.

10.5 Distribution of Homogeneous versus Heterogeneous Computers

This section discusses the third of the three dimensions of the distributed computing cube, which represents the nature of the computers in the system. Creating a distributed system using computers of a single type is considerably easier than creating one that will transparently handle a heterogeneous collection of computers. Few companies are willing to accept the limitation of homogeneous distribution, however. Most companies have an assortment of computers to begin with, and even if they have uniform hardware they at least would like to have the negotiating position that they could easily switch hardware vendors if prices are not competitive. Companies also have a variety of computing needs that are difficult to meet if they are restricted to a single hardware vendor.

If each person in an organization spoke a different language, accomplishing cooperative tasks would be extremely difficult. This corresponds to a major problem with the development of distributed computing in the past—there has been no standard way of communicating information among the objects in the system. Now that a limited number of distributed object communication standards exist, as discussed in the next section, the stage is set for a rapid expansion of distributed computing.

The transparency needed for a heterogeneous system is not limited to hardware considerations and operating systems. Language transparency is also required for many organizations. The potential savings in not having to duplicate software in multiple languages are significant, even if one restricts the duplication to the most popular two languages.

10.6 Conformance to Standards: OMG Standardization

Anyone who has ever tried to remove a quarter-inch bolt with a set of metric wrenches has an appreciation of the need for a single standard. Even the existence of two competing standards, such as the English and metric systems of measurement, has caused enormous extra costs and lost opportunities for manufacturers engaged in international trade. Similarly, in the software industry, the lack of a standard for the portability of applications has caused constant expenditure of time and effort to convert differing languages, operating systems, and hardware requirements.

Distributed object management (DOM) is a term used to describe the new computing paradigm that couples client/server and object-oriented technologies (Johnston, 1992). The primary unifying force in the development of DOM technology has been the Object Management Group (OMG), a broad-based consortium of software and hardware vendors and end-users formed in 1989 to alleviate many of the problems in the object-oriented portion of the software industry related to the lack of standardization.

The OMG created an overall architecture for the evolution of a series of standards related to the interoperability of software components and portability of distributed object-oriented applications. The OMG Object Management Architecture (OMA) (OMG, 1993) defines an abstract foundation for systematic integration of the components of object technology with emphasis on distributed computing.

The OMA includes the OMG Object Model (OMG/OM), which provides design portability for object interactions. The model is intended to evolve in an orderly fashion by adding profiles to the Core Component already established; these profiles (collections of components) are standards related to technology domains.

The Core Component of the OMG/OM provides a foundation that can be used for object request brokers, object database systems, and other object-oriented applications. It defines objects in the manner one would expect, which is consistent with the object-oriented paradigm. Objects are instances of types and have a state and have behaviors specified as operations. Types are organized in a specialization hierarchy of subtypes and supertypes.

Consistent with the emphasis on distributed object management, the first of the profiles to be created by the OMG was the CORBA (Common Object Request Broker Architecture) standard (OMG TC Document, 1991), which provides a common definition for how object interfaces are to be handled in a language-neutral manner, thus providing portability of source code. CORBA defines the interfaces and services of the Object Request Broker (ORB) that provide the mechanism that allows transparency of the location of objects. CORBA defines a metalanguage called the Interface Definition Language (IDL) that defines the public interface for applications using ORBs. It also defines an application programming interface, the Basic Object Adapter (BOA).

Unfortunately, there are competing standards for distributed processing. The Open Software Foundation's Distributed Computing Environment (OSF DCE) provides for product interoperability, but does not use an object model. Thus OSF DCE lacks the benefits of object technology described in Section 1.3 and is in only indirect competition with the CORBA standard. Hewlett-Packard's ORB Plus attempts to bridge the incompatibility between OSF DCE by layering an ORB on top of DCE (Ewald & Roy, 1994).

Microsoft's COM (Common Object Manager) is a competitor to the CORBA standard for distributed object management. Choosing between CORBA and COM is an important management decision that may have major long-term consequences. CORBA is clearly the broader and more stable standard and has many advantages. The one major advantage (and disadvantage) of the COM standard is that it is an incremental extension of Microsoft standards. The need to continue to rely on Microsoft products may be an overriding consideration for many users. Mowbray (1994) provides a detailed discussion of the pros and cons of the two standards. This article or others like it are "must reads" before any decision is made between COM and CORBA—the stakes are high.

A distributed object standard must deal well with both distribution and objects. The OSF/DCE standard is strong on distribution but weak on objects. The COM standard is moderately strong on objects but weak on distribution. Because the CORBA standard is strong in both areas, it is the putative lingua franca of the distributed computing world for distributed objects. Fortunately, the CORBA standard is general enough that it can be used as a common standard that encompasses other standards. CORBA can be used as a superstandard that will allow interoperability between products created according to CORBA and Microsoft's COM. Digital Equipment Corporation (DEC) is working on achieving capability between the two.

Those who choose the CORBA standard have an increasing number of implementations of the standard from which to choose. Organizations already using IBM's System Object Model (SOM) will undoubted wish to use IBM's Distributed System Object Model (DSOM). Many organizations not already using SOM may want to use SOM and DSOM for distributed computing because it is robust, has diverse platform support, and is designed for enterprise-wide applications (Czukkermann & Spera, 1995); however, DSOM is quite complex. All other organizations have a much more difficult choice considering the variety of implementations now available. See Taylor (1994) for further information on the development of CORBA and vendor support for it.

10.7 Database Management on a Distributed Computing System

A distributed DBMS is composed of multiple cooperating DBMSs that are located on different nodes (Loomis, 1992b). The objective is achieving efficient use of computing resources in a manner that is convenient for the users, allowing them to access objects transparently from any client as if there were a single local database.

In a fully distributed computing system, the user need not be concerned about the location and format of the data, regardless of the type of computer and location of the database management systems on the network. Accomplishing this and maintaining the transparency essential to a distributed system represents a formidable challenge to the industry.

Considering that the CORBA standard provides a foundation for distributing objects, it is a legitimate question as to what more a distributed ODBMS adds beyond that of distributed object management. Part of the answer is that an ODBMS can provide all of the specific data management features that an RDBMS provides, including most of the features discussed in the previous chapter.

The rest of the answer is that an ODBMS operates on a lower level of granularity than does a DOM. A DOM is designed to manipulate course-grained entities, such as application programs, like a word processor, and large objects, like a chapter in a book. The limiting aspect of CORBA is that it does not define implementation details like caching techniques. Without dealing with low-level efficiency concerns, management of objects according to CORBA requires significant access times for interobject communications. ODBMSs can provide the detailed object manipulation techniques to allow efficient in-memory processing speed needed for intensive calculations among small objects.

Thus, an ideally distributed system is to some extent only a bare foundation with a great deal of potential on which to build. For many applications, a database management system is needed to turn this potential into a full production environment.

By putting the information into a DBMS environment, several advantages are gained over a file system, such as: recovery from failures, integrity, concurrency, scalability, and query processing (Wade, 1994). Relational database management systems have provided this capability with great success in many areas. RDBMSs have not provided a convenient and efficient means of managing most types of data, however.

One of the primary advantages of an object-oriented approach to database management is that it makes it much easier to transparently distribute both data and its semantics over a network. The ability to retain the meaning of the data when storing and distributing it allows one to accomplish more complex modeling tasks with comparative ease.

On the other hand, the emphasis of the object-oriented paradigm on encapsulation and the emphasis of a database management system of sharing data create a tension between two competing goals of an ODBMS. Simultaneously achieving encapsulation and shared use requires considerable foresight. As the number of anticipated applications increases, the harder it is to find behaviors of an object that are common to all applications. Thus one should tend to use simpler objects in an ODBMS than one might in an individual application.

10.8 The Internet and Java

The Internet needs true distributed computing, just as local and wide area networks do. We have a way to go before the Internet can act like one big computer, but progress is being made in this direction. One implication of this trend is that many consumers may choose to use inexpensive terminal-type PCs instead of more expensive hardware. This kind of PC, which has been referred to as an Internet appliance, could allow access to most of the capabilities and software that we now have with current closed systems. It is unlikely that this concept will displace sophisticated PC hardware, but advances in distributed computing may well open a new market for such minimal-capability computers. Furthermore, it may have a major impact on the entire software market, with companies that make large software packages feeling the impact (Yourdon, 1996).

Currently, most Web pages on the Internet are written in HTML (HyperText Markup Language), which is limited in capabilities even after applying the CGI (Common Gateway Interface) extensions. The Java language by SunSoft is a new object-oriented language that is well designed to overcome current limitations on what can be accomplished on the Internet. A typical use of Java programming is to create small programs called *Applets* that are embedded in Web pages. The Applets are downloaded to the client (e.g., the user's computer) and executed there instead of having the application logic executed on the server. When such application logic involves displaying large amounts of data on the client machine, the time involved can be orders of magnitude less than the time it would have taken to transfer the same server-calculated data by modem.

Java's feature list is impressive even when compared to a much more complex language like C++. Java has syntax similar to that of C++, but was developed without the constraint of having to maintain compatibility with the C language. This allowed the creation of a streamlined language with small memory requirements. Java also adds some critical capabilities that C++ lacks. Most important of these are garbage collection, portability, multithreading, and security.

Garbage collection improves the reliability of the software. Portability is essential on the Internet because the creator of a Web page cannot know what platforms may be accessing it. Multithreading, which allows multiple processes to run concurrently, is important so that users can spend less time waiting for a response from the network; rather, they can be running other processes. Java's security features, which prevent distributed objects from transmitting viruses, are essential for a language for the Internet that allows interactive Web pages. The lack of pointers in Java contributes greatly to both reliability and security. After explaining to my wife what an Applet was and then proceeding to tout Java's security features to her, she said, "I understand, an Applet a day keeps the virus away." Java, by the way, is not an acronym; in particular, it does *not* stand for "just another vague acronym."

Because Java is easier to learn than C++ and has the type-checking capability that Smalltalk lacks, Java has a bright future not only with distributed computing, but also as a general-purpose language. At the time of this writing, Java is very slow compared to the other general-purpose languages and this must be addressed before it can be used in time-critical applications. It is typical of new languages that compiler optimization efforts are seriously addressed only after the language has become quite popular. Therefore, I expect major improvements in efficiency will have occurred by the time this is published. On the other hand, as an Internet language Java is extremely fast compared to using HTML and CGI for interactive transactions. This because it allows a balanced client/server architecture instead of depending on the server to perform the application's logical operations.

For those interested in learning more about Java, the *Internet World 60 Minute Guide to Java* (Tittel & Gaither, 1995) is a good introduction that has more depth than one might expect from the title. Not surprisingly, many World Wide Web sites provide a wealth of information about Java. *Hooked on Java* (Van Hoff, Shaio, & Starbuck, 1996) provides a list of such sites.

10.9 Summary

It is no simple matter to make a system of computers with no shared memory appear to the user as if they were a single computer. Some forms of transparency have been addressed by nonobject-oriented methods, but object technology is needed to address other transparency problems. To accomplish this, distributed systems have been evolving from centralized, relational, homogeneous systems toward decentralized, object-oriented, heterogeneous systems. Table 10.1 summarizes the usual advantages of the latter over the former; the Table values assume that the application requires dealing with complex objects in a complex environment. For simple systems a minimally distributed architecture may be preferable.

The Object Management Group has helped direct the course of this evolution. The OMG was formed in 1989 to promote object technology and to "boost the software industry by increasing productivity, enhancing reusability, and allowing portability and interoperability" (Ben-Natan, 1995). It has done a remarkably good job in achieving widespread acceptance of the standards that make these goals possible. The OMG created an underlying Object Model on which extensions, called profiles, are built to achieve design level portability. The profile most essential to distributed computing, the Object Request Broker, is defined by the CORBA standard.

Achieving a balance in the use of resources by using a distributed system is of great value in many areas. The real estate company example in this chapter is just one example of this. The Internet is certainly another area in which distributed computing offers enormous opportunities. Stikeleather (1994) sums up the value of distributed object computing in yet another application area as follows: "Distributed object computing is the proper and, perhaps, the only technology available to implement information systems that enable the reengineering of a company" (p. 37).

For most businesses, the Internet is too rich an information source and to valuable a marketing tool to ignore. Managers need to make many decisions relative to the use of the Internet regarding utilization, marketing, and security. The main points of this chapter, with regard to these decisions, are in the area of security and platform transparency. Java supplies security and platform transparency, and no other viable contenter for Java's role on the Internet exists. (Other solutions

Table 10.1 *Comparison of a Minimally Distributed to a Fully Distributed Architecture*

Item Compared	Centralized, Relational, Homogeneous	Decentralized, Object-oriented, Heterogeneous
Cost:	Higher	Lower
Reliability:	Lower	Higher
Distribution:	Data	Data + Functionality
Coupling:	High	Low
Number of Platforms:	Single	Multiple
Language:	Dependent on	Independent of

exist but lack sufficient support from a broad spectrum of corporations). Furthermore, Java has numerous other features that make it an excellent programming language. Managers involved with the Internet need to assess the potential of Java in their enterprise. The critical role of the object-oriented paradigm in distributed computing is one more reason why managers need to understand object technology.

10.10 References

Ben-Natan, R. (1995). *CORBA: A Guide to Common Object Request Broker Architecture.* New York: McGraw-Hill.

Berson, A. (1992). *Client/server architecture.* New York: McGraw-Hill.

The Common Object Request Broker: Architecture and specification. (1991, December 6) OMG TC Document Number 91.12.1, Revision 1.1.

Czukkermann, J. L., & Spera, P.G. (1995). Distributing objects, an enterprise perspective. *Object Magazine, 5*(3),33–38.

Ewald, A., & Roy, M. (1994). Should you use DCE RPC or an ORB? *Object Magazine, 4*(5),24–26.

Johnston, M. (1992). Client/server computing. *Object Magazine, 2*(3),52.

Loomis, M. E. S. (1992a). Client-server architecture. *Journal of Object-Oriented Programming, 4*(9), 000–000.

Loomis, M. E. S. (1992b). Making objects persistent. *Journal of Object-Oriented Programming, 5*(6),25–28.

Mowbray, T. J. (1994). Choosing between OLE/COM and CORBA, *Object Magazine, 4*(7),39–46.

Object Management Group. (1993). *Object management architecture guide.* New York: John Wiley.

Stikeleather, J. (1994). Why distributed object computing is inevitable. *Object Magazine, 4*(1),37.

Tanenbaum, A. S. (1992). *Modern operating systems* (p. 382). Englewood Cliffs, NJ: Prentice Hall.

Taylor, D. A. (1994). Objects for the Enterprise. *Object Magazine. 4*(8):65–70, 75–76.

Tittel, E., & Gaither, M. (1995). *Internet world 60 minute guide to Java.* Foster City, CA: IDG Books Worldwide.

Van Hoff, A., Shaio, S., & Starbuck, O. (1996). *Hooked on Java.* Reading, MA: Addison-Wesley.

Wade, A. (1994). Databases and distributed objects. *Object Magazine, 4*(1),47–52.

Yourdon, E. (1996). Java and the new wave of internet programming languages. In *Corporate Internet Strategies.* Arlington, MA: Cutter Information Corp.

Chapter 11

Managing Object Technology

Chapter 2 addressed the question of committing to object technology. Chapter 4 described the development process. We now assume that a decision has been made to implement the process. This chapter assumes that the reader is familiar with software project management and is mainly interested in what is different about managing an object-oriented project. However, some traditional software management is discussed for background and to avoid gaps in the topics being discussed. Managing object technology involves much more than can be covered here. Therefore, I have selected some issues related to the topic that I feel are either particularly important or frequently overlooked. Upper-level managers who desire a more detailed discussion of the topics discussed here, particularly those relating to organizational issues in object technology projects, will profit by reading Goldberg and Rubin's (1995) *Succeeding with Objects.*

11.1 Preparing for Transition

The transition to object technology is a major undertaking. A gradual approach is feasible, but by the time the first significant project is completed, almost every technical and managerial aspect of the project will be affected to some degree. Let's look at what this transition entails.

11.1.1 Management Commitment

An organization usually becomes involved in object technology for one of two reasons, the software engineers become convinced of the technical merits of the approach, or management initiates the change for competitive reasons. Occasionally both groups become interested in object technology at the same time; which is most desirable. This normally happens only when an outside organization is invited in to introduce both groups to the technology. Although training organizations are very good at this, they may raise expectations too high.

It is possible to initiate and execute a transition of a project to object technology primarily from the bottom up. Nevertheless, software engineers attempting this must obtain a level of commitment from management that is substantially beyond, "Okay, you can use an object-oriented approach." No matter how enthusiastic software engineers may be about object technology, it is questionable whether an object-oriented effort should be undertaken at all with management that is indifferent to the technology (Figure 11.1).

Management needs to understand that the object-oriented approach invests more time in analysis and possibly design (unless reuse of earlier analysis and design is feasible) in order to reduce the time eventually spent in maintenance. Without this understanding, budget allocations will be malapportioned and deadlines will be missed. Management needs to understand that a major investment in training and consulting is required initially and that organizational and procedural changes will be needed.

Figure 11.1 *Indifference breeds surprises.*

These include creating a reuse support group, modifying personnel job descriptions, and changes in review procedures and testing methods. As with any software development effort, a budget for a support environment is needed [e.g., computer-aided software engineering (CASE) tools, configuration management tools, and interactive development environment].

If management does not understand the key differences between the object-oriented approach and other methods, the consequences can be serious. This can include serious misunderstanding between management and both the developers and customers. With a bottom-up approach, the developers tend to be in a position of constantly defending the technology against a dubious management; this can be quite stressful to the developers and detract from their focusing on technical problems. If customers monitor progress by how much code is being written, they may be disappointed at how long the analysis takes and not appreciate the later benefits that may include reduced programming and testing time, more reliable code, quick response to changing requirements, and reduced maintenance.

Initiation of object technology from the top down also has problems. Software engineers may feel threatened by the imposition of a new technology that is initially confusing to almost all new initiates. The problem is compounded if the management understands only the benefits of object technology and not the difficulties of a very steep learning curve and the need for fundamental changes in the way software is developed. Everyone involved in an object-oriented project needs to have realistic expectations about what they will be able to accomplish with a new technology. The benefits of object technology are small in the short term and only in the long term do they become apparent. Along with realistic expectations one needs a realistic budget. Training costs and the cost of organizational and procedural adjustment create initial costs that will take some time to amortize. The eventual return on investment for an individual project comes only later mainly in reduced maintenance costs. When multiple projects use the object-oriented approach additional savings due to reuse can become quite significant.

11.1.2 Personnel

The personnel assigned to the transition team should be the company's best. A football coach does not put in his second string for the first quarter because he is not sure he can win the game; doing so would only portend defeat. Transitions to a new technology are difficult and require people who can adapt to new ideas. These people will form the nucleus for the conversion of additional projects to object technology, so leaders are needed.

A person's first thought when a need to develop software arises may be that programmers are needed. Programming has typically represented only about 20% or less of the total software development effort for major projects, however. Furthermore, object technology and software development tools are shrinking this fraction to about 10%. The potential exists to automate the process and shrink the faction to zero for many types of projects. Proper analysis and design procedures shrink the task of the programmer and tend to make it mechanical; in fact, the main impediment left to generating code from design specifications for many applications is the problem of creating efficient code. I find it surprising how much more frequently one sees job postings for object-oriented programmers than the other positions, considering that programming should only require such a small fraction of the development time in an object-orientated project. This indicates to me that many managers do not understand the importance of analysis, design, and testing in the development of software.

The remainder of the effort besides programming tends to be about half analysis and design and half testing (when quality assurance and project management are allocated to these areas). The implication of this is that a manager should be more concerned about the obtaining analysts, designers, and testing experts than programmers. Of the four, good programmers are probably the easiest type of employee to find. With respect to the difficulty of filling these positions, Lee (1993, p. 49) writes, "My informal sampling of software engineers produces a distribution that peaks in the middle, with program design and coding, and falls off in both directions, with good analysts and testers being the most rare."

The personnel needed for an object-oriented project include the usual positions of code architect, assistant code architects, domain experts, analysts, designers, quality-assurance personnel, testers, programmers, system administrators, and tool experts. In addition, a reuse librarian is needed for most projects. The size of the project determines how many people are needed for each position or how many positions are merged into a single position.

The new position of the reuse librarian requires locating and evaluating commercial class libraries for use in the project and providing the expertise needed to use and extend them. The importance of this role should not be underestimated because the cost of reinventing an existing class library or even modifying an ill-chosen one can constitute a major expenditure. The reuse librarian also catalogs and maintains application specific libraries created in-house.

The roles of the analysts and designers may change somewhat with object technology, because it is more likely that the roles will be combined. This is because object-oriented analysis and design share a common notation and are more tightly coupled than with traditional methods, despite the fact that the purpose of the two phases is still quite distinct. Thus, it makes sense, for example, if one has two analyst/designers and two subsystems, to assign one individual to each subsystem rather than one individual to the analysis of both subsystems and the other to the design of both subsystems. In many application areas the time involved in learning the domain of the subsystem is more significant than the time it takes to cross train analysts and designers.

Whether a company hires permanent employees or contracts out some of the positions is dependent on the corporate culture. At least initially, however, most projects will need outside consultants for training and mentoring. Analysis and design experts are the most likely positions that need to be filled by outside contractors; it is essential that their skills be transferred to company employees—otherwise, program maintenance and future development efforts will suffer. Object-oriented programming skills should usually be developed in-house with outside assistance. The number of programmers trained should be the number for whom there will be continuing work in the language. Outside contractors can provide programmers for peaks in programming activity. Tool specialists include CASE tool experts and maintainers and developers of reusable libraries; this should usually be an in-house responsibility.

It is easier to determine the quality of a programmer than an analyst or designer because it is not difficult to determine if a program is readable and locally well structured. If the testing process on previous work was comprehensive, it is not difficult to tell if a programmer writes code that works. On the other hand, it is not easy to evaluate the performance of the other types of software developers. The people most capable of determining if the analysts and designers have performed an excellent job or a merely adequate one are people who are experts in analysis and design. Poor design is generally obvious to anyone trying to maintain the code; however, it may be the unfortunate programmers who get blamed for requiring considerable time to make "simple" changes to the software. The fault may well lie in a design that has high coupling and low cohesion, the reverse of two fundamental principles of design.

Managers need to understand how software personnel think and react in general to understand the psychological implications of a transition to object technology. Yourdon (1992) has a chapter on "Peopleware" that provides a good starting point and contains additional references and how to motivate people.

11.1.3 Choosing Consultants

The roles of an object-oriented consultant include formal training and mentoring to educate management and staff. Training of management focuses on creating a realistic understanding of the benefits, challenges, and risks of object technology and on changes in the nature of each phase of the software life cycle. Training of staff is specific to job type, but all involved need to understand the basic concepts of the object-oriented paradigm. Analysts and designer must understand at least one object-oriented methodology. The consultant who trains them should understand multiple methodologies. Designers need to understand the concepts and capabilities of object-oriented programming languages; programmers need to understand the syntax as well as the semantics of the chosen language.

Because of the multiple roles of the consultant, obtaining consultants who are specialized in the various areas of management education, analysis and design, implementation, and testing may be desirable for large projects. The technology is new and it is difficult to find consultants with 5 years' experience in each of the areas of a technology that didn't really get going until the 1980s for programming and the 1990s for analysis and design. Don't assume that experts in an object-oriented language know much about object-oriented analysis and design or vice versa.

Look for a consultant willing to commit to a long-term relationship (at least the life of the initial project). Build assurance that the consultant will provide continuing support into the contract by weighting payments toward the end of the project. Even though a consultant acting as a mentor may be doing most of the training, the people he or she is training are providing incidental training for him or her in their field. A company cannot afford to waste this training if the consultant decides that management is not taking his or her advice and walks out.

The biggest problem with finding a consultant is to determine the quality of the consultant. Anyone can claim to be a consultant, and some who claim to be object-oriented experts will show a very superficial understanding of the technology. In addition to the usual process for selecting consultants, a company can hire an expert from a different consulting organization to review the candidates to assure their understanding of object technology.

It can pay to shop around—you never know how hungry even top talent may be at a given moment. I was surprised to discover from a colleague who is an extremely well-known expert in object technology that he had a cash-flow problem because several government contracts dried up at once. Situations like this give companies a great opportunity to get quality and still be able to negotiate on price, even when true experts are generally scarce.

11.1.4 Training

Taylor (1994, p. 20) points out that "training has a demonstrated return on investment of more than twice that of capital equipment," but training is usually shortchanged anyway. Rather than shortchange object-oriented training, it would be best to simply forget about making the transition to object technology. Attempting to use a complex technology without understanding it is an invitation to disaster. For example, the inheritance capability provided by object technology is a two-edged sword. It can allow tremendous leveraging of existing capabilities, or, if abused, can result in the need for massive structural changes to make simple changes. Just as one should not put a race-car driver at the controls of a commercial jet without additional training, one should not put a software engineer in control of inheritance structures without training.

Training does not just refer to training programmers in an object-oriented language. It does not just refer to training analysts and designers in object technology. It refers to training everyone involved, particularly managers. Training does not just refer to classroom lectures, classroom exercises, or even pilot projects. Training refers to these plus long-term mentoring and consulting support for at least the life of the initial project. Mentoring implies on-the-job training in which a substantial portion of time is spent not just in getting the job done, but in understanding the technology.

Don't assume that people with a lot of previous and analysis and design experience will not require much training. For someone learning a software paradigm for the first time, the object-oriented methods are more natural and easier to learn, because we grow up thinking in terms of objects much more than in terms of procedures. Nevertheless, object-oriented methods may be more difficult for people experienced in structured techniques to learn than for unschooled people to learn, because of difficulty inherent in unlearning something.

The need for object-oriented training has been discussed by many other authors. I would like to focus now on how to make training cost effective. A key to effective education is that people learn best by doing. Actually attempting to accomplish a real goal is very motivating and provides the environment that stimulates the student to ask the right questions and remember the answers. For example, suppose I tell you that you should always check that the return value from the "new" function in a C++ program to assure that the memory was actually allocated. How long will you remember this advice compared to how well you will remember if you write a program in which you fail to do this, and then you discover that the lack of the check caused your program to crash?

I therefore make the following suggestion, which is a heresy to object-oriented training companies and will also seem strange coming from someone who offers a class in object-oriented analysis and design (OOAD). I suggest that bringing in outside trainers to conduct a basic week-long class in OOAD, although quite worthwhile, is an expensive approach to training. Let me suggest the following alternative, which starts with a self-help program and is later supplemented with outside expertise.

The rationale for this approach is the following. Any trainer is likely to possess less knowledge about object technology than the sum of all knowledge documented in numerous books. Furthermore, people can read faster than someone can speak. Therefore, reading should be a more efficient means of learning than listening. The hook, however, is that reading may not be as stimulating and motivating as listening and occasionally interacting with an instructor. The main value of a class is twofold. First, it provides extra motivation. Second, it forces everyone to devote full time to the topic. An alternative method must deal with these issues.

It is definitely important to force concentrated attention to the task of understanding object technology. Therefore, I would schedule a "class" and meet just as if an outside trainer were going to teach a course, and I would require attendance of the target group. However, their assignment would simply be to read an assortment of books on object technology. Groups of three to five people should be assigned the same book to read. Periodically, the groups will present their understanding of the material to the other groups. Yes, the understanding will be primitive and an instructor could clarify a lot of questions, but the point of the discussion is mainly to stimulate interest. Discussions should be frequent, but the time devoted to discussion should be quite limited and a time limit strictly enforced, with most of the time devoted to individual study. Yes, it is the blind leading the blind, but all participants will end up with some degree of understanding. Approximately the same amount of learning will occur as if an instructor had presented material. There will be more unanswered questions, but this is not bad at this stage, if fact, it may be advantageous because it will stimulate further investigation.

Several weeks of this method can be productive. At some point questions and disagreements will accumulate within the group. At this time bringing in a mentor can prove extremely productive; the students are well motivated by internal disagreements and have the foundation for understanding the mentor's advice. Actually, the mentor should be involved earlier to help set up (but not participate in) the self-help sessions.

My point is not that external training is not needed—quite the contrary. External support is very important to the efficient transition to object technology. This support is expensive, however, and a company should try to get the most out of their investment. Having a mentor sit down with students and answer well-prepared questions is a much more effective learning technique than lectures. Training is needed the most during the actual development of the software. The training should be integrated into the project and a mentor should be committed to and support the project from start to finish. Any company that provides object-oriented training of the hit-and-run variety without providing continuing support and that gives the customer the impression that the training alone is adequate for using object technology is inviting disaster and will contribute to giving object technology a bad name. It is perfectly legitimate for a company to specialize in training only, but it is that company's responsibility to advise the customer to seek continued expert assistance. Training should be focused around a real, but not a large project, and sufficient technical resources must be made available. In addition to a mentor, make sure that training resources include a reference library of at least a dozen different books on object-oriented analysis and design.

Make sure that programmers learn the basic principles of object-oriented analysis and design, not just an object-oriented programming language. Otherwise the OO programming language will be used to create non-object-oriented programs. To train C programmers in C++, consider using Smalltalk or Java as an initial introduction to object-oriented programming instead of C++, even if C++ is to be used for most of the language training and the project. Because Smalltalk is a "pure" object-oriented language, in that all variables are objects, it helps break the procedural mind-set. Whereas Java syntax resembles C++, Java semantics resemble those of Smalltalk. To train analysts and designers this is not necessary, but it is still not a bad idea.

11.1.5 Budget and Schedule

The easiest part of estimating the cost of an initial object-oriented project is determining the cost of the software needed to support the object-oriented approach, such as the cost of compilers, CASE tools, commercially available reusable libraries, and interactive development environments. The cost of modifying existing standard operating procedures can be reasonably well estimated based on past experience once the methodology is selected. The cost of training is easy to estimate if one considers only formal training.

The most difficult part of the estimate is determining the magnitude of the additional cost of having to complete the educational process of learning object-oriented analysis, design, and programming as development proceeds. It is simply not feasible to completely train personnel independently of the actual project work and expect them to be fully productive on the first project; every part of the process will be slower the first time through. Unfortunately, this is affected by the nature of the application, the size and complexity of the solution, the methodology selected, the quality of personnel, tools and frameworks available for the application domain, and other factors, so that there is no way to predict how much the drag of this hidden learning curve will cost. It will probably cost more than most might expect and the budget should make a very generous allotment to account for this factor.

Cost-estimate formulae are not very effective when implementing any new technology. Only actual experience will allow accurate estimates to be made; therefore, if at all possible, a pilot project should be undertaken and productivity data accumulated and evaluated. A subsystem of the real system may make a good pilot project. A medium-sized project is best. If the pilot project is too small, it may appear to succeed despite a chaotic development process and the lack of proper application of object-orientation techniques. Independent monitoring of the project is needed to determine the quality of the work done. Because the pilot project requires a considerable investment to be effective for budget estimation and training, the project needs to be of real use.

Fortunately, the object-oriented approach makes it very feasible to break a system into subsystems and to complete one subsystem independently of the others. This approach is the most effective way of making an estimate for the rest of the project. Although counting classes and methods completed is a poor way of evaluating personal performance, it is quite useful in making schedule estimates.

Adjustments need to be made to scale the results of the pilot project to the real project because much of the hidden learning curve problem will have been worked out on the pilot, so personnel should be more productive on the real project. Also, although costs with traditional methods increase more than linearly as size and complexity increase; because of reuse, costs may be less than linear with increasing size and complexity, as mentioned in Section 1.3.5. However, do not count on this unless the pilot project measured the extra cost of developing reusable code and unless it is quite apparent what can be reused from one subsystem to another.

I am sorry that all of this in not more quantitative; however, any attempt to be quantitative would simply be illusory. Statistics have been recorded for demonstration projects, but these can not account for many important parameters that are specific to the application.

The budget can virtually be guaranteed not to be too large nor the schedule too generous because there is so much people need to learn about object technology; any "extra" time spent will pay off in future projects. A tight budget and schedule will simply detract from the learning process that needs to occur if subsequent projects are to be more successful, and, if too tight, may lead to project failure. Do not make the first object-oriented project one requiring a low budget and tight schedule. Managers need to view the first project more as an object-technology training project that happens to produce a useful product than as project to produce a product that happens to use object technology.

Part of budget planning is planning on how to keep funds in the budget; that is, how to keep the funder of the project happy enough not to terminate the project. If frameworks or reusable code from earlier projects exist, then prototypes can be developed rapidly to impress the funder. If no reuse is feasible, prototypes showing the user interface can still be developed quickly compared to the rest of the project, at least for projects that are not user interface intensive.

11.1.6 Scheduling

Scheduling considerations require careful consideration of the order in which the requirements specifications are determined. For example, performance requirements may affect the hardware to be purchased for the project and the software language to be used. Therefore, performance requirements may need to be among the first requirements determined to assure the hardware is available when needed. The language to be used should be determined early if training in the selected language will take place early in the project. This is likely when the use of concurrent development allows each subsystem to be small so that some coding work can begin early (see Section 4.1.4).

The use of a modern life cycle as discussed in Chapter 3 allows taking advantage of the opportunities that the object-oriented approach provides for better partitioning of the system and overlapping of work in different phases of the software life cycle. This allows much more flexibility in scheduling. Careful scheduling with concurrent engineering will allow analysts, designers, and programmers to keep equally busy. While the analysis of the initial partition is taking place, programmers can be assisting the tool, reuse, and quality-assurance experts in searching for reusable classes, installing CASE tools, setting up configuration management, and documenting procedures. Early identification of utility classes requiring customized programming can help keep programmers busy during the early part of the project. Even the work of the testers, whose job supposedly takes place at the end of the life cycle, can be overlapped with the rest if the overlapping partitions are small enough. In addition, before the first partition is ready for testing, the testers will have plenty of work to do planning the testing for all of the partitions undergoing analysis. If the domain experts are not part of the project or under the management of the customer, pay particular attention to getting a commitment and schedule for them. Avoid the situation in which the analysts have to go around begging for domain experts to spend some time with them.

11.2 Building the Foundation

A methodology is needed to provide a foundation for the development effort. The choice of a programming language also can have a major impact on the success of the project for some applications.

11.2.1 Choosing a Methodology

The task of choosing a methodology was discussed in Chapter 7. The following summarizes the conclusions of that chapter. Most important issues in choosing a methodology are the nature of the application, the current level of training of personnel in object technology and software engineering in general, whether the application is user-interface intensive, and the amount of control logic in the application. For most applications one should make sure the methodology includes something like use cases or else plan to add them separately to the methodology.

11.2.2 Language Selection

What are the important things we need to know about the language? Most important, we need to know if it is an object-oriented language—this has a significant impact on design. We will assume we are using an object-oriented language rather than a procedure-based language to implement a project using object-oriented analysis and design; these days it would be rare to do otherwise. (Object-oriented languages can be considered procedural as well as object oriented, which is why I referred to a procedure-based rather than procedural language.)

One could do all of the analysis and the language-independent part of the design without knowing the implementation language. However, we must know the language before completing the design because detailed design is language dependent. The main reason for knowing the language early in the project is for planning purposes. Another reason for deciding on the language early is that one may wish to use the language as a tool for defining the specification; for example, if the implementation is to be done in only one language, one may use the actual language instead of pseudocode for describing complex logic requirements.

Users of a particular language tend to become passionate advocates of that language. Therefore, let me warn the user that my language expertise is in C++ and Java. However, I do not consider these clearly superior to other languages or even superior at all for many applications. Let's consider only the six most popular object-oriented languages in this discussion, Eiffel, C++, Smalltalk, Ada-95, OO COBOL, and CLOS, plus the newcomer to the field, Java.

I have seen many statements that Eiffel is the best of these languages. I am only casually acquainted with Eiffel, but from what I know I will not dispute this. The use of Eiffel is particularly worth investigating for any company without programmers already experienced in C, C++ or Smalltalk. Certainly Eiffel has more general features than C++ including a good library, garbage collection (whose absence in C++ makes memory leaks a major concern), and persistence. Efforts in improving C++ will somewhat reduce Eiffel's lead in features. C++ bests Eiffel mainly in the area of encapsulation features, and of course, in leveraging off the existing widely used C language. Eiffel is good in terms of portability as the language and development environment are centrally controlled by a consortium. The merger of the two major vendors of Smalltalk should soon take care of the existing incompatibilities between the two major versions of the language.

C++ is a difficult language to learn and is not a good language for C programmers to use to make the break with procedural programming, but it is marvelously flexible. C++ has multiple inheritance whereas Smalltalk does not; this gives C++ the advantage and risk of being able to create complex inheritance lattices. C++ is particularly appropriate for distributed computing. C++'s encapsulation and type-checking features also are better than those of Smalltalk. C++ has major portability problems because of the lack of a standard development environment or even major class libraries as an extension of the language. For example, the two best-known libraries for C++, Borland's Object Window Library (OWL) and Microsoft's Foundation Class Library are on no better speaking terms than their respective companies.

Smalltalk is an easier language to use and provides its own comprehensive development environment. Smalltalk has had an advantage over C++ in allowing programmers to be productive quickly because of its excellent development environment; however, this advantage is rapidly disappearing as equivalent C++ tools are developed. Smalltalk has been gaining on C++'s speed advantage with the development of more efficient Smalltalk compilers, but Smalltalk will always be slower than C++ because of the former's universal application of polymorphism. This may make Smalltalk a poor choice for real-time systems development; however, the efficiency difference is small, so this should be used as a major selection criterion only where time is critical. Smalltalk's lack of safe type checking may also argue against its use in mission-critical applications. On the other hand, C++'s lack of garbage collection and resulting reliability problems could similarly argue against its being used in critical applications. Smalltalk sacrifices type checking for the flexibility of universal polymorphism; C++'s polymorphism is restricted to within user-created inheritance hierarchies. On the other hand, C++ is fundamentally more flexible than Smalltalk, so that with considerable effort one can create a framework with C++ that models the way Smalltalk works. The reverse is not feasible.

Despite a late start, the Ada language can be considered the first "official" object-oriented language by being the first to receive approval by the ISO and ANSI committees. Ada-83 was already an object-based language, lacking only inheritance, dynamic binding, and polymorphism to qualify as an object-oriented language. The addition of these features to the Ada-95 language make it fully object oriented. Because Ada already had strong support for concurrency, the capabilities of the language have leap-frogged those of the object-orientation languages lacking concurrency support. This makes Ada very attractive for applications requiring object-oriented features and multitasking capabilities. However, the advantage is mainly in having a standard for concurrency; "unofficial" versions of the other OO languages exist that allow multiple threads of control. Java is another language that should be considered when concurrency is a requirement.

OO COBOL is of interest to existing COBOL programmers. The main value of OO COBOL is to effect a gradual transition of legacy

COBOL code into object-oriented code. If conversion of legacy code is not an overriding concern, then anyone seriously considering using OO COBOL should look at Smalltalk as a possible alternative because of Smalltalk's greater maturity.

Those interested in artificial intelligence (AI) and knowledge based systems (KBSs) will want to look at CLOS (Common Lisp Object System) rather than the others, although CLOS capabilities by no means limit it to these applications. See Srinivasan and Jayaraman (1994) for a case in which CLOS was selected for a computer-integrated manufacturing system (CIMS) application. Nevertheless, most non-AI, non-KBS object-oriented projects will probably use one of the other languages mentioned.

For anyone developing Internet applications, Java is the object-oriented language of choice. Because it has some of the best features of the other languages (without some of the legacy baggage that C++ has in maintaining compatibility with C), Java is a strong contender for many other applications outside of the Internet. Section 10.9 discussed some of these features.

Aside from these brief guidelines I will not get involved in the language wars; plenty has been written by advocates favoring each of these languages and pointing out the faults of the others. Those interested in more details about the various object-oriented languages will find examples of the fervor of language supporters in the May 1995 issue of *Object Magazine.* The issue contains articles that discuss C++, OO COBOL, Smalltalk, Eiffel, and Ada. The choice of languages may best be made by application developers who have no biases rather than experts who do. The assistance of a consultant is desirable if one can be found who is equally familiar with all of the candidate languages. Focus on the nature of the application and the existing skills of the programming staff when making the decision.

11.3 Gathering Resources

Building custom code is terribly inefficient compared to using high-quality existing code. Therefore, early in the project one needs to determine what resources exist that may be obtained at a small fraction of the price of developing it in-house. Many needed capabilities will simply not be available; others will require modification; some will be relatively expensive but still cheap compared to reinventing them; some will be free.

It fact it is quite amazing how much software one can obtain at essentially no cost. For example, the Linux operating system, a Unix clone, is free except for the cost a company will charge for distributing it, which is as little as $25 for 4 CD-ROMs. This includes not just the comprehensive operating system with full networking capability but additional software like the GNU C++ compiler. Just because this is freeware, don't assume that it is not reliable. By all reports it is much more reliable and better documented than a very popular commercial operating system. I am referring to Windows 3.x and its habit of requiring one to reboot the system when certain errors occur. Although all this is related to object technology mainly because of the availability of a free C++ compiler, the point is that bargains exist that should be researched rather than assuming that the more money spent on a product, the better it is.

11.3.1 Object-Oriented Building Blocks

Objects and classes, being nicely encapsulated units of data and functionality, form discrete building blocks from which a software application can be created. Just as one can build a building faster with concrete blocks or prefabricated units than with bricks, coarser granularities of software building blocks are needed to speed development. The next level of granularity above classes involve an interacting collection of classes or objects to satisfy some complex behavior beyond that of individual classes and methods. Frameworks provide a still higher level of building block that uses collections of classes to create a fairly comprehensive set of services for a specific application domain. At the highest level of granularity a framework can consist of other frameworks and classes that allow the creation of an entire program by assembling parts rather than doing traditional programming. Frameworks are of primary interest in this chapter as major resources for achieving productivity and reliability.

11.3.2 Frameworks

A framework provides the classes, class relationships, and classification hierarchies needed to construct a domain (subsystem). The easiest way to relate to the significance of a framework is to consider the most common and widely used framework, the graphical user interface (GUI). Users of applications designed for Microsoft Windows or the X Window System are familiar with the results of using a GUI framework and know how convenient they are to use compared to text-based user interfaces. Builders of these applications are familiar with the productivity that GUI frameworks make possible in developing windows applications. Creating windowing capabilities like a dialog box from scratch in a language like C++ involves a huge amount of programming. Creating one using a framework can be as simple as clicking and dragging with a mouse button to select and position the dialog box and similarly creating control objects like buttons, text boxes, and scroll bars and typing in title information. All of the hard programming was done by the framework creators and is simply reused.

Frameworks have been developed in many application areas. The application areas that have received the most attention have been areas that have wide applicability and have predictable requirements. GUIs certainly have these characteristics. Frameworks evolved quickly in database applications because of their high demand and well-established behavior. Borland's Paradox for Windows and Microsoft's Foxpro are examples of object-based frameworks for database applications.

Portability frameworks are also popular and can provide two productivity multiplying factors. For example, multiplatform GUIs are portability frameworks that provide the productivity increase of a GUI times the productivity increase of being able to port the code to a variety of platforms. Liant's C++/Views, InMark's zApp, XVT Software's XVT, and Zinc's Zinc Application Framework are examples of dual GUI and portability frameworks.

These frameworks are now being threatened by the inherent portability of the Java language, which contains its own portable Abstract Windows Toolkit. Even though the Java GUI capability is more primitive than its more mature competitors, the universality and automatic portability of Java makes it an extremely attractive alternative.

Two very general frameworks evolved out of operating systems: Next Computer's NEXTSTEP, which was mentioned earlier, and Taligent's CommonPoint, which Adrian Bowles (1995, p. 22) describes as "the most advanced technical framework-based environment on the commercial horizon."

No company developing a general application these days would consider building their own GUI from scratch, but would simply choose one of many existing GUI frameworks. Similarly, any large company with an ongoing software development effort should consider buying or developing a framework for their application domain rather than recreating all of the basic coding each time they create a new application. Frameworks have been developed and are being development for many application domains. These include, among others, hospital patient management, office automation, banking, international monetary transactions, and telecommunications. If no suitable framework exists for sale, then a company should try to develop a framework for their application domain that achieves the kind of productivity increases that have been achieved in the GUI domain.

Paradoxically, the biggest problem with frameworks is that they are extremely valuable. Not only is much greater productivity achieved, but the all-important time to market is reduced correspondingly. This has encouraged the production and general availability of front-end type domains that can be used by multiple industries, because it is profitable to produce and sell such frameworks. The problem with the availability of frameworks in specific industries is the expertise for creating them usually lies within the industry, and a company that creates one generates a major competitive advantage for itself. It is not likely to sell its advantage to its competitors. However, it is possible for major companies to cooperate to create a framework as demonstrated by the insurance industry (Stewart, 1995).

11.3.3 Design Patterns for Specification Reusability

Design patterns are a valuable resource for achieving reuse of specifications. As mentioned before, the reuse of code accomplishes only part of the potential of the object-oriented approach for achieving reusability. Much more reuse can be accomplished if the analysis and design is also made reusable. Although this can be accomplished to some extent simply by saving past analysis and design work, a more disciplined approach can make this much more effective and allow reuse of designs created outside the organization. Currently there is great interest and effort underway in implementing such an approach to specification reuse through the concept of design patterns.

The foundation work for creating design patterns was written in 1977 by Christopher Alexander, and had nothing to do with software

(Alexander, 1977). Alexander describes the use of design patterns to record the wisdom of great architects so that others may reproduce building designs that have been proven to be of high quality. Alexander's work sufficiently impressed the software-engineering community about how to think about systems in general that it was adopted as a guideline to the creation of software architectural patterns.

Just as bricks and mortar alone do not create a beautiful building, classes and objects do not create a good object-oriented design. It is an intuition about organization and structure that create a quality product. And just as painters study the works of great painters, software engineers need to study the patterns common to the architecture of the best software products.

How does one go about creating a building that is a work of art? How does one create a painting that is a work of art? How does one create a software product that is a work of art? Have you created a software design or a program or a part of a program that you felt was a work of art? If so, you've said to yourself, this is an elegant solution or this design fits beautifully into the rest of the program. The question is how do we create works of art in software consistently? Or, if we cannot create works of art, how do we at least create reasonably good facsimiles of software designs that have been done well before? These questions are what the concept of design patterns attempts to answer.

Despite the use of the word design in design patterns, design patterns also cover the analysis of the problem. Not only does the design pattern describe the problem and its solution, but it provides hints and examples to assist in implementation. One can think of patterns as prefabricated solutions. They provide a structure for the solution and document the tricks of the trade. Design patterns make it easier for everyone to create good analysis and design models by creating patterns of successful designs.

The study of patterns is a fairly new topic in object-oriented analysis and design, but it is an important one, because understanding patterns is a fast route toward understanding object-oriented design. Instead of considering each application to be unique and creating a solution from scratch, one can borrow most of the solution from a pattern developed by an expert or by one's own previous work. People who are experts at doing object-oriented design are experts largely because they know what has worked successfully in the past and they know how to reuse their knowledge in slightly different situations. Because problems and their solutions tend to fall into similar groups, a pattern can be developed to model the best solution for a particular group of problems. Once we recognize the pattern and its implications, we can solve any number of similar problems fairly quickly.

The premier book describing this concept as applied to software engineering is *Design Patterns: Elements of Reusable Object-Oriented Software* by Erich Gamma, Richard Helm, Ralph Johnson, and John Vlissides (1995). The development and categorizing of design patterns begun in Gamma et al.'s book is continuing very actively on the Internet. This existing conceptual repository of object-oriented design information should be a starting point for any development effort. One can subscribe by sending a request to patterns-request@cs.uiuc.edu, or use anonymous ftp to obtain pattern documents in directory /pub/patterns/papers at st.cs.uiuc.edu.

A *pattern language* is a group of cooperating design patterns that are directed at a particular problem domain. Richard Gabriel (1994), in an article entitled "The Failure of Pattern Languages," tells that Alexander was quite disappointed in the results obtained by others who attempted to apply his design patterns. They simply did not create the great architecture that was characteristic of the original work on which the design patterns were based. The implication of this on software development may be that design patterns do not avoid the need for brilliance to achieve the best of designs. A more realistic hope for software design patterns may simply be to avoid the need for developers to start over from first principles when attacking a problem, to speed the development process, and to produce reasonably good designs.

11.3.4 Tools

The number-one tool for all object-oriented projects should be an old-fashioned library of books and magazines on object technology and software engineering in general. The return on this investment should exceed all others because of the low cost. One can create a good library for the cost of the airfare for bringing in a consultant. The cost is also small compared to purchasing a single PC or CASE tool, and quite small compared to a single one-week class.

Bilow (1995) recommends five current and ten all-time classes in object technology, and his choices are excellent. The September issues of the *Journal of Object-Oriented Programming* contain a focus-on-books section that can help in the selection. Both the *Journal of Object-Oriented Programming* and *Object Magazine* provide reviews of books related to object technology. Even if the project has already chosen a methodology, books describing other methodologies provide valuable insights. Order back issues of *Object Magazine* and the *Journal of Object-Oriented Programming* and a publication for the language to be used (e.g., *The C++ Report, The Smalltalk Report,* the *C/C++ Users Journal,* or the *Java Report*). For a more general software engineering reading list see Yourdon (1992, Appendix B).

Software tools include languages, class libraries, compilers, debuggers, editors, browsers, testing tools, frameworks, configuration management tools, project management tools, reverse engineering tools, CASE tools, and integrated development environments to name a few. Some of these tools are obviously essential for all projects and others, such as CASE tools, are almost essential for large projects. Nevertheless, tools are of no use unless one knows how to use them, and I mean not just mechanically but conceptually. Training is more important than tools; with training one can improve tools; with tools and no knowledge of the object-oriented principles behind their use, one can only waste time playing when them. Substantial training should be completed before heavily investing in tools. Actually beginning the project and doing some work that could be done by tools is not a bad idea. This will help assure that the tools selected actually meet the real needs of the project. Don't just buy a very expensive CASE tool with the assumption that it somehow substitutes for investing in training.

Browsers are particularly needed with an object-oriented approach because when one is looking at a class that is part of an inheritance hierarchy one is not seeing the entire picture of class capabilities. One needs to be able to easily determine the entire interface of the class including inherited parts that are not apparent from looking at the class itself. The best browsers provide the option to view a class as it would appear by merging in the inherited data and operations of all ancestor classes.

The great variety of object-oriented tools and vendors makes tool selection difficult. Once a methodology and language are selected, the possibilities are reduced somewhat, but many options still exist. Discussion of specific tools is beyond the scope of this book; depend on your consultant to get you started in the selection process and develop a tool specialist to help review the tools and become the local guru in the ones selected.

11.4 The Effect of Object Technology on Software Management

Object technology has a profound effect on software development management in several areas and a lesser, but still significant effect in other areas. The most important effects are the need to change to an iterative and incremental development process and to make software development an enterprise-wide endeavor to gain the maximum benefits from reuse.

11.4.1 The Development Process

Chapter 4 discussed the development process in detail; this section highlights issues related to the process that should be of particular interest to managers.

11.4.1.1 Managing Iterative and Incremental Development

A successful development effort requires both innovation and discipline. Without innovation, the system under development will lack a cohesive architectural vision, possibly resulting in an overly complex solution to the problem, poor communications within the code and among the developers, duplication, and inefficiency. Without discipline exactly the same problems can occur. A rigid development process model such as the waterfall model provides discipline but discourages innovation. The anarchy of the code-and-fix model encourages innovation, but only at a very local level, and provides no discipline. Increasingly, object-oriented methodologists are achieving both contending requirements by using an iterative and incremental development process.

Iteration refers to gradual refinement of the a part of the model. This iteration occurs at all levels from refining the overall architecture to refining individual classes and methods.

Incremental development refers to the gradual addition of new capabilities to existing capabilities. This is like one form of prototyping—not the kind in which one creates throwaway prototypes, but the one in which one carefully plans the development of a series of permanent prototypes with increasing functionality. This approach has a major advantage over the waterfall model in that it is much easier to monitor progress so as to avoid unexpected late-stage integration problems. The iterative and incremental approach does not eliminate the need for careful planning. It does make planning a continuous part of the process.

Booch (1994) describes this approach in terms of a macroprocess that defines the strategic direction of the development effort and a microprocess that defines the tactical day-to-day activities of the process. The macroprocess provides the overall control to assure that the microprocess remains consistent with the architectural vision. For both processes Booch describes formal steps with milestones and measures to assure that the innovation that is encouraged by the process is evaluated and the implementation is controlled. As one example of the use of a measure, Booch uses the degree of stability of the data dictionary as an indication of whether the development team has achieved focus.

Even when using a methodology with a well-defined sequence of steps, it is important for managers to recognize that an iterative and incremental process is desirable. Rather than resisting when software engineers want to use this process, the manager should adapt to it by modifying a rigid methodology to allow more iteration and innovation and compensating for the freer approach with counterbalancing activities, such as increasing risk-assessment activities, monitoring progress more often using informal methods, and depending on peer review to keep the effort on track. Software engineers should not be allowed to use the iterative and incremental philosophy to justify a reduced amount of documentation. The incremental approach shows progress faster and is both motivational to software engineers and reassuring to the customer. It counters the greater proportion of time that is spent in analysis compared to programming with the OO approach by not attempting to finish the analysis and design for the entire project before implementation begins.

11.4.1.2 Group Collaboration

Techniques for getting users and systems analysts and designers to collaborate closely in project development are neither new or unique to object technology. Such communication is facilitated by object technology's use of terminology that is consistent for both users and developers, however.

This kind of collaboration is as important in object technology as it ever was and bears mentioning here because integrating the collaboration techniques with object technology requires understanding both. These techniques go by a couple of commonly used names: joint application design (or development) (JAD) and rapid application development (RAD).

JAD and RAD bring together users and system analysts to work on the analysis and design of a system. JAD is one of Yourdon's (1992) 11 silver pellets in his book, *The Decline and Fall of the American Programmer.* Let me give the background on silver pellets. In the classic book, *The Mythical Man Month,* Brooks (1982) describes problems with managing large projects and says that there is no silver bullet with which to solve them. Later Brad Cox wrote an article saying there was a silver bullet and it is object-oriented computing. Yourdon's book says that there is not a silver bullet but that there are many silver pellets that together can subdue the werewolf of the software crisis that is still with us. Object technology is, of course, one of these silver pellets.

As important as it is to keep up with technological change, one must avoid the "silver-bullet" psychology in which, as Jacobson puts it, people "shop for 'silver-bullet' panaceas rather than systematically reengineer their development processes" (Jacobson & Jacobson, 1995, p. 241).

If you compare working individually and working together, presumably everyone's ideas together result in a much better understanding of issues. It can also be argued that individuals with a vision will produce a more coherent product than a group. There is room for both approaches in a development project. JAD is particularly useful in establishing requirements. Design consistency can be maintained by having a responsible code architect who provides the vision but who is stimulated and challenged by the group.

JAD requires having someone in charge who will keep the group focused and who will, at an appropriate time, see that a decision is made. It is very easy to argue forever about fine points that are not critical to the success of the task, and some people prefer talking indefinitely rather than having to go back and do some work by themselves. But once the major decisions are made, people usually have to do the actual details individually.

A prime value of JAD is that most errors will come to light quickly, because people enjoy pointing out other people's errors. I know there aren't many things that my kids enjoy more than being able to pounce on me when I make a mistake.

RAD extends JAD by adding the use of component software and, frequently, CASE tools. Examples of RAD software tools include XVT Software's XVT Development Solution for C++, Magec Software's Magec RAD (for COBOL), and Gupta's SQLWindows. The most important components of these tools are GUI components. Database components are another common component of RAD software tools.

RAD uses a prototyping software life-cycle model but is almost always weak in methodology. RAD has had considerable success in small projects. It has even successfully produced enterprise wide applications (Weston, 1995). However, there is great danger in assuming that RAD can handle any project. First of all, the needed components simply do not exist for most other application areas. Second, the probability of success using RAD, without extending its typical simple prototyping methodology, is reduced as the size and complexity of the application increases. RAD is good for creating external interfaces but, at least so far, not at creating an internal architecture that makes applications scalable.

The ability of RAD to work with little in the way of a methodology is similar to the ability of programmers to write small programs well without writing down anything in the way of a formal design. Because RAD uses component software, much larger programs can be written without using a formal design. Roughly the same amount of thought is required and the resulting product is of equivalent complexity whether one spends a month writing lines of source code or assembling components. This is true even though the assembled components may represent 20 times as many lines of source code. Therefore, when using RAD with component software there is no problem with exercising minimal effort in design and creating programs say 20 times as big as one can without using components.

However, managers need to remember that the writing of large programs without a methodology resulted in a software crisis that has lasted for decades. The use of component software has changed nothing in this respect other than the size of the building blocks. One can stack a pile of concrete slabs much higher than one can stack a pile of bricks. However, just because one can accomplish a lot more with less effort, this does not mean there has been a fundamental improvement in the construction process. If one is stacking bricks or blocks on a foundation of sand, there are definite limits on how high one can go. A methodology provides the foundation and mortar needed to assure that the product will not collapse when more growth is needed or when the system is otherwise stressed.

RAD is a very useful tool, but like most tools it can be misused. It is safest to view RAD as a communication mechanism like JAD plus some tools, not a methodology or a substitute for a methodology. The danger of thinking of it as a substitute for a methodology is that one then tends to assume that it can substitute for a methodology on any large project. RAD has worked well for many large GUI and database projects, but even in these areas caution is warranted as project size increases. For most application areas, the use of a methodology is essential to achieve robustness, performance, scalability, and maintainability for large projects.

11.4.1.3 Contingency Planning

One does not plan to fail but one should plan in case of failure. This implies minimizing the damage if a project does not succeed. This planning can affect the order of the development effort. For example, some argue that given the choice of beginning with either the application logic or the user interface, one should start with the essential part of the problem, the application logic. Others argue that one should do the user interface first, because this helps in the derivation of user requirements and assures that the user will be happy with how he will interact with the code. The later method makes use of prototypes and reduces the chance of failure through incremental development, creating a dummy application logic behind the user interface and gradually filling in the details. The counterargument is that the user interface is generally straightforward, at least conceptually, and that the real danger of failure is in the application logic—the problem might not even be feasible to solve. This view implies doing the highest risk items first and working toward the lower risk items.

Which view is right? No general rule can be given. One needs to understand the risks involved and make a decision based on the probabilities. An application like creating the software for strategic defense has high application logic risk and is an obvious candidate for attacking the application logic first. An application like making a user-friendly graphical interface to update and retrieve information from a database favors the user-interface prototype approach. Areas between these extremes require an assessment of all risks and an understanding of the nature of the two options.

11.4.1.4 Enterprise-Level Effort

Object technology has many benefits for individual projects. With management approval and some support, applying object technology to a single project can be quite successful, but it's contribution to the capabilities of the enterprise as a whole will be limited to the product plus having trained a group of object-oriented developers. What is lost is the opportunity to expand the benefits of reuse to other projects. Reuse can be highly effective only by combining the development efforts of multiple development groups. An enterprise-level effort needs to be planned and executed according to a long-range plan for fully utilizing specification and code reuse.

11.4.2 Reuse

Reuse is potentially the most valuable contribution of object technology; however, it also creates the most difficult new challenge for management. The benefits of reuse are neither free nor immediate. Don't expect great gains in productivity when you start using object technology. (However, do expect to produce a higher quality product, even on your first try.) Considerable improvements in productivity will come in time, but only if you plan for reuse and invest in it.

Software reuse can be accomplished by directly using previously created classes and their documentation. However, frequently such classes do not provide exactly the right functionality needed on a new project. Therefore, it is common to achieve reuse by extending classes or classification hierarchies of classes with specialized classes that inherit the capabilities of the original ancestor classes. Creating specialized classes that extend existing capabilities usually involves a small fraction of the amount of work that creating the original capability required.

A reuse library containing classes and their documentation must be maintained. Procedures must be established that will encourage library growth, utility, quality, convenience, and usage. The hardest part of this is to establish incentives and funding for library growth.

11.4.2.1 What to Reuse

A company should definitely buy rather than build basic class libraries whenever possible. The fundamental libraries that are available for purchase from multiple sources include the following. Basic utility classes include strings, date, time, and simple extensions of numeric classes. Geometry class utilities include points, lines, circles, and all manner of shapes that may be moved and rotated. Mathematical classes include classes like complex numbers, vectors, matrices, and much more complex and specialized classes. Input/output classes include stream I/O packages that are not part of the C++ language itself but are almost certain to be included with any C++ compiler. Object manipulation classes are provided by extensions to these iostream packages that allow persistent storage of objects. Object manipulation classes also include shallow and deep object-copying capabilities. (A shallow copy copies only the immediate object, whereas a deep copy copies the object plus all those it refers to through any number of levels of indirection.) Container classes include such classes as lists, linked lists, sets, bags, arrays, and dictionaries. User interface classes are usually a set of classes comprising a GUI framework. Database classes include those provided by various object-oriented database management systems as discussed in Chapter 8.

With Smalltalk, Java, and Eiffel, some of these come as part of the development environment inherent in the language. With C++ some may come as an interactive development environment associated with a particular compiler. All the above classes are available for purchase or even at no cost, so there is no reason to build them. It will require some investment in time to understand the libraries and how to use and extend them.

Libraries for some higher level domains have been developed, but most likely these will have been done by a company's competitors. Therefore these usually must be created in-house. One needs to be selective about what classes are made reusable as extra cost is involved in creating, testing, cataloging, and making available reusable classes. Classes that have broad applicability within an application domain should be the primary candidates. For example, one would choose a class like an employee class in a business application rather than a class to represent the dozen mathematicians who understand the proof of Fermat's last theorem. (Yes, if you missed the news, it has been proven.)

Reuse does not just refer to reusing code. Every effort should be made to reuse the analysis, design, testing, and documentation as well. Treating each class as a unit of reusability with these different aspects encourages full reusability. This can be made simpler by having a system that allows each class to have each of these aspects to be associated with it. As an example of one of the benefits of this, if the input for testing and results obtained for various versions of a class are encapsulated with the class, this greatly simplifies retesting. This is particularly valuable for regression testing because of a change in an ancestor class in an inheritance structure, because the only effort required may be rerunning the test cases and checking results with earlier results. Even if the class itself is significantly changed, the test cases will provide a foundation for a new set of test cases. This extension of the encapsulation of classes into the domain of configuration management can provide quality-assurance benefits.

11.4.2.2 Organizing for Reuse

It can be considerably more expensive to develop reusable software compared to task-specific software. Most problematic, reuse spans organizational boundaries and funding sources. Reuse requires an initial investment and the rewards of reuse are not only delayed, they are misplaced. They are misplaced in the sense that the project doing the extra work of making classes reusable is not usually the project that benefits from reuse. This is the root of the nontechnical difficulties in achieving reuse. It is difficult to determine a fair means of paying for the extra effort required to create reusable subsystems. If the individual projects are responsible for creating reusable code, it is difficult to provide them with an incentive to divert effort from their project to benefit other subsequent projects.

Reuse is the aspect of OO development that most changes the nature of management involvement in software development. To be properly addressed, the issue of reuse must be addressed by high-level management, not by individual project management. The full potential of reuse can be achieved only though coordination and commitment throughout the company. The difficulty of gaining management support and the difficulty of implementing any type of company-wide cooperation is a significant impediment to reuse.

11.4.2.3 Funding Reuse

One of several alternative means of developing reusable software and funding its development must be selected. The alternative selected depends on the nature of the organization, its customers, and its funding sources.

The most straightforward and most efficient method is to create a separate reuse group devoted to developing, maintaining, testing, and distributing reusable code. This group will need company-level funding initially, but later could charge projects for reusable code that has been accumulated. The reuse group can assist projects in identifying reuse opportunities and in creating more reusable code. Credit can be given for code submitted to the group's library by the projects, provided they are of sufficient quality and general utility to be worth developing into robust, generally reusable software.

This method is appropriate for large companies with a commitment to object technology. It may not be appropriate for a small company or a small organization in a company that is not committed to object technology.

I suggest the following alternative for small companies and companies unable or unwilling to make the initial investment. This can be described as an incremental value-added approach. Although it is still much better to have at least a minimal reuse group to coordinate efforts, it is possible with this technique to extract some reuse by having simple requirements on all projects, such as the following.

By the end of a project, a list of potential reusable classes must be posted and distributed among other projects. Any project wishing to use and modify an existing class or hierarchy must agree to maintain its existing capabilities, add capabilities needed for its own purposes, and improve the reusability of the software. As long as the savings by use of the original code results in a net gain, there will be no problem with having to charge the customer for the extra effort in creating the reusable code. Again, it is definitely preferable to have as much support as possible for an independent reuse group. Benefits are very limited without someone who is aware of overall company needs who directs reuse efforts into the most productive areas. This method does allow for some reuse by administrative action only, however.

It is probably not very realistic to expect software engineers struggling to make a success of their first object-oriented project to have the time, knowledge, and presence of mind to worry about future projects as well. They will be doing well to create inheritance hierarchies that will be extensible within their own project and simplify their own software maintenance without figuring out how to do this for everyone else.

Therefore, my advice on one's first object-oriented project is to use good object-oriented techniques that improve software extensibility and make reuse easier, but not to attempt to have any specific reuse goals to help future projects. After the project is completed and before the next project, one can identify reuse candidates from the first project; at this point personnel will better understand the OO approach and do a better job on creating reusable class hierarchies. This also has the advantage that the first project does not have to pay the costs of developing highly reusable software along with all other initial costs.

11.4.7.4 Avoiding Reinvention

Effort must be made to help people locate reusable code. A means is needed to ensure the robustness of the reusable code and to convince people that the code really is safe to use. In other words, the "not-invented-here" syndrome that causes people to reinvent rather than reuse must be overcome.

The procedural paradigm lent itself to the creation of the reusable procedures only, such as mathematical libraries, not to the creation of reusable objects. Therefore, software engineers have become great at reinvention. Lacking reusable code outside this narrow band, programmers have written and rewritten the same code all over the world ad nauseam. Object technology has broken this limitation and provides the opportunity to create reusable classes, not just reusable procedures. The potential here is that virtually an entire code might be assembled from reusable objects instead of just being able to use bits and pieces of procedural code.

11.5 A Hand on the Pulse

A manager needs to know how a project is going at all times. Here are a few traditional methods for a manager to keep his hand on the pulse of the project with a discussion of how object technology affects the methods used.

11.5.1 The Specification As a Contract

The requirements specification has more uses than just describing what must be accomplished. It also acts as the manager's basis for measuring progress. It is particularly useful in this manner when the project has been partitioned in an object-oriented manner that lends itself to incremental completion of the requirements. When this approach is used a manager needs to pay particular attention to the need to treat the specification as a contract.

When designers encounter a problem with the requirements, either with consistency or omissions, the temptation exists simply to design around the problem or make assumptions as to what the requirements should be. This is particularly the case with any kind of incremental development method. Because the object-oriented approach lends itself to incremental development and to rapid prototyping, one may encounter the problem more frequently with object technology than before.

There are many reasons that designers should not attempt to fix a requirements problem during design. The designer may lack needed expertise in the problem domain. The practice dangerously subverts the review process. Finally, it can cause serious traceability problems.

Managers need to make the following policy clear. The analysis specification should be considered a contract that the designer must adhere to or else renegotiate with the analyst and client to change. The designer must report the problem, and only after the people responsible for the analysis change the specification and appropriate review and approval have been obtained, can the designer adjust the design in accordance with the new specification. Managers can encourage adherence to this policy by assuring that procedures are in place that allow problems with the specification to be quickly remedied. Without a process that allows for timely correction of the problem, designers will probably find a way to undermine the process.

11.5.1.1 Measuring Success

The measure of success in one's first object-oriented project should be completing the project with a reasonable degree of efficiency, learning the technology, and creating a higher quality product than with traditional methods. Productivity is not a reasonable criterion for the first project. Only if the project is very large, so that one can generate significant reuse with the project itself, might one expect to have improved productivity.

11.5.1.2 Measuring Productivity

Managers will want to know the benefits of object technology with respect to productivity, because quality and usefulness of software is difficult to quantify. Any attempt at measuring the productivity of an OO project must (1) discount the initial learning phase because it will be amortized over the length of the employee's employment; (2) include the entire life cycle of the project, particularly including the maintenance phase, where the object-oriented method will shine; (3) count the value of reusable code created for the project and used in other projects; and (4) make sure not to compare a high-quality, highly useful object-oriented product with a lower-quality, less useful nonobject-oriented product.

Probably the most popular traditional metric for determining programming productivity is the number of lines of code produced per unit time. Use of this for measurement with traditional software approaches had some problems, but measuring productivity by the number of lines of coding created in an object-oriented project is definitely counterproductive. Good object-oriented design should reduce the number of lines of coding because of the use of inheritance, whereas bad design will tend to increase it, so that in the case of object-oriented software, an inverse relationship exists between size and quality. Taylor (1996) mentions a project in which a system that was reconstructed using object technology required only 9.5% as many lines of source code as the original. Byard (1994) compares the practice of counting lines to the measurement of brain capacity in the 19th century and the drawing of the conclusion that men were more intelligent than women because of their large brain size.

Counting the number of methods created might be an improvement over counting the number of lines produced, but evaluating software engineers with such a crude tool would only accomplish distorting the design by encouraging the creating of a lot of small methods even when larger ones might be more appropriate. Furthermore, it certainly does not encourage concise solutions over complex solutions.

Byard makes two important points. The first is that there is minimal correlation between most attributes that have been proposed as metrics for object-oriented software and the value or quality of the product. The second is that people, and not just those of the 19th century, tend to measure well but draw poor conclusions about the significance of what they measure.

Current state of the art in productivity measurement in traditional software is inadequate, and object technology provides no solution to the problem. Individual productivity measurement is simply not possible without understanding the technology and examining the details—gross measurements do not work. Reviews of the individual contributions of the developers during the process give a better idea than counting numbers of methods and classes or any other measure yet devised. Traditional techniques of understanding the technology, understanding the personnel, concentrating on the development process, and testing the product are still the best tools the manager has to measure quality, utility, and productivity.

Although direct measurements using source code statistics are of questionable value, keeping track of test results, error reports, and verified defects is an essential and valuable activity. Concentrating the use of metrics in this area can detect general patterns of problems that can lead to general remedial action as well as immediate response to the problems. Metrics should include more than keeping track of errors and corrections, it should include monitoring how well satisfied customers are with the quality and responsiveness of the solutions.

11.5.2 Evaluating Personnel

To be good at evaluating personnel, a manager must first understand the fundamentals of the technology. He can casually test a developer's knowledge, for example, to determine if he knows particularly important facts such as the fact that using inheritance increases coupling. Managers can pick a topic the software engineers should know about, study it, and ask the developers questions. The software engineers should still know a lot more than the manager, but he can determine whether they talk intelligently about a particular subject, such as the advantages and disadvantages of multiple inheritance. However, the manager should not assume he knows the answers; if questions arise, he should consult with experts or invest the time himself to determine the facts.

I know a software engineer who got a new technical monitor and department manager at about the same time. The technical monitor, who knew little about software engineering, suggested to the manager (who was two levels above the engineer) that the engineer, who I'll call Tom, might not be technically competent. The manager ordered an independent review, not of Tom's work, but of a code for which he had inherited responsibility. The report was highly critical of the code; it was the reviewer's job to find problems and Tom willingly told the reviewer what the problems were. The manager assumed that because Tom was responsible for the code, any problems with it were his fault. He interrogated Tom and, in the process, showed a total lack of understanding of software-engineering principles. Tom argued technical issues with him without really convincing him he was wrong. However, the manager was diligent enough to pursue determining the truth of the disputed points, so that Tom was eventually vindicated. The moral of the story is that managers must invest enough effort in understanding technical issues or else they could end up firing the competent and hiring incompetent smooth talkers who don't argue with them. Hire the best, verify their competence, and let them do their jobs.

11.6 Important Technical Considerations

This section summarizes some important technical considerations in managing object technology that require careful attention.

11.6.1 Inheritance Structures

Management needs to pay particular regard to assuring that the potential benefits of the use of inheritance are achieved and that the pitfalls are avoided. The advantages of having a well thought out stable inheritance hierarchy are that one does not have to retest, redebug, and redocument all of the coding that a new class inherits. The misuse of inheritance can not only miss the advantages but can create major maintenance problems.

Although general principles should be followed that make extensibility easier, one cannot create an inheritance structure that is generally extensible in all directions. Extensibility can only be achieved by knowing in what ways a hierarchy may need to be extended. Although software engineers must be trained in creating extensible inheritance hierarchies, management needs to inform the developers of plans for future expansion of the project.

The use of inheritance results in bigger units of coding being coupled because an entire inheritance structure has high coupling. Any change in the ancestor classes can impact all descendant classes. Therefore, it is very important that the base of inheritance hierarchies be stable. A good stable inheritance structure allows extremely effective leveraging of coding, increasing productivity, and avoiding retesting of ancestor classes when specialized classes are added. However, an inheritance structure in which the ancestor classes are constantly being changed or the structure itself is being changed necessitates retesting of entire tree structures of classes.

Therefore, management oversight and review needs to focus very heavily on assuring that structural hierarchies are stable and extensible. Object-oriented techniques do make it much easier to modify the code, but this depends on doing a good job of creating the structures originally. It is critical to get the structure right during analysis and design, so use design reviews before beginning implementation. Once part of the system is programmed and a need arises to insert new classes in the middle of an inheritance structure, a lot of extra work is created. On the other hand, adding new specializations at the bottom of the existing inheritance hierarchy is quite easy.

Analysts and designers needed to be challenged by their peers and possibly outside consultants to ensure the quality of inheritance hierarchies; the quality of aggregation hierarchies should also be reviewed. Obviously the review process must be conducted with care. Analysts and designers may be quite proud of their architecture and sensitive to criticism. Encouraging informal discussion during development and obtaining a group consensus early rather than depending on later reviews can greatly alleviate this problem.

Reviewers should make sure that the classes used in inheritance structures model the physical nature underlying the application, not a computer-oriented solution to the problem. Basing the classes on the application domain, which should not change much compared to the solution domain, creates a more stable structure that will better withstand the impact of changes to the requirements. By keeping the structure of the software hierarchies consistent with the underlying reality while molding them to specific requirements, one can avoid having to make drastic structural changes later.

11.6.2 How to Tell Good from Bad Solutions

If you are an Aristotelian philosophically, then you may feel that there is one best solution to a problem. This may be true, but with any complex problem no one will ever find this best solution, and even if he or she did, not everyone would ever agree that it is the best. It would be very nice for managers to be able give a problem to a group of analysts and have each one come up with the same solution. Unfortunately, even if they all use the same methodology they will each produce different solutions. These solutions may be vastly different in quality.

This fact can be dealt with in two ways, both of which should be employed. The best thing one can do with internal resources is to do the work as a group, with a lot of ideas input from a lot of different viewpoints, and debate the merits. This pooling of resources normally will produce a much better product. While sharing ideas should be a team effort, this does not imply that the decision-making responsibility should be shared; the ultimate decision should be the responsibility of the code architect who has the vision of how the entire system should fit together, subject only to the rare intervention of management for managerial, not technical reasons. In addition to this, bringing in an outside consultant or even someone from another project who can take an independent and dispassionate look at a proposed solution may bring unexpected problems to light.

11.6.3 Safety First

To make a program safe, that is to assure its integrity, one needs to build in many checks, such as to make sure the program values are within a narrow range of acceptable values. The more constraints we place into the coding, the safer the code is, but the harder it is to extend it if the requirements change. The encapsulation of the object-orientation approach lends itself to preserving the integrity of objects by controlling how the state of the object is allowed to change. Managers should check that this object-oriented capability is fully utilized to ensure code reliability.

11.6.4 Efficiency

Many programmers are efficiency enthusiasts. Sometimes this is out of necessity and sometimes it is just part of the game—an intriguing puzzle to delight in solving. Managers need to make sure that the effort devoted to programming efficiency is worthwhile. The flexibility of the object-oriented approach can be compromised if designers and programmers disregard good software practice for the sake of run-time efficiency where it is not needed. Making coding more efficient may require making it less general purpose. When you consider efficiency, consider not only run-time efficiency but development-time efficiency as well. Greater development flexibility, meaning making the design more extensible and maintainable, may reduce the development costs with negligible effect on execution time.

11.7 Summary

The following is an enumeration of some important points to remember about managing object technology. They include items from early sections as well as this section.

- Training in the object-oriented approach is needed for those experienced in traditional techniques every bit as much as for novice developers.
- Proportionally more time is needed for analysis and possibly design compared to programming than with traditional development.
- The use of a modern life-cycle model with iterative and incremental development is important.
- Achieving extensive reuse requires an enterprise-level effort that involves commitment from top management.
- The use of frameworks is a fast route to profiting from the potential for reuse in object technology.
- Look for design patterns to allow reuse of specifications.
- If maintenance is not reduced in an object-oriented project, then something is seriously wrong with the application of the technology.
- When selecting an object-oriented language, be sure to evaluate Java as well as the older languages.
- Make a conscious decision on the relative importance of run-time efficiency versus development and maintenance efficiency.
- The most important single technical consideration in design reviews is the quality of the specialization (inheritance) structures.
- Make sure that constraints are built into the software to assure reliability.

We have discussed a broad spectrum of issues related to object technology that I hope has been of interest to upper managers, technical managers, and developers. Many issues that are important to only one of these groups were omitted. Therefore, each of these audiences will need to further pursue their specialties if an object-oriented project is undertaken.

Developers need to understand the technical details to implement the technology. They also need to understand the manager's problems and point of view so that they can better support managers in making technical decisions.

Technical managers need to understand the concepts and principles of software development well enough to recognize quality when they see it. Otherwise, they are ill-prepared to make either technical decisions or personnel decisions involving the technical quality of their employees.

Upper managers must weigh the risks versus the benefits of using object technology; if they choose to utilize a new technology, they must deal with many new challenges. Managers who are brave enough to adopt new technology must also be wise enough to make some adjustments to management policies if their efforts are to be highly successful.

Switching to object technology should not be taken lightly nor undertaken half-heartedly. Considerable financial and intellectual investment is required. Companies with a long-range vision and considerable determination will be the ones to profit by meeting the challenges and opportunities with which technology is constantly confronting us.

I hope this book has provided you with some insights about the nature of object technology. I have enjoyed writing it and hope it will help make your projects more successful.

11.8 References

Alexander, C. (1977). *A pattern language*. New York: Oxford University Press.

Byard, C. (1994). Software beans: Class metrics and the mismeasure of software. *Journal of Object-Oriented Programming, 7*(5), 32–34.

Bilow, S. C. (1995). Five for '95: This year's hot new books. *Journal of Object-Oriented Programming, 8*(5),43–46.

Booch, G. (1994). *Object oriented design with applications*. Redwood City, CA: Benjamin/Cummings.

Bowles, A. (1995). Modeling business abstractions. *Object Magazine, 5*(4),22.

Brooks, F. P. (1982). *The Mythical Man-Month.* Reading, MA: Addison-Wesley.

Gabriel, R. P., (1994). The failure of pattern languages. *Journal of Object-Oriented Programming, 5*(9),84–88.

Gamma, E., Helm, R., Johnson, R., & Vlissides, J. (1995). *Design patterns: Elements of reusable object-oriented software.* Reading, MA: Addison-Wesley.

Goldberg, A., & Rubin, K. S. (1995) *Succeeding with objects: Decision frameworks for project management.* Reading, MA: Addison-Wesley.

Jacobson, I., & Jacobson, S. (1995). Beyond methods and CASE: The software engineering process with its integral support environment. *Object Magazine, 4*(8),24.

Lee, M. M. (1993) Object-oriented analysis in large-scale projects. *Object Magazine, 3*(4),49.

Srinivasan, K., & Jayaraman, S. (1994). Comparison of object-oriented programming languages: The enterprise modeling framework perspective. *Journal of Object-Oriented Programming, 7*(3),27–32.

Stewart, M. K. (1995). Executive brief. *Object Magazine, 5*(7),10.

Taylor, D. A. (1994). Managing your first object project. *Object Magazine, 4*(2),20.

Taylor, D. A. (1996). The use and abuse of reuse. *Object Magazine. 6*(2):18.

Weston, R. (1995). Pushing the limits of RAD. *Open Computing, 12*(6), 30–35.

Yourdon, E. (1992). *Decline and fall of the American programmer.* Englewood Cliffs, NJ: Yourdon Press.

Appendix A

Keeping Concepts Straight

This appendix is for readers who desire a more detailed discussion of object-oriented terminology; it differentiates between closely related terms and constructs.

A.1 Types and Classes

Cardelli and Wagner (1985, p. 474) informally describes a type as "a set of clothes (or a suit of armor) that protects an underlying untyped representation from arbitrary or unintended use." Thus a type is an encapsulation concept that requires different types to interact in a manner restricted to the rules of the types. A class is an implementation of a type that should include implementing these constraints. The concept of a type is applicable to analysis, design, and programming; class is strictly a design and programming construct that may or may not implement the type concept. In strongly typed languages like C++, classes enforce type consistency; in untyped languages like Smalltalk, classes do not enforce type consistency.

A.2 Abstract Types and Abstract Data Types

The term *abstract data type* is a synonym for type and is also known as a *user-defined type*, although the later excludes built-in types like integer and character. Abstract data types should not be confused with abstract types, which are types that are not instantiated themselves but that are used to create concrete types (ones that have instances). These abstract types make it easier to extract common information from a set of types for the purpose of sharing it in a specialization hierarchy without having to create a type that must be useful by itself.

A.3 Classes and Objects

Classes are templates for creating objects in their own image. Classes exist at compile time; objects exist at execution time. Both may have variables associated with them—a class variable is one that is common to all objects of the class. Although an object usually refers to an instance of a class, sometimes the word object is used to mean either instance or class.

A.4 Classification and Generalization

Classification includes the process of sorting similar objects into classes. For some definitions it also includes the creation of generalization hierarchies. The following discussion assumes a definition of classification that does not include the idea of generalization.

Classification and generalization are similar in that they both extract common characteristics from a group of similar entities. Classification identifies the common characteristics of a collection of objects. Generalization extracts the common characteristics of a collection of types. Generalization and specialization are the same concept just looked at from different directions.

In classification one looks at a set of objects and creates a type so that each of the objects is an instance of the type. In generalization one looks at a set of types and creates a supertype so that the objects of each of the types are also objects of the supertype. Classification uses inductive reasoning on object similarities, whereas generalization uses inductive reasoning on type similarities. Another way of looking at the choice between classification and generalization is that it is the choice between using objects or using subtypes to represent specialized entities.

A.5 Is A

An aggregation can be referred to as an *is-a-part-of* or a *has-a* relationship. There is no confusion with this. However, a specialization relationship is frequently referred to as an *is-a* relationship. This is quite common but several methodologists, including Graham and Firesmith, take issue with this. They say, and I agree, that a specialization relationship should be referred to as an *is-a-kind-of* relationship, whereas an *is-a* relationship should refer to classification exclusive of specialization. For example, "Fido is a dog" shows the classification of the object "Fido" as being an object of the class "Dog." The sentence "A dog is a kind of a mammal," shows the specialization relationship in which a dog is a subtype of mammal. We would not say that "Fido is a kind of a dog" (unless perhaps we were trying to insult him). We might say that "A dog is a mammal," but this would really just be an abbreviation of what we really mean, that a dog is a type of mammal. Therefore, it would be best to use *is a part of* for aggregation, *is a kind of* for specialization or inheritance, and *is a* for classification of objects into types. However, the use of *is a* for specialization is so widespread that it leaves a dilemma as to whether to try to standardize to the most popular terminology or to the more enlightening terminology.

A.6 Methods and Operations

Frequently the words method and operation are used interchangeably. Both words always have the meaning that some object is performing work for another. In all definitions, an operation is the implementation of a behavior of a type or class. However, there are alternative ways of making fuller use of the words by differentiating their meanings. For both of the options below, "operation" is a more general term than "method."

The most common way to differentiate between the two is to use method to mean the implementation of an operation. This means an operation can have multiple methods that implement it. This can occur when an operation is a general description of what work needs to be done within an inheritance hierarchy. For example, suppose we have an operation like *getTotalBudget()* that represents the work to be done within an inheritance hierarchy that consists of class company with subclass department that has a subclass group. Then the methods are the different *getTotalBudget()* definitions for each of the three kinds of classes involved. Each of the *getTotalBudget()* methods implements the same operation using different coding for the different classes.

This is, of course, an example of the use of polymorphism. The form of the implementation of the operation and method is the same for polymorphic functions. That is, both have the same signatures (name, arguments, and return value types).

Another way in which the words are given different meanings is to consider an operation to include both methods and other procedures. That is, methods and procedures are two different kinds of operations. Methods must be associated with a class; other procedures do not need to be associated with a class. A method corresponds to a member function in C++. A procedure corresponds to a nonmember function in C++.

A.7 Messages and Methods

Although messages and methods are frequently considered synonymous, if they really were then we would only need one of the words. If we picked the word "method," then we would say things like "the client sends a method to a server;" although we really should say message. If we picked the word "message," we would have to say things like "the class's behavior is implemented by a message." Of course this is the opposite of what we normally would say, so clearly there is some difference between these words. A message and a method can be considered as two parts of the same communication event during execution viewed from different perspectives. The message is the part of the communication viewed from the sender; the method is the part of the communication viewed by the receiver.

Both methods and messages are specified by describing their name, parameters, and return values; however, a method also requires processing instructions as part of its specification. A message is different from a method because a message is a request for a method to be applied rather than being the method itself. In particular, a message is different from a method in that the method is represented by coding in the server object, whereas the message is represented by the coding in the client object that requests the invocation of the method.

A.8 Messages and Signals

Jacobson defines a message as an intraprocess communication between objects inside the single process, but this may be very confusing to you if you think of process as a function. Jacobson's use of process refers to an entire program or equivalent. His definition is designed to contrast a message, which takes place within the program, and a signal that is allows communication among programs or relatively independent sections thereof.

A.9 Events and Messages

A message is the means by which software communicates the existence of an event from one object to another. Messages and events both cause objects to react, so what is the difference between an event and a message? An event is a slightly more abstract concept than a message. The difference is that an event is a generalized request for a behavior or state transition, whereas a message is a specific request. An event may cause the sending of many different messages or one message to many objects. For example, the event that a police car behind you turns on its siren may result in your mind generating several messages. Foot—put on the break. Hands—steer to the side of the road. Adrenal glands—start pumping. Sweat glands—start pouring.

Although a message is a specific request, it may still represent more than one event because a message may be bidirectional in that it may return a value. Events are unidirectional and therefore a message with a return value represents two events.

A.10 Polymorphism and Overloading

If you are already somewhat familiar with object-oriented programming, don't confuse overloading with polymorphism. For polymorphism we must have the same operation signature sent to different classes. For overloading, we must send different signatures, typically to the same object. Actually, overloading is a form of ad hoc polymorphism, but in common usage it is not considered polymorphism (Cardelli & Wegner, 1985).

A.11 References

Cardelli, L., & Wegner P. (1985). On understanding types, data abstraction, and Polymorphism. *Computing Surveys, 17*(4),474, 475.

Appendix B

Application Experiences

Regardless of how many theoretical reasons there may be why object technology is a superior approach, only actual experience can verify this. This Appendix provides evidence that projects using object technology can be quite successful. Of course, the selection is not a random sampling of projects. Those involved in unsuccessful projects are not as likely to want to publish their experiences.

The sampling given in Table B.1 shows a wide variety of applications and may provide some hints as to a methodology to select for a particular type of application. Most successful projects would probably have been successful using a different methodology, however. It is the quality of the management and the developers that is most important to the success of a project.

One particular project report warrants some additional discussion. In particular, the article describing the second example, a real-time project using OMT, was highly critical of the methodology. Although most of the criticisms were valid, the authors' expectations of the methodology seemed unrealistically high for that time period in the evolution of the technology. Object-oriented methodologies are still evolving, and at the time of this project none had yet evolved to include a full life-cycle process. The title of Rumbaugh's book that was the guide for the project indicates the intent to discuss modeling and design; it did not claim to provide a cradle-to-grave process for object-oriented projects. Considerable effort is underway now to provide methodologies with a comprehensive development process and supporting environment. The authors also apparently expected Rumbaugh's book to explain everything they needed to know about object-oriented concepts. There are still no books that will do this, including this one. Software developers who wish to develop a deep understanding of the technology need to study many sources to achieve this. I also got the impression that this was a "go-it-alone" project without the assistance of outside consultants and mentors. If this was the case, then their confusion about object-oriented concepts is not surprising.

Table B-1. *Project Experiences for Various Application Domains*

Application domain: Telecommunications — **Reference:** DeJesus (1995)
Methodology: Shlaer-Mellor — **Language:** C++

Project description

Company: GTE

Nature of project: software for asynchronous transfer mode switch

Size: very large

Development environment: BridgePoint 3.0, Cadre's ObjectTeam

Reason for using object technology: not even feasible to do project otherwise

Reason for methodology selection: to take advantage of the automatic translation of analysis to code and to allow easy upgrading of the system every 6 months

Evaluation: highly successful

Lessons learned

Switching to object technology involves massive retraining in many areas.

Devoting most of the development effort to the analysis phase paid off.

Management support and understanding of the technology was essential to success.

The use of outside consultants was essential.

Choosing an initial development team of forward-thinking people was important.

Tool support enhanced productivity greatly.

The Shlaer-Mellor methodology was well suited to this type of project.

Application domain: Real Time	**Reference:** Fayad, Tsa, Anthony, and Fulghum (1994)
Methodology: OMT	**Language:** Ada

Project description

Company: McDonnell Douglas

Nature of project: mission file for self-guided cruise missile

Development environment: Cadre's Teamwork; comments on others looked at

Reason for methodology selection: applicable to Ada, previous experience with Colbert and Shlaer-Mellor methodologies, and CASE tool support

Evaluation: not stated—the article focused on the problems with the methodology so one gets the impression that the project itself did not go well

Lessons learned

The report of the study was highly critical of OMT. Many of the criticisms are addressed in OMT-2; therefore, I am including only some of those criticisms that I believe are not well address by OMT-2. See the text at the start of this Appendix.

OMT documentation does not make clear by itself all of the important concepts one needs to understand to implement an object-oriented project.

OMT does not provide adequate guidance on object-oriented testing or maintaining traceability.

Application domain: Office automation and networking	**Reference:** Guttman and Matthews (1992)
Methodology: Home-grown methods	**Language:** C++

Project description

Company: NCR

Nature of project: an integrated set of office automation software on a LAN/WAN network

Size: very large (over 100 software engineers involved)

Development environment: minimal

Reason for using OT: prototype indicated the value of the object-oriented approach

Reason for methodology selection: task started in 1989 when no methodology was available

Evaluation: slightly behind schedule but otherwise highly successful; productivity on the initial object-oriented project was estimated to be 200% higher than expected with traditional approaches

Lessons learned

Conversion of a hierarchical management structure to a matrix-style management structure is recommended.

Consultants were essential to the task; an individual consultant could either be used as a worker or as a consultant, but not both.

Designing for reuse is difficult and reviews are valuable in creating reusable classes.

It is best to conduct reviews as a continuous process rather than just a final step in the process.

Many of the best ideas will come late in the first project; this makes the first one difficult but bodes well for future projects.

The response of personnel to the new technology varied widely; those who finished the project could not imagine going back to the old ways.

Application Domain: Civil Engineering
Methodology: Booch
Reference: Kirkpatrick (1994)
Language: Smalltalk

Project description

Company: Haestad Methods Inc.

Nature of project: hydrology and hydraulics applications with a GUI

Development environment: Digitalk's Smalltalk/V with Envy/Developer from Object Technology International and WindowBuilder from ObjectShare

Reason for language selection: past bad experience with complexity of C++ class libraries

Reason for methodology selection: project leader familiarity with the methodology

Evaluation: highly successful with fewer bugs, faster prototyping, and more robust design

Lessons learned

Smalltalk can be used for numerically intensive engineering applications; however, this requires a significant optimization effort that adversely affects portability.

Smalltalk allowed the creation of a workable version much faster than C++ would have.

Some of the time saved in the early stages of development was lost in the optimization effort and creating a small executable file.

Application Domain: Medical diagnostics
Methodology: Shlaer-Mellor
Reference: Ladd (1994)
Language: C

Project description

Company: Abbott Laboratories

Nature of project: blood analysis

Reason for language selection: no experience in C++ and lack of confidence in C++ compilers for the embedded processors

Evaluation: very successful with better documentation, understanding of the problem, and team communications

Lessons learned

The emphasis of the Shlaer-Mellor methodology on complete analysis made code generation easy despite the limited capabilities and overoptimistic vendor claims about the CASE tools. The following are important: formal training, starting with a small pilot project, thorough documentation, thorough analysis and design before beginning coding, and understanding that the conversion to object technology will be difficult.

B.1 References

DeJesus, E. X. (1995). Big OOP, no oops. *Byte, 20*(8),74–78.

Fayad, M. E., Tsai, W., Anthony, R. L., & Fulghum, M. L. (1994). Object modeling technique (OMT): Experience report. *Journal of Object-Oriented Programming, 7*(7),46–58.

Guttman, M. K., & Matthews, J. R. (1992). Managing a large project: Case study of a long-term project at NCR. *Object Magazine, 2*(4),75–78,81.

Kirkpatrick, D. (1994). Developing a commercial engineering application in Smalltalk. *Object Magazine, 4*(6),33–38.

Ladd, J. (1994). Developing a medical diagnostic system with OOA/RD. *Object Magazine, 4*(7),48–52.

Index